# THE CHILDREN OF THE POOR

TCB CLASSICS

*Immigrant family in the baggage room of Ellis Island*
*Source: Lewis Hine, 1905, Wikimedia Commons*

# THE CHILDREN OF THE POOR

## A CHILD WELFARE CLASSIC

*Special Illustrated Edition*

**Jacob A. Riis**

**TCB CLASSICS**

Pittsburgh, Pennsylvania

**TCB CLASSICS**

An imprint of TCB Research & Indexing LLC

Pittsburgh, Pennsylvania

www.tcbinfosci.com

First published by Charles Scribner's Sons in 1892.

ISBN 978-0-9996604-0-9 (hardcover)

ISBN 978-0-9996604-1-6 (paperback)

ISBN 978-0-9996604-2-3 (ebook)

Library of Congress Control Number 2017961179

All original photographs and illustrations are in the public domain.

Front cover based on *Halka* (1891), painting by Olga Boznańska
in the National Museum, Poznań, Poland.

Unless otherwise noted, photographs and illustrations appeared in the 1908
Scribner's edition of *The Children of the Poor* by Jacob A. Riis.

Book design, editorial content, derived images, and index by Tanja Bekhuis.

Printed in the United States of America.

# CONTENTS

# ILLUSTRATIONS

# Foreword

*The Children of the Poor* (1892) is a classic study of immigrant children living in the slums of New York City. Jacob August Riis (1849–1914) wrote this exposé as a companion to his influential book titled *How the Other Half Lives: Studies among the Tenements of New York* (1890). Riis was one of the first investigative journalists to adopt flash photography. His photographs were not intended as works of art. Rather, they were used as undeniable evidence of misery in the tenements, sweat shops, alleys and streets. His photojournalism and illustrated books subsequently inspired social reforms during the Progressive Era.

Portrayals of children in this book are moving and yet may be offensive to modern readers. Although Riis clearly cared about the children he wrote about, he used racial and ethnic stereotypes to broadly characterize groups of immigrants. The reader will have to weigh the historical value of this book against occasionally offensive language.

This special edition includes a subject index written by a social scientist. It is a navigational aid for scholars and general readers, particularly those interested in the history of child welfare, immigration, and urban slums. A short biography of Riis along with a list of resources for further study may be found at the end of the book. The illustrations, mainly photographs appearing in the 1908 Scribner's edition, were resized, trimmed and optimized for print. Hyphenation, capitalization, and punctuation were modernized, but the content is otherwise unchanged.

*Tanja Bekhuis, PhD*
*TCB Classics*
*Pittsburgh, Pennsylvania*
*December 2017*

# Preface

To my little ones, who, as I lay down my pen, come rushing in from the autumn fields, their hands filled with flowers "for the poor children," I inscribe this book. May the love that shines in their eager eyes never grow cold within them; then they shall yet grow up to give a helping hand in working out this problem which so plagues the world today. As to their father's share, it has been a very small and simple one, and now it is done. Other hands may carry forward the work. My aim has been to gather the facts for them to build upon. I said it in *How the Other Half Lives*, and now, in sending this volume to the printer, I can add nothing. The two books are one. Each supplements the other. Ours is an age of facts. It wants facts, not theories, and facts I have endeavored to set down in these pages. The reader may differ with me as to the application of them. He may be right and I wrong. But we shall not quarrel as to the facts themselves, I think. A false prophet in our day could do less harm than a careless reporter. That name I hope I shall not deserve.

To lay aside a work that has been so long a part of one's life, is like losing a friend. But for the one lost I have gained many. They have been much to me. The friendship and counsel of Dr. Roger S. Tracy, of the Bureau of Vital Statistics, have lightened my labors as nothing else could save the presence and the sympathy of the best and dearest friend of all, my wife. To Major Willard Bullard, the most efficient chief of the Sanitary Police; Rabbi Adolph M. Radin; Mr. A. S. Solomons, of the Baron de Hirsch Relief Committee; Dr. Annie Sturges Daniel; Mr. L. W. Holste, of the Children's Aid Society; Colonel George T. Balch, of the Board of Education; Mr. A. S. Fairchild, and to Dr. Max L. Margolis, my thanks are due and here given. Jew and Gentile, we have sought the truth together. Our reward must be in the consciousness that we have sought it faithfully and according to our light.

*J. A. R., Richmond Hill, Long Island, October 1, 1892*

1

# THE PROBLEM OF THE CHILDREN

THE PROBLEM OF THE CHILDREN is the problem of the State. As we mould the children of the toiling masses in our cities, so we shape the destiny of the State which they will rule in their turn, taking the reins from our hands. In proportion as we neglect or pass them by, the blame for bad government to come rests upon us. The cities long since held the balance of power; their dominion will be absolute soon unless the near future finds some way of scattering the population which the era of steam power and industrial development has crowded together in the great centres of that energy. At the beginning of the century the urban population of the United States was 3.97 percent of the whole, or not quite one in twenty-five. Today it is 29.12 percent, or nearly one in three. In the lifetime of those who were babies in arms when the first gun was fired upon Fort Sumter it has all but doubled. A million and a quarter live today in the tenements of the American metropolis. Clearly, there is reason for the sharp attention given at last to the life and the doings of the other half, too long unconsidered. Philanthropy we call it sometimes with patronizing airs. Better call it self-defense.

In New York there is all the more reason because it is the open door through which pours in a practically unrestricted immigration, unfamiliar with and unattuned to our institutions; the dumping ground where it rids itself of its burden of helplessness and incapacity, leaving the procession of the strong and the able free to move on. This sediment forms the body of our poor, the contingent that lives, always from hand to mouth, with no provision and no means of providing for the morrow. In the first generation it preempts our slums; [1] in the second, its worst elements, reinforced by the influences that prevail there, develop the tough, who confronts society with the claim that the world owes him a living and that he will collect it in his own way. His plan is a practical application of the spirit of our free institutions as his opportunities have enabled him to grasp it.

Thus it comes about that here in New York to seek the children of the poor one must go among those who, if they did not themselves come over the sea, can rarely count back another generation born on American soil. Not that there is far to go. Any tenement district will furnish its own tribe, or medley of many tribes. Nor is it by any means certain that the children when found will own their alien descent. Indeed, as a preliminary to gaining their confidence, to hint at such a thing would be a bad blunder. The ragged Avenue B boy, whose father at his age had barely heard, in his corner of the Fatherland, of America as a place where the streets were paved with nuggets of gold and roast pigeons flew into mouths opening wide with wonder, would, it is safe to bet, be as prompt to resent the insinuation that he was a "Dutchman," as would the little "Mick" the Teuton's sore taunt. Even the son of the immigrant Jew in his virtual isolation strains impatiently at the fetters of race and faith, while the Italian takes abuse philosophically only when in the minority and bides his time until he too shall be able to prove his title by calling those who came after him names. However, to quarrel with the one or the other on that ground would be useless. It is the logic of the lad's evolution, the way of patriotism in the slums. His sincerity need not be questioned.

Many other things about him may be, and justly are, but not

that. It is perfectly transparent. His badness is as spontaneous as his goodness, and for the moment all there is of the child. Whichever streak happens to prevail, it is in full possession; if the bad is on top more frequently than the other, it is his misfortune rather than his design. He is as ready to give his only cent to a hungrier boy than he if it is settled that he can "lick" him, and that he is therefore not a rival, as he is to join him in torturing an unoffending cat for the common cheer. The penny and the cat, the charity and the cruelty, are both pregnant facts in the life that surrounds him, and of which he is to be the coming exponent. In after years, when he is arrested by the officers of the Society for the Prevention of Cruelty to Animals for beating his horse, the episode adds but to his confusion of mind in which a single impression stands out clear and lasting, viz., that somehow he got the worst of it as usual. But for the punishment, the whole proceeding must seem ludicrous to him. As it is he submits without comprehending. *He* had to take the hard knocks always; why should not his horse?

In other words, the child is a creature of environment, of opportunity, as children are everywhere. And the environment here has been bad, as it was and is in the lands across the sea that sent him to us. Our slums have fairly rivalled, and in some respects outdone, the older ones after which they patterned. Still, there is a difference, the difference between the old slum and the new. The hopelessness, the sullen submission of life in East London as we have seen it portrayed, has no counterpart here; neither has the child born in the gutter and predestined by the order of society, from which there is no appeal, to die there. We have our Lost Tenth to fill the trench in the Potter's Field; quite as many wrecks at the finish, perhaps, but the start seems fairer in the promise. Even on the slums the doctrine of liberty has set its stamp. To be sure, for the want of the schooling to decipher it properly, they spell it license there, and the slip makes trouble. The tough and his scheme of levying tribute are the result. But the police settle that with him, and when it comes to a choice, the tough is to be preferred to the born pauper any day. The one has the making of something in him, unpromising as he looks; seen in a certain light he may even be considered a hopeful symptom. The other is just so much dead loss. The tough is not born: he is made. The all-important point is the one at which the manufacture can be stopped.

So rapid and great are the changes in American cities, that no slum has yet had a chance here to grow old enough to distil its deadliest poison. New York has been no exception. But we cannot always go at so fast a pace. There is evidence enough in the crystallization of the varying elements of the population along certain lines, no longer as uncertain as they were, that we are slowing up already. Any observer of the poor in this city is familiar with the appearance among them of that most distressing and most dangerous symptom, the home-feeling for the slum that opposes all efforts at betterment with dull indifference. Pauperism seems to have grown faster of late than even the efforts put forth to check it. We have witnessed this past winter a dozen times the spectacle of beggars extorting money by threats or violence without the excuse which a season of exceptional distress or hardship might have furnished. Further, the raid in the last Legislature upon the structure of law built up in a generation to regulate and keep the tenements within safe limits, shows that fresh danger threatens in the alliance of the slum with politics. Only the strongest public sentiment, kept always up to the point of prompt action, avails to ward off this peril. But public sentiment soon wearies of such watch duty, as instanced on this occasion, when several bills radically remodelling the tenement house law and repealing some of its most beneficent provisions, had passed both houses and were in the hands of the Governor before a voice was raised against them, or anyone beside the politicians and their backers seemed even to have heard of them. And this hardly five years after a special commission of distinguished citizens had sat an entire winter under authority of the State considering the tenement house problem, and as the result of its labors had secured as vital the enactment of the very law against which the raid seemed to be chiefly directed!

The tenement and the saloon, with the street that does not always divide them, form the environment that is to make or unmake the child. The influence of each of the three is bad. Together they have power to overcome the strongest resistance. But the child born under their evil spell has none such to offer. The testimony of all to whom has fallen the task of undoing as much of the harm done by them as may be, from the priest of the parish school to the chaplain of the penitentiary, agrees upon this point, that even the tough, with all his desperation, is weak rather than vicious. He promises well, he even means well; he is as downright sincere in his repentance as he was in his wrong doing, but it doesn't prevent him from doing the very same evil deed over again the minute he is rid of restraint. He would rather be a saint than a sinner, but somehow he doesn't keep in the *rôle* of saint, while the police help perpetuate the memory of his wickedness. After all, he is not so very different from the rest of us. Perhaps that, with a remorseful review of the chances he has had, may help to make a fellow-feeling for him in us.

That is what he needs. The facts clearly indicate that from the environment little improvement in the child is to be expected. There has been progress in the way of building the tenements of late years, but they swarm with greater crowds than ever— good reason why they challenge the pernicious activity of the politician, and the old rookeries disappear slowly. In the relation of the saloon to the child there has been no visible improvement, and the street is still his refuge. It is, then, his opportunities outside that must be improved if relief is to come. We have the choice of hailing him man and brother or of being slugged and robbed by him. It ought not to be a hard choice, despite the tatters and the dirt, for which our past neglect is in great part to blame. Plenty of evidence will be found in these pages to show that it has been made in the right spirit already, and that it has proved a wise choice. No investment gives a better return today on the capital put out than work among the children of the poor.

A single fact will show what is meant by that. Within the lifetime of the Children's Aid Society, in the thirty years between 1860 and 1890, while the population of this city was doubled, the commitments of girls and women for vagrancy fell off from 5,880 to 1,980, while the commitments of girl thieves fell between 1865 and 1890 from 1 in 743 to 1 in 7,500. [2] Stealing and vagrancy among boys has decreased too, if not so fast, yet at a gratifying rate.

Enough has been written and said about the children of the poor and their sufferings to make many a bigger book than this. From some of it one might almost be led to believe that one-half of the children are worked like slaves from toddling infancy, while the other half wander homeless and helpless about the streets. Their miseries are great enough without inventing any that do not exist. There is no such host of child outcasts in New York as that. Thanks to the unwearied efforts of the children's societies in the last generation, what there is is decreasing, if anything. As for the little toilers, they will receive attention further on. There are enough of them, but as a whole they are anything but a repining lot. They suffer less, to their own knowledge, from their wretched life than the community suffers for letting them live it, though it, too, sees the truth but in glimpses. If the question were put to a vote of the children tomorrow, whether they would take the old life with its drawbacks, its occasional starvation, and its everyday kicks and hard knocks, or the good clothes, the plentiful grub, and warm bed, with all the restraints of civilized society and the "Sunday-school racket" of the other boy thrown in, I have as little doubt that the street would carry the day by a practically unanimous vote as I have that there are people still to be found— too many of them—who would endorse the choice with a sigh of relief and dismiss the subject, if it could be dismissed that way, which, happily, it cannot.

The immediate duty which the community has to perform for its own protection is to school the children first of all into good Americans, and next into useful citizens. As a community it has not attended to this duty as it should, but private effort has stepped in and is making up for its neglect with encouraging success. The outlook that was gloomy from the point of view of the tenement, brightens when seen from this angle, however toilsome the road yet ahead. The inpouring of alien races no longer darkens it. The problems that seemed so perplexing in the light of freshly formed prejudices against this or that immigrant, yield to this simple solution that discovers all alarm to have been groundless. Yesterday it was the swarthy Italian, today the Russian Jew, that excited our distrust. Tomorrow it may be the Arab or the Greek. All alike they have taken, or are taking, their places in the ranks of our social phalanx, pushing upward from the bottom with steady effort, as I believe they will continue to do unless failure to provide them with proper homes arrests the process. And in the general advance the children, thus firmly grasped, are seen to be a powerful moving force. The one immigrant who does not keep step, who, having fallen out of the ranks, has been ordered to the rear, is the Chinaman, who brought neither wife nor children to push him ahead. He left them behind that he might not become an American, and by the standard he himself set up he has been judged.

# 2

# THE ITALIAN SLUM CHILDREN

WHO AND WHERE ARE THE SLUM CHILDREN of New York today? That depends on what is understood by the term. The moralist might seek them in Hell's Kitchen, in Battle Row, and in the tenements, east and west, where the descendants of the poorest Irish immigrants live. They are the ones, as I have before tried to show, upon whom the tenement and the saloon set their stamp soonest and deepest. The observer of physical facts merely would doubtless pick out the Italian ragamuffins first, and from his standpoint he would be right. Irish poverty is not picturesque in the New World, whatever it may have been in the Old. Italian poverty is. The worst old rookeries fall everywhere in this city to the share of the immigrants from Southern Italy, who are content to occupy them, partly, perhaps, because they are no worse than the hovels they left behind, but mainly because they are tricked or bullied into putting up with them by their smarter countrymen who turn their helplessness and ignorance to good account. Wherever the invasion of some old home section by the tide of business has left ramshackle tenements falling into hopeless decay, as in the old "Africa," in the Bend, and in many other places in the downtown wards, the Italian sweater landlord is ready with his offer of a lease to bridge over the interregnum, a lease that takes no account of repairs or of the improvements the owner sought to avoid. The crowds to make it profitable to him are never wanting. The bait he holds out is a job at the ash dump with which he connects at the other end of the line. The house, the job, and the man as he comes to them fit in well together, and the copartnership has given the Italian a character which, I am satisfied from close observation of him, he does not wholly deserve. At all events, his wife does not. Dirty as *he* seems and is in the old rags that harmonize so well with his surroundings, there is that about her which suggests not only the capacity for better things, but a willingness to be clean and to look decent, if cause can be shown. It may be a bright kerchief, a bit of old-fashioned jewelry, or the neatly smoothed and braided hair of the wrinkled old hag who presides over the stale bread counter. Even in the worst dens occupied by these people, provided that they had not occupied them too long, I have found this trait crop out in the careful scrubbing of some piece of oilcloth rescued from the dump and laid as a mat in front of the family bed or in a bit of fringe on the sheet or quilt, ragged and black with age though it was, that showed what a fruitful soil proper training and decent housing would have found there.

I have in mind one Italian "flat" among many, a half underground hole in a South Fifth Avenue yard, reached by odd passageways through a tumbledown tenement that was always full of bad smells and scooting rats. Across the foul and slippery yard, down three steps made of charred timbers from some worse wreck, was this "flat," where five children slept with their elders. How many of those there were I never knew. There were three big family beds, and they nearly filled the room, leaving only patches of the mud floor visible. The walls were absolutely black with age and smoke. The plaster had fallen off in patches and there was green mould on the ceiling. And yet, with it all, with the swarm of squirming youngsters that were as black as the floor they rolled upon, there was evidence of a desperate, if hopeless, groping after order, even neatness. The beds were made up as nicely as they could be with the old quilts and pieces of carpet that served for covering. In Poverty Gap, where an Italian would be stoned as likely as not, there would have been a heap of dirty straw instead of beds, and the artistic arrangement of tallow dips stuck in the necks of bottles about the newspaper cut of a saint on the corner shelf would have been missing altogether, fervent though the personal regard might be of Poverty Gap for the saint. The bottles would have been the only part of the exhibition sure to be seen there.

I am satisfied that this instinct inhabits not only the more aristocratic Genoese, but his fellow countryman from the southern hills as well, little as they resemble each other or agree in most things. But the Neapolitan especially does not often get a chance to prove it. He is so altogether uninviting an object when he presents himself, fresh from the steamer, that he falls naturally the victim of the slum tenement, which in his keep becomes, despite the vigilance of the sanitary police, easily enough the convenient depot and halfway house between the garbage dump and the bone factory. Starting thus below the bottom, as it were, he has an uphill journey before him if he is to work out of the slums, and the promise, to put it mildly, is not good. He does it all the same, or, if not he, his boy. It is not an Italian sediment that breeds the tough. Parental authority has a strong enough grip on the lad in Mulberry Street to make him work, and that is his salvation. "In seventeen years," said the teacher of the oldest Italian ragged school in the city that, day and night, takes in quite six hundred, "I have seen my boys work up into decent mechanics and useful citizens almost to a man, and of my girls only two I know of have gone astray." I had observed the process often enough myself to know that she was right. It is to be remembered, furthermore, that her school is in the very heart of the Five Points district, and takes in always the worst and the dirtiest crowds of children.

Within a year there has been, through some caprice of immigration, a distinct descent in the quality of the children, viewed from even the standard of cleanliness that prevails at the Five Points. Perhaps the exodus from Italy has worked farther south, where there seems to be an unusual supply of mud. Perhaps the rivalry of steamship lines has brought it about. At any rate, the testimony is positive that the children that came to the schools after last vacation, and have kept coming since, were the worst seen here since the influx began. I have watched with satisfaction, since this became apparent, some of the bad old tenements, which the newcomers always sought in droves, disappear to make room for great factory buildings. But there are enough left. The cleaning out of a Mulberry Street block left one lopsided old rear tenement that had long since been shut in on three sides by buildings four stories higher than itself, and forgotten by all the world save the miserable wretches who burrowed in that dark and dismal pit at the bottom of a narrow alley. Now, when the fourth structure goes up against its very windows, it will stand there in the heart of the block, a survival of the unfittest, that, in all its disheartening dreariness, bears testimony, nevertheless, to the beneficent activity of the best Board of Health New York has ever had—the onward sweep of business. It will wipe that last remnant out also, even if the law lack the power to reach it.

Shoals of Italian children lived in that rookery, and in those the workmen tore down, in the actual physical atmosphere of the dump. Not a gunshot away there is a block of tenements, known as the Mott Street Barracks, in which still greater shoals are—I was going to say housed, but that would have been a mistake. Happily they are that very rarely, except when they are asleep, and not then if they can help it. Out on the street they may be found tumbling in the dirt, or up on the roof lying stark naked, blinking in the sun—content with life as they find it. If they are not a very cleanly crew, they are at least as clean as the frame they are set in, though it must be allowed that something has been done of late years to redeem the buildings from the reproach of a bad past. The combination of a Jew for a landlord and a saloonkeeper—Italian, of course—for a lessee, was not propitious, but the buildings happen to be directly under the windows of the Health Board, and something, I suppose, was due to appearances. The authorities did all that could be done, short of tearing down the tenement, but though comparatively clean, and not nearly as crowded as it was, it is still the old slum. It is an instructive instance of what can and cannot be done with the tenements into which we invite these dirty strangers to teach them American ways and the self-respect of future citizens and voters. There are five buildings—that is, five front and four rear houses, the latter a story higher than those on the street; that is because the rear houses were built last, to "accommodate" this very Italian immigration that could be made to pay for anything. Chiefly Irish had lived there before, but they moved out then. There were 360 tenants in the Barracks when the police census was taken in 1888, and 40 of them were babies. How many were romping children I do not know. The "yard" they had to play in is just 5 feet 10 inches wide, and a dozen steps below the street level. The closets of all the buildings are in the cellar of the rear houses and open upon this "yard," where it is always dark and damp as in a dungeon. Its foul stenches reach even the top floor, but so also does the sun at midday, and that is a luxury that counts as an extra in the contract with the landlord. The rent is nearly one-half higher near the top than it is on the street level. Nine dollars above, six and a half below, for one room with windows, two without, and with barely space for a bed in each. But water pipes have been put in lately, under orders from the Health Department, and the rents have doubtless been raised. "No windows" means no ventilation. The rear building backs up against the tenement on the next street; a space a foot wide separates them, but an attempt to ventilate the bedrooms by windows on that was a failure.

When the health officers got through with the Barracks in time for the police census of 1891, the 360 tenants had been whittled down to 238, of whom 47 were babies under five years. Persistent effort had succeeded in establishing a standard of cleanliness that was a very great improvement upon the condition prevailing in 1888. But still, as I have said, the slum remained and will remain as long as that rear tenement stands. In the four years fifty-one funerals had gone out from the Barracks. The white hearse alone had made thirty-five trips carrying baby coffins. This was the way the two standards showed up in the death returns at the Bureau of Vital Statistics: in 1888 the adult death rate, in a population of 320 over five years old, was 15.62 per 1,000; the baby death rate, 325.00 per 1,000, or nearly one-third in a total of 40. As a matter of fact 13 of the 40 had died that year. The adult death rate for the entire tenement population of more than a million souls was that year 12.81, and the baby death rate 88.38. Last year, in 1891, the case stood thus: Total population, 238, including 47 babies. Adult death rate per 1,000, 20.94; child death rate (under five years) per 1,000, 106.38. General adult death rate for 1891 in the tenements, 14.25; general child death rate for 1891 in the tenements, 86.67. It should be added that the reduced baby death rate of the Barracks, high as it was, was probably much lower than it can be successfully maintained. The year before, in 1890, when practically the same improved conditions prevailed, it was twice as high. Twice as many babies died.

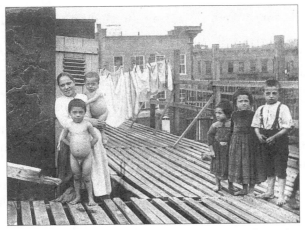

*Mother and children on a Mott Street Barracks roof*

I have referred to some of the typical Italian tenements at some length to illustrate the conditions under which their children grow up and absorb the impressions that are to shape their lives as men and women. Is it to be marvelled at, if the first impression of them is sometimes not favorable? I recall, not without amusement, one of the early experiences of a committee with which I was trying to relieve some of the child misery in the East Side tenements by providing an outing for the very poorest of the little ones, who might otherwise have been overlooked. In our anxiety to make our little charges as presentable as possible, it seems we had succeeded so well as to arouse a suspicion in our friends at the other end of the line that something was wrong, either with us or with the poor of which the patrician youngsters in new frocks and with clean faces, that came to them, were representatives. They wrote to us that they were in the field for the "slum children," and slum children they wanted. It happened that their letter came just as we had before us two little lads from the Mulberry Street Bend, ragged, dirty, unkempt, and altogether a sight to see. Our wardrobe was running low, and we were at our wits' end how to make these come up to our standard. We sat looking at each other after we had heard the letter read, all thinking the same thing, until the most courageous said it: "Send them as they are." Well, we did, and waited rather breathlessly for the verdict. It came, with the children, in a note by return train, that said: "Not *that* kind, please!" And after that we were allowed to have things our own way.

The two little fellows were Italians. In justice to our frightened friends, it should be said that it was not their nationality, but their rags, to which they objected; but not very many seasons have passed since the crowding of the black-eyed brigade of "guinnies," as they were contemptuously dubbed, in ever increasing numbers, into the ragged schools and the kindergartens, was watched with regret and alarm by the teachers, as by many others who had no better cause. The event proved that the children were the real teachers. They had a more valuable lesson to impart than they came to learn, and it has been a salutary one. Today they are gladly welcomed. Their sunny temper, which no hovel is dreary enough, no hardship has power to cloud, has made them universal favorites, and the discovery has been made by their teachers that as the crowds pressed harder their schoolrooms have marvellously expanded, until they embrace within their walls an unsuspected multitude, even many a slum tenement itself, cellar, "stoop," attic, and all. Every lesson of cleanliness, of order, and of English taught at the school is reflected into some wretched home, and rehearsed there as far as the limited opportunities will allow. No demonstration with soap and water upon a dirty little face but widens the sphere of these chief promoters of education in the slums. "By 'm by," said poor crippled Pietro to me, with a sober look, as he labored away on his writing lesson, holding down the paper with his maimed hand, "I learn t' make an Englis' letter, maybe my fadder he learn too." I had my doubts of the father. He sat watching Pietro with a pride in the achievement that was clearly proportionate to the struggle it cost, and mirrored in his own face every grimace and contortion the progress of education caused the boy. "Si! Si!" he nodded, eagerly. "Pietro he good a boy, make Englis', Englis'!" and he made a flourish with his clay pipe, as if he too were making the English letter that was the object of their common veneration.

Perhaps it is as much his growing and well-founded distrust of the middleman, whose unresisting victim he has heretofore been, and his need of some other joint to connect him with the English-speaking world that surrounds him, as any personal interest in book learning, that impels the illiterate Italian to bring his boy to school early and see that he attends it. Greed has something to do with it too. In their anxiety to lay hold of the child, the charity schools have fallen into a way of bidding for him with clothes, shoes, and other bait that is never lost on Mulberry Street. Even sectarian scruples yield to such an argument, and the parochial school, where they get nothing but on the contrary are expected to contribute, gets left.

In a few charity schools where the children are boarded they have discovered this, and frown upon Italian children unless there is the best of evidence that the father is really unable to pay for their keep and not simply unwilling. But whatever his motive, the effect is to demonstrate in a striking way the truth of the observation that real reform of poverty and ignorance must begin with the children. In his case, at all events, the seed thus sown bears some fruit in the present as well as in the coming generation of toilers. The little ones, with their new standards and new ambitions, become in a very real sense missionaries of the slums, whose work of regeneration begins with their parents. They are continually fetched away from school by the mother or father to act as interpreters or go-betweens in all the affairs of daily life, to be conscientiously returned within the hour stipulated by the teacher, who offers no objection to this sort of interruption, knowing it to be the best condition of her own success. One cannot help the hope that the office of trust with which the children are thus invested may, in some measure, help to mitigate their home hardships. From their birth they have little else, though Italian parents are rarely cruel in the sense of abusing their offspring.

It is the home itself that constitutes their chief hardship. It is only when his years offer the boy an opportunity of escape to the street, that a ray of sunlight falls into his life. In his backyard or in his alley it seldom finds him out. Thenceforward most of his time is spent there, until the school and the shop claim him, but not in idleness. His mother toiled, while she bore him at her breast, under burdens heavy enough to break a man's back. She lets him out of her arms only to share her labor. How well he does it anyone may see for himself by watching the children that swarm where an old house is being torn down, lugging upon their heads loads of kindling wood twice their own size and sometimes larger than that. They come, as crows scenting carrion, from every side at the first blow of the axe. Their odd old-mannish or old-womanish appearance, due more to their grotesque rags than to anything in the children themselves, betrays their race even without their chatter. Be there ever so many children of other nationalities nearer by—the wood gatherers are nearly all Italians. There are still a lot of girls among them who drag as big loads as their brothers, but since the sewing machine found its way, with the sweater's mortgage, into the Italian slums also, little Antonia has been robbed to a large extent even of this poor freedom, and has taken her place among the wage earners when not on the school bench. Once taken, the place is hers to keep for good. Sickness, unless it be mortal, is no excuse from the drudgery of the tenement. When, recently, one little Italian girl, hardly yet in her teens, stayed away from her class in the Mott Street Industrial School so long that her teacher went to her home to look her up, she found the child in a high fever, in bed, sewing on coats, with swollen eyes, though barely able to sit up.

But neither poverty nor hard knocks has power to discourage the child of Italy. His nickname he pockets with a grin that has in it no thought of the dagger and the revenge that come to solace his after years. Only the prospect of immediate punishment eclipses his spirits for the moment. While the teacher of the sick little girl was telling me her pitiful story in the Mott Street school, a characteristic group appeared on the stairway. Three little Italian culprits in the grasp of Nellie, the tall and slender Irish girl who was the mentor of her class for the day. They had been arrested "fur fightin'" she briefly explained as she dragged them by the collar toward the principal, who just then appeared to inquire the cause of the rumpus, and thrust them forward to receive sentence. The three, none of whom was over eight years old, evidently felt that they were in the power of an enemy from whom no mercy was to be expected, and made no appeal for any. One scowled defiance. He was evidently the injured party.

"He hit-a me a clip on de jaw," he said in his defense, in the dialect of Mott Street with a slight touch of "the Bend." The aggressor, a heavy browed little ruffian, hung back with a dreary howl, knuckling his eyes with a pair of fists that were nearly black. The third and youngest was in a state of bewilderment that was most ludicrous. He only knew that he had received a kick on the back and had struck out in self-defense, when he was seized and dragged away a prisoner. He was so dirty—school had only just begun and there had been no time for the regular inspection—that he was sentenced on the spot to be taken down and washed, while the other two were led away to the principal's desk. All three went out howling.

I said that the Italians do not often abuse their children downright. The padrone has had his day; the last was convicted seven years ago, and an end has been put to the business of selling children into a slavery that meant outrage, starvation, and death; but poverty and ignorance are fearful allies in the homes of the poor against defenseless childhood, even without the child-beating fiend. Two cases which I encountered in the East Side tenements, in the summer of 1891, show how the combination works at its worst. Without a doubt they are typical of very many, though I hope that few come quite up to their standard. The one was the case of little Carmen, who last March died in the New York Hospital, where she had lain five long months, the special care of the Society for the Prevention of Cruelty to Children. One of the summer corps doctors found her in a Mott Street tenement, within stone throw of the Health Department office, suffering from a wasting disease that could only be combated by the most careful nursing. He put her case into the hands of the King's Daughters' Committee that followed in the steps of the doctor, and it was then that I saw her. She lay in a little back room, up two flights and giving upon a narrow yard where it was always twilight. The room was filthy and close, and entirely devoid of furniture, with the exception of a rickety stool, a slop pail, and a rusty old stove, one end of which was propped up with bricks. Carmen's bed was a board laid across the top of a barrel and a trunk set on end. I could not describe, if I would, the condition of the child when she was raised from the mess of straw and rags in which she lay. The sight unnerved even the nurse, who had seen little else than such scenes all summer.

Loathsome bedsores had attacked the wasted little body, and in truth Carmen was more dead than alive. But when, shocked and disgusted, we made preparations for her removal with all speed to the hospital, the parents objected and refused to let us take her away. They had to be taken into court and forced to surrender the child under warrant of law, though it was clearly the little sufferer's only chance for life, and only the slenderest of chances at that.

Carmen was the victim of the stubborn ignorance that dreads the hospital and the doctor above the discomfort of the dirt and darkness and suffering that are its everyday attendants. Her parents were no worse than the Monroe Street mother who refused to let the health officer vaccinate her baby, because her crippled boy, with one leg an inch shorter than the other, had "caught it"—the lame leg, that is to say—from his vaccination. She knew it was so, and with ignorance of that stamp there is no other argument than force. But another element entered into the case of a sick Essex Street baby. The tenement would not let it recover from a bad attack of scarlet fever, and the parents would not let it be taken to the country or to the seashore, despite all efforts and entreaties. When their motive came out at last, it proved to be a mercenary one. They were behind with the rent, and as long as they had a sick child in the house the landlord could not put them out. Sick, the baby was to them a source of income, at all events a bar to expense, and in that way so much capital. Well, or away, it would put them at the mercy of the rent collector at once. So they chose to let it suffer. The parents were Jews, a fact that emphasizes the share borne by desperate poverty in the transaction, for the family tie is notoriously strong among their people.

No doubt Mott Street echoed with the blare of brass bands when poor little Carmen was carried from her bed of long suffering to her grave in Calvary. Scarce a day passes now in these tenements that does not see some little child, not rarely a newborn babe, carried to the grave in solemn state, preceded by a band playing mournful dirges and followed by a host with trailing banners, from some wretched home that barely sheltered it alive. No suspicion of the ludicrous incongruity of the show disturbs the paraders. It seems as if, but one remove from the dump, an insane passion for pomp and display, perhaps a natural reaction from the ash barrel, lies in wait for this Italian, to which he falls a helpless victim. Not content with his own national and religious holidays and those he finds awaiting him here, he has invented or introduced a system of his own, a sort of communal celebration of proprietary saints, as it were, that has taken Mulberry Street by storm. As I understand it, the townsmen of some Italian village, when there is a sufficient number of them within reach, club together to celebrate its patron saint, and hire a band and set up a gorgeous altar in a convenient backyard. The fire escapes overlooking it are draped with flags and transformed into reserved-seat galleries with the taste these people display under the most adverse circumstances. Crowds come and go, parading at intervals in gorgeous uniforms around the block. Admission is by the saloon door, which nearly always holds the key to the situation, the saloonist who prompts the sudden attack of devotion being frequently a namesake of the saint and willing to go shares on the principle that he takes the profit and the saint the glory.

The partnership lasts as long as there is any profit in it, sometimes the better part of the week, during which time all work stops. If the feast panned out well, the next block is liable to be the scene of a rival celebration before the first is fairly ended. As the supply of Italian villages represented in New York is practically as inexhaustible as that of the saloons, there is no reason why Mulberry Street may not become a perennial picnic ground long before the scheme to make a park of one end of it gets under way. From the standpoint of the children there can be no objection to this, but from that of the police there is. They found themselves called upon to interfere in such a four days' celebration of St.

Rocco last year, when his votaries strung cannon firecrackers along the street the whole length of the block and set them all off at once. It was at just such a feast, in honor of the same saint, that a dozen Italians were killed a week later at Newark in the explosion of their fireworks.

It goes without saying that the children enter into this sort of thing with all the enthusiasm of their little souls. The politician watches it attentively, alert for some handle to catch his new allies by and affect their "organization." If it is a new experience for him to find the saloon put to such use, he betrays no surprise. It is his vantage ground, and whether it serve as the political bait for the Irishman, or as the religious initiative of the Italian, is of less account than that its patrons, young and old, in the end fall into his trap. Conclusive proof that the Italian has been led into camp came to me on last St. Patrick's Day through the assurance of a certain popular clergyman, that he had observed, on a walk through the city, a number of hand organs draped in green, evidently for the occasion.

This dump of which I have spoken as furnishing the background of the social life of Mulberry Street, has lately challenged attention as a slum annex to the Bend, with fresh horrors in store for defenseless childhood. To satisfy myself upon this point I made a personal inspection of the dumps along both rivers last winter and found the Italian crews at work there making their home in every instance among the refuse they picked from the scows. The dumps are wooden bridges raised above the level of the piers upon which they are built to allow the discharge of the carts directly into the scows moored under them. Under each bridge a cabin had been built of old boards, oilcloth, and the like, that had found its way down on the carts; an old milk can had been made into a fireplace without the ceremony of providing stovepipe or draught, and here, flanked by mountains of refuse, slept the crews of from half a dozen to three times that number of men, secure from the police, who had grown tired of driving them from dump to dump and had finally let them alone. There were women at some of them, and at four dumps, three on the North River and one on the East Side, I found boys who ought to have been at school, picking bones and sorting rags.

*Italian home under a dump*

They said that they slept there, and as the men did, why should they not? It was their home. They were children of the dump, literally. All of them except one were Italians. That one was a little homeless Jew who had drifted down at first to pick cinders. Now that his mother was dead and his father in a hospital, he had become a sort of fixture there, it seemed, having made the acquaintance of the other lads.

Two boys whom I found at the West Nineteenth Street dumps sorting bones were as bright lads as I had seen anywhere. One was nine years old and the other twelve. Filthy and ragged, they fitted well into their environment—even the pig I had encountered at one of the East River dumps was much the more respectable, as to appearance, of the lot—but were entirely undaunted by it. They scarcely remembered anything but the dump. Neither could read, of course. Further down the river I came upon one seemingly not over fifteen, who assured me that he was twenty-one. I thought it possible when I took a closer look at him. The dump had stunted him. He did not even know what a letter was. He had been there five years, and garbage limited his mental as well as his physical horizon.

*Child of the dump*

Enough has been said to show that the lot of the poor child of the Mulberry Street Bend, or of Little Italy, is not a happy one, courageously and uncomplainingly, even joyously, though it be borne. The stories of two little lads from the region of Crosby Street always stand to me as typical of their kind. One I knew all about from personal observation and acquaintance; the other I give as I have it from his teachers in the Mott Street Industrial School, where he was a pupil in spells. It was the death of little Giuseppe that brought me to his home, a dismal den in a rear tenement down a dark and forbidding alley. I have seldom seen a worse place. There was no trace there of a striving for better things—the tenement had stamped that out—nothing but darkness and filth and misery. From this hole Giuseppe had come to the school a mass of rags, but with that jovial gleam in his brown eyes that made him an instant favorite with the teachers as well as with the boys. One of them especially, little Mike, became attached to him, and a year after his cruel death shed tears yet, when reminded of it. Giuseppe had not been long at the school when he was sent to an Elizabeth Street tenement for a little absentee. He brought her, shivering in even worse rags than his own; it was a cold winter day.

"This girl is very poor," he said, presenting her to the teacher, with a pitying look. It was only then that he learned that she had no mother. His own had often stood between the harsh father and him when he came home with unsold evening papers. Giuseppe fished his only penny out of his pocket—his capital for the afternoon's trade. "I would like to give her that," he said. After that he brought her pennies regularly from his day's sale, and took many a thrashing for it. He undertook the general supervision of the child's education, and saw to it that she came to school every day. Giuseppe was twelve years old.

There came an evening when business had been very bad, so bad that he thought a bed in the street healthier for him than the Crosby Street alley. With three other lads in similar straits he crawled into the iron chute that ventilated the basement of the post office on the Mail Street side and snuggled down on the grating. They were all asleep, when fire broke out in the cellar. The three climbed out, but Giuseppe, whose feet were wrapped in a mailbag, was too late. He was burned to death.

The little girl still goes to the Mott Street school. She is too young to understand, and marvels why Giuseppe comes no more with his pennies. Mike cries for his friend. When, some months ago, I found myself in the Crosby Street alley, and went up to talk to Giuseppe's parents, they would answer no questions before I had replied to one of theirs. It was thus interpreted to me by a girl from the basement, who had come in out of curiosity:

"Are youse goin' to give us any money?" Poor Giuseppe!

My other little friend was Pietro, of whom I spoke before. Perhaps of all the little life stories of poor Italian children I have come across in the course of years—and they are many and sad, most of them—none comes nearer to the hard everyday fact of those dreary tenements than his, exceptional as was his own heavy misfortune and its effect upon the boy. I met him first in the Mulberry Street police station, where he was interpreting the defense in a shooting case, having come in with the crowd from Jersey Street, where the thing had happened at his own door. With his rags, his dirty bare feet, and his shock of tousled hair, he seemed to fit in so entirely there of all places, and took so naturally to the ways of the police station, that he might have escaped my notice altogether but for his maimed hand and his oddly grave yet eager face, which no smile ever crossed despite his thirteen years. Of both, his story, when I afterward came to know it, gave me full explanation. He was the oldest son of a laborer, not "borned here" as the rest of his sisters and brothers. There were four of them, six in the family besides himself, as he put it: "2 sisters, 2 broders, 1 fader, 1 modder," subsisting on an unsteady maximum income of $9 a week, the rent taking always the earnings of one week in four. The home thus dearly paid for was a wretched room with a dark alcove for a bedchamber, in one of the vile old barracks that until very recently preserved to Jersey Street the memory of its former bad eminence as among the worst of the city's slums. Pietro had gone to the Sisters' school, blacking boots in a haphazard sort of way in his off-hours, until the year before, upon his mastering the alphabet, his education was considered to have sufficiently advanced to warrant his graduating into the ranks of the family wage earners, that were sadly in need of recruiting. A steady job of "shinin'" was found for him in an Eighth Ward saloon, and that afternoon, just before Christmas, he came home from school and putting his books away on the shelf for the next in order to use, ran across Broadway full of joyous anticipation of his new dignity in an independent job. He did not see the streetcar until it was fairly upon him, and then it was too late. They thought he was killed, but he was only crippled for life. When, after many months, he came out of the hospital, where the company had paid his board and posed as doing a generous thing, his bright smile was gone, his "shining" was at an end, and with it his career as it had been marked out for him. He must needs take up something new, and he was bending all his energies, when I met him, toward learning to make the "Englis' letter" with a degree of proficiency that would justify the hope of his doing something somewhere at sometime to make up for what he had lost. It was a far-off possibility yet. With the same end in view, probably, he was taking nightly writing lessons in his mother tongue from one of the perambulating schoolmasters who circulate in the Italian colony, peddling education cheap in lots to suit. In his sober, submissive way he was content with the prospect. It had its compensations. The boys who used to worry him, now let him alone. "When they see this," he said, holding up his scarred and misshapen arm, "they don't strike me no more." Then there was his fourteen-months-old baby brother who was beginning to walk, and could almost "make a letter." Pietro was much concerned about his education, anxious evidently that he should one day take his place. "I take him to school sometime," he said, piloting him across the floor and talking softly to the child in his own melodious Italian. I watched his grave, unchanging face.

*Pietro learning to make an Englis' letter*

"Pietro," I said, with a sudden yearning to know, "did you ever laugh?"

The boy glanced from the baby to me with a wistful look.

"I did wonst," he said, quietly, and went on his way. And I would gladly have forgotten that I ever asked the question, even as Pietro had forgotten his laugh.

# 3

# IN THE GREAT EAST SIDE TREADMILL

I F THE SIGHTSEER FINDS LESS to engage his interest in Jewtown than in the Bend, outside of the clamoring crowds in the Chasir—the Pig Market—he will discover enough to enlist his sympathies, provided he did not leave them behind when he crossed the Bowery. The loss is his own then. There is that in the desolation of child life in those teeming hives to make the shrivelled heart ache with compassion for its kind and throb with a new life of pain, enough to dispel some prejudices that are as old as our faith, and sometimes, I fear, a good deal stronger. The Russian exile adds to the offence of being an alien and a disturber of economic balances the worse one of being a Jew. Let those who cannot forgive this damaging fact possess their souls in patience. There is some evidence that the welcome he has received in those East Side tenements has done more than centuries of persecution could toward making him forget it himself.

The Italian who comes here gravitates naturally to the oldest and most dilapidated tenements in search of cheap rents, which he doesn't find. The Jew has another plan, characteristic of the man. He seeks out the biggest ones and makes the rent come within his means by taking in boarders, "sweating" his flat to the point of police intervention. That that point is a long way beyond human decency, let alone comfort, an instance from Ludlow Street, that came to my notice while writing this, quite clearly demonstrates. The offender was a tailor, who lived with his wife, two children, and two boarders in two rooms on the top floor. [It is always the top floor; in fifteen years of active service as a police reporter I have had to climb to the top floor five times for every one my business was further down, irrespective of where the tenement was or what kind of people lived in it. Crime, suicide, and police business generally seem to bear the same relation to the stairs in a tenement that they bear to poverty itself. The more stairs the more trouble. The deepest poverty is at home in the attic.] But this tailor, with his immediate household, including the boarders, he occupied the larger of the two rooms. The other, a bedroom eight feet square, he sublet to a second tailor and his wife; which couple, following his example as their opportunities allowed, divided the bedroom in two by hanging a curtain in the middle, took one-half for themselves and let the other half to still another tailor with a wife and child. A midnight inspection by the sanitary police was followed by the arrest of the housekeeper and the original tailor, and they were fined or warned in the police court, I forget which. It doesn't much matter. That the real point was missed was shown by the appearance of the owner of the house, a woman, at Sanitary Headquarters, on the day following, with the charge against the policeman that he was robbing her of her tenants.

The story of inhuman packing of human swarms, of bitter poverty, of landlord greed, of sweater slavery, of darkness and squalor and misery, which these tenements have to tell, is equalled, I suppose, nowhere in a civilized land. Despite the prevalence of the boarder, who is usually a married man, come over alone the better to be able to prepare the way for the family, the census[3] shows that fifty-four percent of the entire population of immigrant Jews were children, or under age. Every steamer has added to their number since, and judging from the sights one sees daily in the office of the United Hebrew Charities, and from the general appearance of Ludlow Street, the proportion of children has suffered no decrease. Let the reader who would know for himself what they are like, and what their chances are, take that street some evening from Hester Street down and observe what he sees going on there. Not that it is the only place where he can find them. The census I spoke of embraced forty-five streets in the Seventh, Tenth, and Thirteenth Wards. But at that end of Ludlow Street the tenements are taller and the crowds always denser than anywhere else. Let him watch the little pedlars hawking their shoestrings, their matches, and their penny paper pads, with the restless energy that seems so strangely out of proportion to the reward it reaps; the half-grown children staggering under heavy bundles of clothes from the sweater's shop; the ragamuffins at their fretful play, play yet, discouraged though it be by the nasty surroundings—thank goodness, every year brings its Passover with the scrubbing brigade to Ludlow Street, and the dirt is shifted from the houses to the streets once anyhow; if it does find its way back, something may be lost on the way—the crowding, the pushing for elbow room, the wails of bruised babies that keep falling downstairs, or rolling off the stoop, and the raids of angry mothers swooping down upon their offspring and distributing thumps right and left to pay for the bruises, an eye for an eye, a tooth for a tooth. Whose eye, whose tooth, is of less account in Jewtown than that the capital put out bears lawful interest in kind. What kind of interest may society some day expect to reap from ghettos like these, where even the sunny temper of childhood is soured by want and woe, or smothered in filth? It is a long time since I have heard a good honest laugh, a child's gleeful shout, in Ludlow Street. Angry cries, jeers, enough. They are as much part of the place as the dirty pavements; but joyous, honest laughs, like soap and water, are at a premium there.

But children laugh because they are happy. They are not happy in Ludlow Street. Nobody is except the landlord. Why should they be? Born to toil and trouble, they claim their heritage early and part with it late. There is even less time than there is room for play in Jewtown, good reason why the quality of the play is poor. There is work for the weakest hands, a step for the smallest feet in the vast treadmill of these East Side homes. A thing is worth there what it will bring. All other considerations, ambitions, desires, yield to that. Education pays as an investment, and therefore the child is sent to school. The moment his immediate value as a worker overbalances the gain in prospect by keeping him at his books, he goes to the shop. The testimony of Jewish observers, who have had quite unusual opportunities for judging, is that the average age at which these children leave school for good is rather below twelve than beyond it, by which time their work at home, helping their parents, has qualified them to earn wages that will more than pay for their keep. They are certainly on the safe side in their reckoning, if the children are not. The legal age for shop employment is fourteen. On my visits among the homes, workshops, and evening schools of Jewtown, I was always struck by the number of diminutive wage earners who were invariably "just fourteen." It was clearly not the child which the tenement had dwarfed in their case, but the memory or the moral sense of the parents.

If, indeed, the shop were an exchange for the home, if the child quit the one upon entering the other, there might be little objection to make, but too often they are two names for the same thing; where they are not, the shop is probably preferable, bad as that may be. When, in the midnight hour, the noise of the sewing machine was stilled at last, I have gone the rounds of Ludlow and Hester and Essex Streets among the poorest of the Russian Jews, with the sanitary police, and counted often four, five, and even six of the little ones in a single bed, sometimes a shakedown on the hard floor, often a pile of half-finished clothing brought home from the sweater, in the stuffy rooms of their tenements. In one I visited very lately, the only bed was occupied by the entire family lying lengthwise and crosswise, literally in layers, three children at the feet, all except a boy of ten or twelve, for whom there was no room. He slept with his clothes on to keep him warm, in a pile of rags just inside the door. It seemed to me impossible that families of children could be raised at all in such dens as I had my daily and nightly walks in. And yet the vital statistics and all close observation agree in allotting to these Jews even an unusual degree of good health. The records of the Sanitary Bureau show that while the Italians have the highest death rate, the mortality in the lower part of the Tenth Ward, of which Ludlow Street is the heart and type, is the lowest in the city. Even the baby death rate is very low. But for the fact that the ravages of diphtheria, croup, and measles run up the record in the houses occupied entirely by tailors—in other words, in the sweater district, where contagion always runs riot [4] —the Tenth Ward would seem to be the healthiest spot in the city, as well as the dirtiest and the most crowded. The temperate habits of the Jew and his freedom from enfeebling vices generally must account for this, along with his marvellous vitality. I cannot now recall ever having known a Jewish drunkard. On the other hand, I have never come across a Prohibitionist among them. The absence of the one renders the other superfluous.

*"Slept in that cellar four years"*

It was only last winter I had occasion to visit repeatedly a double tenement at the lower end of Ludlow Street, which the police census showed to contain 297 tenants, 45 of whom were under five years of age, not counting 3 pedlars who slept in the mouldy cellar, where the water was ankle deep on the mud floor. The feeblest ray of daylight never found its way down there, the hatches having been carefully covered with rags and matting, but freshets often did. Sometimes the water rose to the height of a foot, and never quite soaked away in the dryest season. It was an awful place, and by the light of my candle the three, with their unkempt beards and hair and sallow faces, looked more like hideous ghosts than living men. Yet they had slept there among and upon decaying fruit and wreckage of all sorts from the tenement for over three years, according to their own and the housekeeper's statements. There had been four. One was then in the hospital, but not because of any ill effect the cellar had had upon him. He had been run over in the street and was making the most of his vacation, charging it up to the owner of the wagon, whom he was getting ready to sue for breaking his leg. Upstairs, especially in the rear tenement, I found the scene from the cellar repeated with variations. In one room a family of seven, including the oldest daughter, a young woman of eighteen, and her brother, a year older than she, slept in a common bed made on the floor of the kitchen, and manifested scarcely any concern at our appearance. A complaint to the Board of Health resulted in an overhauling that showed the tenement to be unusually bad even for that bad spot; but when we came to look up its record, from the standpoint of the vital statistics, we discovered that not only had there not been a single death in the house during the whole year, but on the third floor lived a woman over a hundred years old, who had been there a long time. I was never more surprised in my life, and while we laughed at it, I confess it came nearer to upsetting my faith in the value of statistics than anything I had seen till then. And yet I had met with similar experiences, if not quite so striking, often enough to convince me that poverty and want beget their own power to resist the evil influences of their worst surroundings. I was at a loss how to put this plainly to the good people who often asked wonderingly why the children of the poor one saw in the street seemed generally such a thriving lot, until a slip of Mrs. Partington's discriminating tongue did it for me: "Manured to the soil." That is it. In so far as it does not merely seem so—one does not see the sick and suffering—that puts it right.

Whatever the effect upon the physical health of the children, it cannot be otherwise, of course, than that such conditions should corrupt their morals. I have the authority of a distinguished rabbi, whose field and daily walk are among the poorest of his people, to support me in the statement that the moral tone of the young girls is distinctly lower than it was. The entire absence of privacy in their homes and the foul contact of the sweaters' shops, where men and women work side by side from morning till night, scarcely half clad in the hot summer weather, does for the girls what the street completes in the boy. But for the patriarchal family life of the Jew that is his strongest virtue, their ruin would long since have been complete. It is that which pilots him safely through shoals upon which the Gentile would have been inevitably wrecked. It is that which keeps the almshouse from casting its shadow over Ludlow Street to add to its gloom. It is the one quality which redeems, and on the Sabbath eve when he gathers his household about his board, scant though the fare be, dignifies the darkest slum of Jewtown.

How strong is this attachment to home and kindred that makes the Jew cling to the humblest hearth and gather his children and his children's children about it, though grinding poverty leave them only a bare crust to share, I saw in the case of little Jette Brodsky, who strayed away from her own door, looking for her papa. They were strangers and ignorant and poor, so that weeks went by before they could make their loss known and get a hearing, and meanwhile Jette, who had been picked up and taken to Police Headquarters, had been hidden away in an asylum, given another name when nobody came to claim her, and had been quite forgotten. But in the two years that passed before she was found at last, her empty chair stood ever by her father's, at the family board, and no Sabbath eve but heard his prayer for the restoration of their lost one. It happened once that I came in on a Friday evening at the breaking of bread, just as the four candles upon the table had been lit with the Sabbath blessing upon the home and all it sheltered. Their light fell on little else than empty plates and anxious faces; but in the patriarchal host who arose and bade the guest welcome with a dignity a king might have envied I recognized with difficulty the humble pedlar I had known only from the street and from the police office, where he hardly ventured beyond the door.

But the tenement that has power to turn purest gold to dross digs a pit for the Jew even through this virtue that has been his shield against its power for evil. In its atmosphere it turns too often to a curse by helping to crowd his lodgings, already overflowing, beyond the point of official forbearance. Then follow orders to "reduce" the number of tenants that mean increased rent, which the family cannot pay, or the breaking up of the home. An appeal to avert such a calamity came to the Board of Health recently from one of the refugee tenements. The tenant was a man with a houseful of children, too full for the official scale as applied to the flat, and his plea was backed by the influence of his only friend in need—the family undertaker. There was something so cruelly suggestive in the idea that the laugh it raised died without an echo.

The census of the sweaters' district gave a total of 23,405 children under six years, and 21,285 between six and fourteen, in a population of something over a hundred and eleven thousand Russian, Polish, and Roumanian Jews in the three wards mentioned; 15,567 are set down as "children over fourteen." According to the record, scarce one-third of the heads of families had become naturalized citizens, though the average of their stay in the United States was between nine and ten years. The very language of our country was to them a strange tongue, understood and spoken by only 15,837 of the fifty thousand and odd adults enumerated. Seven thousand of the rest spoke only German, five thousand Russian, and over twenty-one thousand, could only make themselves understood to each other, never to the world around them, in the strange jargon that passes for Hebrew on the East Side, but is really a mixture of a dozen known dialects and tongues and of some that were never known or heard anywhere else. In the census it is down as just what it is—jargon, and nothing else.

Here, then, are conditions as unfavorable to the satisfactory, even safe, development of child life in the chief American city as could well be imagined; more unfavorable even than with the Bohemians, who have at least their faith in common with us, if safety lies in the merging through the rising generation of the discordant elements into a common harmony. A community set apart, set sharply against the rest in every clashing interest, social and industrial; foreign in language, in faith, and in tradition; repaying dislike with distrust; expanding under the new relief from oppression in the unpopular qualities of greed and contentiousness fostered by ages of tyranny unresistingly borne. Clearly, if ever there was need of moulding any material for the citizenship that awaits it, it is with this; and if ever trouble might be expected to beset the effort, it might be looked for here. But it is not so. The record shows that of the sixty thousand children, including the fifteen thousand young men and women over fourteen who earn a large share of the money that pays for rent and food, and the twenty-three thousand toddlers under six years, fully one-third go to school. Deducting the two extremes, little more than a thousand children of between six and fourteen years, that is, of school age, were put down as receiving no instruction at the time the census was taken; but it is not at all likely that this condition was permanent in the case of the greater number of these. The poorest Hebrew knows—the poorer he is, the better he knows it—that knowledge is power, and power as the means of getting on in the world that has spurned him so long is what his soul yearns for. He lets no opportunity slip to obtain it. Day and night schools are crowded by his children, who are everywhere forging ahead of their Christian school fellows, taking more than their share of prizes and promotions. Every synagogue, every second rear tenement or dark backyard, has its school and its schoolmaster with his scourge to intercept those who might otherwise escape. In the census there are put down 251 Jewish teachers as living in these tenements, a large number of whom conduct such schools, so that, as the children form always more than one-half of the population in the Jewish quarter, the evidence is after all that even here, with the tremendous inpour of a destitute, ignorant people, and with the undoubted employment of child labor on a large scale, the cause of progress along the safe line is holding its own.

*Synagogue school in a Hester Street tenement*

It is true that these tenement schools that absorb several thousand children are not what they might be from a sanitary point of view. It is also true that heretofore nothing but Hebrew and the Talmud have been taught there. But to the one evil the health authorities have recently been aroused; of the other, the wise and patriotic men who are managing the Baron de Hirsch charity are making a useful handle by gathering the teachers in and setting them to learn English. Their new knowledge will soon be reflected in their teaching, and the Hebrew schools become primary classes in the system of public education. The school in a Hester Street tenement that is shown in the picture is a fair specimen of its kind—by no means one of the worst—and so is the backyard behind it, that serves as the children's playground, with its dirty mud puddles, its slop barrels and broken flags, and its foul tenement house surroundings. Both fall in well with the home lives and environment of the unhappy little wretches whose daily horizon they limit. They get there the first instruction they receive in the only tongues with which the teachers are familiar, Hebrew and the jargon, in the only studies which they are competent to teach, the Talmud and the Prophets. Until they are six years old they are under the "Melammed's" rod all day; after that only in the interval between public school and supper. It is practically the only religious instruction the poorest Jewish children receive, but it is claimed by some of their rabbis that they had better have none at all. The daily transition, they say, from the bright and, by comparison, aesthetically beautiful public schoolroom to these dark and inhospitable dens, with which the faith that has brought so many miseries upon their race comes to be inseparably associated in the child's mind as he grows up, tends to reflections that breed indifference, if not infidelity, in the young. It would not be strange if this were so. If the schools, through this process, also help pave the way for the acceptance of the Messiah heretofore rejected, which I greatly doubt, it may be said to be the only instance in which the East Side tenement has done its tenants a good Christian turn.

There is no more remarkable class in any school than that of these Melammedim, [5] that may be seen in session any week day forenoon, save on Saturday, of course, in the Hebrew Institute in East Broadway. Old bearded men struggling through the intricacies of the first reader, "a cow, a cat," and all the rest of childish learning, with a rapt attention and a concentration of energy as if they were devoting themselves to the most heroic of tasks, which, indeed, they are, for the good that may come of it cannot easily be overestimated. As an educational measure it may be said to be getting down to first principles with a vengeance.

When the reader has been mastered, brief courses in the history of the United States, the Declaration of Independence, and the Constitution follow. The test of proficiency in the pupil is his ability to translate the books of the Old Testament, with which he is familiar, of course, from Hebrew into English, and *vice versa*.

*Class of Melammedim learning English*

The Melammed is rarely a dull scholar. No one knows better than he, to whom it has come only in the evening of his hard life, the value of the boon that is offered him. One of the odd group that was deep in the lesson of the day had five children at home, whom he had struggled to bring up on an income of ten dollars a week. The oldest, a bright boy who had graduated with honor, despite the patch on his trousers, from the public school, was ambitious to go to college, and the father had saved and pinched in a thousand ways to gratify his desire. One of the managers of the Institute who knew how the family were starving on half rations, had offered the father, a short time before, to get the boy employment in a store at three dollars a week. It was a tremendous temptation, for the money was badly needed at home. But the old man put it resolutely away from him. "No," he said, "I must send him to college. He shall have the chance that was denied his father." And he was as good as his word. And so was the lad, a worthy son of a worthy father. When I met him he had already proved himself a long way the best student in his class.

In other classrooms in the great building, which is devoted entirely to the cause of Americanizing the young Russian immigrants, hundreds of children get daily their first lessons in English and in patriotism in simultaneous doses. The two are inseparable in the beneficent plan of their instructors. Their effort is to lay hold of the children of the newcomers at once; tender years are no barrier. For the toddlers there are kindergarten classes, with play the street has had no chance to soil. And while playing they learn to speak the strange new tongue and to love the pretty flag with the stars that is everywhere in sight. The night school gathers in as many as can be corralled of those who are big enough, if not old enough, to work. The ease and rapidity with which they learn is equalled only by their good behavior and close attention while in school. There is no whispering and no rioting at these desks, no trial of strength with the teacher, as in the Italian ragged schools, where the question who is boss has always to be settled before the business of the school can proceed. These children come to learn. Even from the Christian schools in the district that gather in their share comes the same testimony. All the disturbance they report was made by their elders, outside the school, in the street. In the Hebrew Institute the average of absence for all causes was, during the first year, less than eight percent of the registered attendance, and in nearly every case sickness furnished a valid excuse. In a year and a half the principal had only been called upon three times to reprove an obstreperous pupil, in a total of 1,500. While I was visiting one of the day classes a little girl who had come from Moscow only two months before presented herself with her green vaccination card from the steamer. She understood already perfectly the questions put to her and was able to answer most of them in English. Boys of eight and nine years who had come over as many months before, knowing only the jargon of their native village, read to me whole pages from the reader with almost perfect accent, and did sums on the blackboard that would have done credit to the average boy of twelve in our public schools. Figuring is always their strong point. They would not be Jews if it was not.

In the evening classes the girls of "fourteen" flourished, as everywhere in Jewtown. There were many who were much older, and some who were a long way yet from that safe goal. One sober-faced little girl, who wore a medal for faithful attendance and who could not have been much over ten, if as old as that, said that she "went out dressmaking" and so helped her mother. Another, who was even smaller and had been here just three weeks, yet understood what was said to her, explained in broken German that she was learning to work at "Blumen" in a Grand Street shop, and would soon be able to earn wages that would help support the family of four children, of whom she was the oldest. The girl who sat in the seat with her was from a Hester Street tenement. Her clothes showed that she was very poor. She read very fluently on demand a story about a big dog that tried to run away, or something, "when he had a chance." When she came to translate what she had read into German, which many of the Russian children understand, she got along until she reached the word "chance." There she stopped, bewildered. It was the one idea of which her brief life had no embodiment, the thing it had altogether missed.

The Declaration of Independence half the children knew by heart before they had gone over it twice. To help them along it is printed in the schoolbooks with a Hebrew translation and another in jargon, a "Jewish-German," in parallel columns and the explanatory notes in Hebrew. The Constitution of the United States is treated in the same manner, but it is too hard, or too wearisome, for the children. They "hate" it, says the teacher, while the Declaration of Independence takes their fancy at sight. They understand it in their own practical way, and the spirit of the immortal document suffers no loss from the annotations of Ludlow Street, if its dignity is sometimes slightly rumpled.

"When," said the teacher to one of the pupils, a little working girl from an Essex Street sweater's shop, "the Americans could no longer put up with the abuse of the English who governed the colonies, what occurred then?"

"A strike!" responded the girl, promptly. She had found it here on coming and evidently thought it a national institution upon which the whole scheme of our government was founded.

It was curious to find the low voices of the children, particularly the girls, an impediment to instruction in this school. They could sometimes hardly be heard for the noise in the street, when the heat made it necessary to have the windows open. But shrillness is not characteristic even of the Pig Market when it is noisiest and most crowded. Some of the children had sweet singing voices. One especially, a boy with straight red hair and a freckled face, chanted in a plaintive minor key the One Hundred and Thirtieth Psalm, "Out of the depths" etc., and the harsh gutturals of the Hebrew became sweet harmony until the sad strain brought tears to our eyes.

The dirt of Ludlow Street is all-pervading and the children do not escape it. Rather, it seems to have a special affinity for them, or they for the dirt. The duty of imparting the fundamental lesson of cleanliness devolves upon a special school officer, a matron, who makes the round of the classes every morning with her alphabet: a cake of soap, a sponge, and a pitcher of water, and picks out those who need to be washed. One little fellow expressed his disapproval of this programme in the first English composition he wrote, as follows:

```
              Indians.
Indians do not want to wash because
they like not water. I wish I was a
Indian.
```

Despite this hint, the lesson is enforced upon the children, but there is no evidence that it bears fruit in their homes to any noticeable extent, as is the case with the Italians I spoke of. The homes are too hopeless, the grind too unceasing. The managers know it and have little hope of the older immigrants. It is toward getting hold of their children that they bend every effort, and with a success that shows how easily these children can be moulded for good or for bad. Nor do they let go their grasp of them until the job is finished. The United Hebrew Charities maintain trade schools for those who show aptness for such work, and a very creditable showing they make. The public school receives all those who graduate from what might be called the American primary in East Broadway.

The smoky torches on many hucksters' carts threw their uncertain yellow light over Hester Street as I watched the children troop homeward from school one night. Eight little pedlars hawking their wares had stopped under the lamp on the corner to bargain with each other for want of cash customers. They were engaged in a desperate but vain attempt to cheat one of their number who was deaf and dumb. I bought a quire of notepaper of the mute for a cent and instantly the whole crew beset me in a fierce rivalry, to which I put a hasty end by buying out the little mute's poor stock—ten cents covered it all—and after he had counted out the quires, gave it back to him. At this act of unheard-of generosity the seven, who had remained to witness the transfer, stood speechless. As I went my way, with a sudden common impulse they kissed their hands at me, all rivalry forgotten in their admiration, and kept kissing, bowing, and salaaming until I was out of sight. "Not bad children," I mused as I went along, "good stuff in them, whatever their faults." I thought of the poor boy's stock, of the cheapness of it, and then it occurred to me that he had charged me just twice as much for the paper I gave him back as for the penny quire I bought. But when I went back to give him a piece of my mind the boys were gone.

# 4

## TONY AND HIS TRIBE

I HAVE A LITTLE FRIEND SOMEWHERE in Mott Street whose picture comes up before me. I wish I could show it to the reader, but to photograph Tony is one of the unattained ambitions of my life. He is one of the whimsical birds one sees when he hasn't got a gun, and then never long enough in one place to give one a chance to get it. A ragged coat three sizes at least too large for the boy, though it has evidently been cropped to meet his case, hitched by its one button across a bare brown breast; one sleeve patched on the under side with a piece of sole leather that sticks out straight, refusing to be reconciled; trousers that boasted a seat once, but probably not while Tony has worn them; two left boots tied on with packing twine, bare legs in them the color of the leather, heel and toe showing through; a shock of sunburnt hair struggling through the rent in the old straw hat; two frank, laughing eyes under its broken brim—that is Tony.

He stood over the gutter the day I met him, reaching for a handful of mud with which to "paste" another hoodlum who was shouting defiance from across the street. He did not see me, and when my hand touched his shoulder his whole little body shrank with a convulsive shudder, as from an expected blow. Quick as a flash he dodged, and turning, out of reach, confronted the unknown enemy, gripping tight his handful of mud. I had a bunch of white pinks which a young lady had given me half an hour before for one of my little friends. "They are yours," I said, and held them out to him, "take them."

Doubt, delight, and utter bewilderment struggled in the boy's face. He said not one word, but when he had brought his mind to believe that it really was so, clutched the flowers with one eager, grimy fist, held them close against his bare breast, and, shielding them with the other, ran as fast as his legs could carry him down the street. Not far, fifty feet away he stopped short, looked back, hesitated a moment, then turned on his track as fast as he had come. He brought up directly in front of me, a picture a painter would have loved, ragamuffin that he was, with the flowers held so tightly against his brown skin, scraped out with one foot and made one of the funniest little bows.

"Thank you," he said. Then he was off. Down the street I saw squads of children like himself running out to meet him. He darted past and through them all, never stopping, but pointing back my way, and in a minute there bore down upon me a crowd of little ones, running breathless with desperate entreaty: "Oh, mister! Give *me* a flower." Hot tears of grief and envy—human passions are much the same in rags and in silks—fell when they saw I had no more. But by that time Tony was safe.

And where did he run so fast? For whom did he shield the "posy" so eagerly, so faithfully, that ragged little wretch that was all mud and patches? I found out afterward when I met him giving his sister a ride in a dismantled tomato crate, likely enough "hooked" at the grocer's. It was for his mother. In the dark hovel he called home, to the level of which all it sheltered had long since sunk through the brutal indifference of a drunken father, my lady's pinks blossomed and, long after they were withered and yellow, still stood in their cracked jar, visible token of something that had entered Tony's life and tenement with sweetening touch that day for the first time. Alas! for the last, too, perhaps. I saw Tony off and on for a while and then he was as suddenly lost as he was found, with all that belonged to him. Moved away— put out, probably—and, except the assurance that they were still somewhere in Mott Street, even the saloon could give me no clue to them.

I gained Tony's confidence, almost, in the time I knew him. There was a little misunderstanding between us that had still left a trace of embarrassment when Tony disappeared. It was when I asked him one day, while we were not yet "solid," if he ever went to school. He said "sometimes," and backed off. I am afraid Tony lied that time. The evidence was against him. It was different with little Katie, my nine-year-old housekeeper of the sober look. Her I met in the Fifty-second Street Industrial School, where she picked up such crumbs of learning as were for her in the intervals of her housework. The serious responsibilities of life had come early to Katie. On the top floor of a tenement in West Forty-ninth Street she was keeping house for her older sister and two brothers, all of whom worked in the hammock factory, earning from $4.50 to $1.50 a week. They had moved together when their mother died and the father brought home another wife. Their combined income was something like $9.50 a week, and the simple furniture was bought on installments. But it was all clean, if poor. Katie did the cleaning and the cooking of the plain kind. They did not run much to fancy cooking, I guess. She scrubbed and swept and went to school, all as a matter of course, and ran the house generally, with an occasional lift from the neighbors in the tenement, who were, if anything, poorer than they. The picture shows what a sober, patient, sturdy little thing she was, with that dull life wearing on her day by day. At the school they loved her for her quiet, gentle ways. She got right up when asked and stood for her picture without a question and without a smile.

"What kind of work do you do?" I asked, thinking to interest her while I made ready.

"I scrubs," she replied, promptly, and her look guaranteed that what she scrubbed came out clean.

*"I scrubs"—Katie, who keeps house in West Forty-ninth Street*

Katie was one of the little mothers whose work never ends. Very early the cross of her sex had been laid upon the little shoulders that bore it so stoutly. Tony's, as likely as not, would never begin. There were earmarks upon the boy that warranted the suspicion. They were the earmarks of the street to which his care and education had been left. The only work of which it heartily approves is that done by other people. I came upon Tony once under circumstances that foreshadowed his career with tolerable distinctness. He was at the head of a gang of little shavers like himself, none over eight or nine, who were swaggering around in a ring, in the middle of the street, rigged out in war paint and hen feathers, shouting as they went: "Whoop! We are the Houston Streeters." They meant no harm and they were not doing any just then. It was all in the future, but it was there, and no mistake. The game which they were then rehearsing was one in which the policeman who stood idly swinging his club on the corner would one day take a hand, and not always the winning one.

The fortunes of Tony and Katie, simple and soon told as they are, encompass as between the covers of a book the whole story of the children of the poor, the story of the bad their lives struggle vainly to conquer, and the story of the good that crops out in spite of it. Sickness, that always finds the poor unprepared and soon leaves them the choice of beggary or starvation, hard times, the death of the breadwinner, or the part played by the growler in the poverty of the home, may vary the theme for the elders; for the children it is the same sad story, with little variation, and that rarely of a kind to improve. Happily for their peace of mind, they are the least concerned about it. In New York, at least, the poor children are not the stunted repining lot we have heard of as being hatched in cities abroad. Stunted in body perhaps. It was said of Napoleon that he shortened the average stature of the Frenchman one inch by getting all the tall men killed in his wars. The tenement has done that for New York. Only the other day one of the best known clergymen in the city, who tries to attract the boys to his church on the East Side by a very practical interest in them, and succeeds admirably in doing it, told me that the drillmaster of his cadet corps was in despair because he could barely find two or three among half a hundred lads verging on manhood, over five feet six inches high. It is queer what different ways there are of looking at a thing. My medical friend finds in the fact that poverty stunts the body what he is pleased to call a beautiful provision of nature to prevent unnecessary suffering: there is less for the poverty to pinch then. It is self-defense, he says, and he claims that the consensus of learned professional opinion is with him. Yet, when this shortened sufferer steals a loaf of bread to make the pinching bear less hard on what is left, he is called a thief, thrown into jail, and frowned upon by the community that just now saw in his case a beautiful illustration of the operation of natural laws for the defense of the man.

Stunted morally, yes! It could not well be otherwise. But stunted in spirits—never! As for repining, there is no such word in his vocabulary. He accepts life as it comes to him and gets out of it what he can. If that is not much, he is not justly to blame for not giving back more to the community of which by and by he will be a responsible member. The kind of the soil determines the quality of the crop. The tenement is his soil and it pervades and shapes his young life. It is the tenement that gives up the child to the street in tender years to find there the home it denied him. Its exorbitant rents rob him of the schooling that is his one chance to elude its grasp, by compelling his enrolment in the army of wage earners before he has learned to read. Its alliance with the saloon guides his baby feet along the well-beaten track of the growler that completes his ruin. Its power to pervert and corrupt has always to be considered, its point of view always to be taken to get the perspective in dealing with the poor, or the cart will seem to be forever getting before the horse in a way not to be understood. We had a girl once at our house in the country who left us suddenly after a brief stay and went back to her old tenement life because "all the green hurt her eyes so." She meant just what she said, though she did not know herself what ailed her. It was the slum that had its fatal grip upon her. She longed for its noise, its bustle, and its crowds, and laid it all to the green grass and the trees that were new to her as steady company.

From this tenement the street offered, until the kindergarten came not long ago, the one escape, does yet for the great mass of children—a Hobson's choice, for it is hard to say which is the most corrupting. The opportunities rampant in the one are a sad commentary on the sure defilement of the other. What could be expected of a standard of decency like this one, of a household of tenants who assured me that Mrs. M—, at that moment under arrest for half clubbing her husband to death, was "a very good, a very decent woman indeed, and if she did get full, he (the husband) was not much." Or of the rule of good conduct laid down by a young girl, found beaten and senseless in the street up in the Annexed District last autumn: "Them was two of the fellers from Frog Hollow," she said, resentfully, when I asked who struck her, "them toughs don't know how to behave theirselves when they see a lady in liquor."

Hers was the standard of the street, the other's that of the tenement. Together they stamp the child's life with the vicious touch which is sometimes only the caricature of the virtues of a better soil. Under the rough burr lie undeveloped qualities of good and of usefulness, rather, perhaps, of the capacity for them, that crop out in constant exhibitions of loyalty, of gratitude, and true-heartedness, a never-ending source of encouragement and delight to those who have made their cause their own and have in their true sympathy the key to the best that is in the children. The testimony of a teacher for twenty-five years in one of the ragged schools, who has seen the shanty neighborhood that surrounded her at the start give place to mile-long rows of big tenements, leaves no room for doubt as to the influence the change has had upon the children. With the disappearance of the shanties—homesteads in effect, however humble—and the coming of the tenement crowds, there has been a distinct descent in the scale of refinement among the children, if one may use the term. The crowds and the loss of home privacy, with the increased importance of the street as a factor, account for it. The general tone has been lowered, while at the same time, by reason of the greater rescue efforts put forward, the original amount of ignorance has been reduced. The big loafer of the old day, who could neither read nor write, has been eliminated to a large extent, and his loss is our gain. The tough who has taken his place is able at least to spell his way through "The Bandits' Cave," the pattern exploits of Jesse James and his band, and the newspaper accounts of the latest raid in which he had a hand. Perhaps that explains why he is more dangerous than the old loafer. The transition period is always critical, and a little learning is proverbially a dangerous thing. It may be that in the day to come, when we shall have got the grip of our compulsory school law in good earnest, there will be an educational standard even for the tough, by which time he will, I think, have ceased to exist from sheer disgust, if for no other reason. At present he is in no immediate danger of extinction from such a source. It is not how much book learning the boy can get, but how little he can get along with, and that is very little indeed. He knows how to make a little go a long way, however, and to serve on occasion a very practical purpose; as, for instance, when I read recently on the wall of the church next to my office in Mulberry Street this observation, chalked in an awkward hand half the length of the wall: "Mary McGee is engagd to the feller in the alley." Quite apt, I should think, to make Mary show her colors and to provoke the fight with the rival "feller" for which the writer was evidently spoiling. I shall get back, farther on, to the question of the children's schooling. It is so beset by lies ordinarily as to be seldom answered as promptly and as honestly as in the case of a little fellow whom I found in front of St. George's Church, engaged in the aesthetic occupation of pelting the Friends' Seminary across the way with mud. There were two of them, and when I asked them the question that estranged Tony, the wicked one dug his fists deep down in the pockets of his blue-jeans trousers and shook his head gloomily. He couldn't read; didn't know how; never did.

"He?" said the other, who could, "He? He don't learn nothing. He throws stones." The wicked one nodded. It was the extent of his education.

But if the three R's suffer neglect among the children of the poor, their lessons in the three D's—Dirt, Discomfort, and Disease—that form the striking features of their environment, are early and thorough enough. The two latter, at least, are synonymous terms, if dirt and discomfort are not. Any dispensary doctor knows of scores of cases of ulceration of the eye that are due to the frequent rubbing of dirty faces with dirty little hands. Worse filth diseases than that find a fertile soil in the tenements, as the health officers learn when typhus and smallpox break out. It is not the desperate diet of ignorant mothers, who feed their month-old babies with sausage, beer, and Limburger cheese, that alone accounts for the great infant mortality among the poor in the tenements. The dirt and the darkness in their homes contribute their full share, and the landlord is more to blame than the mother. He holds the key to the situation which her ignorance fails to grasp, and it is he who is responsible for much of the unfounded and unnecessary prejudice against foreigners, who come here willing enough to fall in with the ways of the country that are shown to them. The way he shows them is not the way of decency. I am convinced that the really injurious foreigners in this community, outside of the walking delegate's tribe, are the foreign landlords of two kinds: those who, born in poverty abroad, have come up through tenement house life to the ownership of tenement property, with all the bad traditions of such a career; and the absentee landlords of native birth who live and spend their rents away from home, without knowing or caring what the condition of their property is, so the income from it suffer no diminution. There are honorable exceptions to the first class, but few enough to the latter to make them hardly worth mentioning.

To a good many of the children, or rather to their parents, this latter statement and the experience that warrants it must have a sadly familiar sound. The Irish element is still an important factor in New York's tenements, though it is yielding one stronghold after another to the Italian foe. It lost its grip on the Five Points and the Bend long ago, and at this writing the time seems not far distant when it must vacate for good also that classic ground of the Kerryman, Cherry Hill. It is Irish only by descent, however; the children are Americans, as they will not fail to convince the doubter. A school census of this district, the Fourth Ward, taken last winter, discovered 2,016 children between the ages of five and fourteen years. No less than 1,706 of them were put down as native born, but only one-fourth, or 519, had American parents. Of the others 572 had Irish and 536 Italian parents. Uptown, in many of the poor tenement localities, in Poverty Gap, in

Battle Row, and in Hell's Kitchen, in short, wherever the gang flourishes, the Celt is still supreme and seasons the lump enough to give it his own peculiar flavor, easily discovered through its "native" guise in the story of the children of the poor.

The case of one Irish family that exhibits a shoal which lies always close to the track of ignorant poverty is even now running in my mind, vainly demanding a practical solution. I may say that I have inherited it from professional philanthropists, who have struggled with it for more than half a dozen years without finding the way out they sought.

There were five children when they began, depending on a mother who had about given up the struggle as useless. The father was a loafer. When I took them the children numbered ten, and the struggle was long since over. The family bore the pauper stamp, and the mother's tears, by a transition imperceptible probably to herself, had become its stock in trade. Two of the children were working, earning all the money that came in; those that were not lay about in the room, watching the charity visitor in a way and with an intentness that betrayed their interest in the mother's appeal. It required very little experience to make the prediction that, shortly, ten pauper families would carry on the campaign of the one against society, if those children lived to grow up. And they were not to blame, of course. I scarcely know which was most to be condemned, when we tried to break the family up by throwing it on the street as a necessary step to getting possession of the children—the politician who tripped us up with his influence in the court, or the landlord who had all those years made the poverty on the second floor pan out a golden interest. It was the outrageous rent for the filthy den that had been the most effective argument with sympathizing visitors. Their pity had represented to him, as nearly as I could make out, for eight long years, a capital of $2,600 invested at six percent, payable monthly. The idea of moving was preposterous;

for what other landlord would take in a homeless family with ten children and no income?

Children anywhere suffer little discomfort from mere dirt. As an ingredient of mud pies it may be said to be not unwholesome. Play with the dirt is better than none without it. In the tenements the children and the dirt are sworn and loyal friends. In his early raids upon the established order of society, the gutter backs the boy up to the best of its ability, with more or less exasperating success. In the hot summer days, when he tries to sneak into the free baths with every fresh batch, twenty times a day, wretched little repeater that he is, it comes to his rescue against the policeman at the door. Fresh mud smeared on the face serves as a ticket of admission which no one can refuse. At least so he thinks, but in his anxiety he generally overdoes it and arouses the suspicion of the policeman, who, remembering that he was once a boy himself, feels of his hair and reads his title there. When it is a mission that is to be raided, or a "Dutch" grocer's shop, or a parade of the rival gang from the next block, the gutter furnishes ammunition that is always handy. Dirt is a great leveller; [6] it is no respecter of persons or principles, and neither is the boy where it abounds. In proportion as it accumulates such raids increase, the Fresh Air Funds lose their grip, the saloon flourishes, and turbulence grows. Down from the Fourth Ward, where there is not much else, this wail came recently from a Baptist Mission Church: "The Temple stands in a hard spot and neighborhood. The past week we had to have arrested two fellows for throwing stones into the house and causing annoyance. On George Washington's Birthday we had not put a flag over the door on Henry Street half an hour before it was stolen. When they neither respect the house of prayer or the Stars and Stripes one can feel young America is in a bad state." The pastor added that it was a comfort to him to know that the "fellows" were Catholics; but I think he was hardly quite fair to them there. Religious enthusiasm very likely had something to do with it, but it was not the moving cause. The dirt was; in other words: the slum.

Such diversions are among the few and simple joys of the street child's life, Not all it affords, but all the street has to offer. The Fresh Air Funds, the free excursions, and the many charities that year by year reach farther down among the poor for their children have done and are doing a great work in setting up new standards, ideals, and ambitions in the domain of the street. One result is seen in the effort of the poorest mothers to make their little ones presentable when there is anything to arouse their maternal pride. But all these things must and do come from the outside. Other resources than the sturdy independence that is its heritage the street has none. Rightly used, that in itself is the greatest of all. Chief among its native entertainments is that crowning joy, the parade of the circus when it comes to town in the spring. For many hours after that has passed, as after every public show that costs nothing, the matron's room at Police Headquarters is crowded with youngsters who have followed it miles and miles from home, devouring its splendors with hungry eyes until the last elephant, the last soldier, or the last policeman vanished from sight and the child comes back to earth again and to the knowledge that he is lost.

If the delights of his life are few, its sorrows do not sit heavily upon him either. He is in too close and constant touch with misery, with death itself, to mind it much. To find a family of children living, sleeping, and eating in the room where father or mother lies dead, without seeming to be in any special distress about it, is no unusual experience. But if they do not weigh upon him, the cares of home leave their mark; and it is a bad mark. All the darkness, all the drudgery is there. All the freedom is in the street; all the brightness in the saloon to which he early finds his way. And as he grows in years and wisdom, if not in grace, he gets his first lessons in spelling and in respect for the law from the card behind the bar, with the big black letters: "No liquor sold here to children." His opportunities for studying it while the barkeeper fills his growler are unlimited and unrestricted.

Someone has said that our poor children do not know how to play. He had probably seen a crowd of tenement children dancing in the street to the accompaniment of a hand organ and been struck by their serious mien and painfully formal glide and carriage—if it was not a German neighborhood, where the "proprieties" are less strictly observed—but that was only because it was a ball and it was incumbent on the girls to act as ladies. Only ladies attend balls. "London Bridge is falling down," with as loud a din in the streets of New York, every day, as it has fallen these hundred years and more in every British town, and the children of the Bend march "all around the mulberry bush" as gleefully as if there were a green shrub to be found within a mile of their slum. It is the slum that smudges the game too easily, and the kindergarten work comes in helping to wipe off the smut. So far from New York children being duller at their play than those of other cities and lands, I believe the reverse to be true. Only in the very worst tenements have I observed the children's play to languish. In such localities two policemen are required to do the work of one. Ordinarily they lack neither spirit nor inventiveness. I watched a crowd of them having a donkey party in the street one night, when those parties were all the rage. The donkey hung in the window of a notion store, and a knot of tenement house children with tails improvised from a newspaper, and dragged in the gutter to make them stick, were staggering blindly across the sidewalk trying to fix them in place on the pane. They got a heap of fun out of the game, quite as much, it seemed to me, as any crowd of children could have got in a fine parlor, until the storekeeper came out with his club. Every cellar door becomes a toboggan slide where the children are around, unless it is hammered full of envious nails; every block a ball ground when the policeman's back is turned, and every roof a kite field; for that innocent amusement is also forbidden by city ordinance "below Fourteenth Street."

It is rather that their opportunities of mischief are greater than those of harmless amusement; made so, it has sometimes seemed to me, with deliberate purpose to hatch the "tough." Given idleness and the street, and he will grow without other encouragement than an occasional "fanning" of a policeman's club. And the street has to do for a playground. There is no other. Central Park is miles away. The small parks that were ordered for his benefit five years ago exist yet only on paper. Games like kiteflying and ballplaying, forbidden but not suppressed, as happily they cannot be, become from harmless play a successful challenge of law and order, that points the way to later and worse achievements. Every year the police forbid the building of election bonfires, and threaten vengeance upon those who disobey the ordinance; and every election night sees the sky made lurid by them from one end of the town to the other, with the police powerless to put them out. Year by year the boys grow bolder in their raids on property when their supply of firewood has given out, until the destruction wrought at the last election became a matter of public scandal. Stoops, wagons, and in one place a showcase, containing property worth many hundreds of dollars, were fed to the flames. It has happened that an entire frame house has been carried off piecemeal, and burned up election night. The boys, organized in gangs, with the one condition of membership that all must "give in wood," store up enormous piles of fuel for months before, and though the police find and raid a good many of them, incidentally laying in supplies of kindling wood for the winter, the pile grows again in a single night, as the neighborhood reluctantly contributes its ash barrels to the cause. The germ of the gangs that terrorize whole sections of the city at intervals, and feed our courts and our jails, may without much difficulty be discovered in these early and rather grotesque struggles of the boys with the police.

Even on the national day of freedom the boy is not left to the enjoyment of his firecracker without the ineffectual threat of the law. I am not defending the firecracker, but arraigning the failure of the law to carry its point and maintain its dignity. It has robbed the poor child of the street band, one of his few harmless delights, grudgingly restoring the hand organ, but not the monkey that lent it its charm. In the band that, banished from the street, sneaks into the backyard, horns and bassoons hidden under bulging coats, the boy hails no longer the innocent purveyor of amusement, but an ally in the fight with the common enemy, the policeman. In the Thanksgiving Day and New Year parades which the latter formally permits, he furnishes them with the very weapon of gang organization which they afterward turn against him to his hurt.

And yet this boy who, when taken from his alley into the country for the first time, cries out in delight, "How blue the sky and what a lot of it there is!"—not much of it at home in his barrack—has in the very love of dramatic display that sends him forth to beat a policeman with his own club or die in the attempt, in the intense vanity that is only a perverted form of pride, capable of any achievement, a handle by which he may be most easily grasped and led. It cannot be done by gorging him *en masse* with apples and gingerbread at a Christmas party. [7] It can be done only by individual effort, and by the influence of personal character in direct contact with the child—the great secret of success in all dealings with the poor. Foul as the gutter he comes from, he is open to the reproach of "bad form" as few of his betters. Greater even than his desire eventually to "down" a policeman, is his ambition to be a "gentleman," as his sister's to be a "lady." The street is responsible for the caricature either makes of the character. On a playbill I saw in an East Side street, only the other day, this *repertoire* set down: "Thursday—The Bowery Tramp; Friday—The Thief." It was a theatre I knew newsboys, and the other children of the street who were earning money, to frequent in shoals. The playbill suggested the sort of training they received there.

I wish I might tell the story of some of these very lads whom certain enthusiastic friends of mine tried to reclaim on a plan of their own, in which the gang became a club and its members "Knights," who made and executed their own laws; but I am under heavy bonds of promises made to keep the peace on this point. The fact is, I tried it once, and my well-meant effort made no end of trouble. I had failed to appreciate the stride of civilization that under my friends' banner marched about the East Side with seven-league boots. They read the magazines down there and objected, rather illogically, to being "shown up." The incident was a striking revelation of the wide gap between the conditions that prevail abroad and those that confront us. Fancy the *Westminster Review* or *The Nineteenth Century* breeding contention among the denizens of East London by any criticism of their ways? Yet even from Hell's Kitchen had I not long before been driven forth with my camera by a band of angry women, who pelted me with brickbats and stones on my retreat, shouting at me never to come back unless I wanted my head broken, or let any other "duck" from the (mentioning a well-known newspaper of which I was unjustly suspected of being an emissary) poke his nose in there. Reform and the magazines had not taken that stronghold of toughdom yet, but their vanguard, the newspapers, had evidently got there.

"It only shows," said one of my missionary friends, commenting upon the East Side incident, "that we are all at sixes and at sevens here." It is our own fault. In our unconscious pride of caste most of us are given to looking too much and too long at the rough outside. These same workers bore cheerful testimony to the "exquisite courtesy" with which they were received every day in the poorest homes; a courtesy that might not always know the ways of polite society, but always tried its best to find them. "In over fifty thousand visits," reports a physician, whose noble life is given early and late to work that has made her name blessed where sorrow and suffering add their sting to bitter poverty, "personal violence has been attempted on but two occasions. In each case children had died from neglect of parents who, in their drunken rage, would certainly have taken the life of the physician had she not promptly run away." Patience and kindness prevailed even with these. The doctor did not desert them, even though she had had to run, believing that one of the mothers at least drank because she was poor and unable to find work; and now, after five years of many trials and failures, she reports that the family is at work and happy and grateful in rooms "where the sun beams in." Gratitude, indeed, she found to be their strong point, always seeking an outlet in expression—evidence of a lack of bringing up, certainly. "Once," she says, "the thankful fathers of two of our patients wished to vote for us, as 'the lady doctors have no vote.' Their intention was to vote for General Butler; we have proof that they voted for Cleveland. They have even placed their own lives in danger for us. One man fought a duel with a woman, she having said that women doctors did not know as much as men. After bar tumblers were used as weapons the question was decided in favor of women doctors by the man. It seemed but proper that 'the lady doctor' was called in to bind up the wounds of her champion, while a 'man doctor' performed the service for the woman."

My friends, in time, by their gentle but firm management, gained the honest esteem and loyal support of the boys whose manners and minds they had set out to improve, and through such means worked wonders. While some of their experiences were exceedingly funny, more were of a kind to show how easily the material could be moulded, if the hands were only there to mould it. One of their number, by and by, hung out her shingle in another street with the word "Doctor" over the bell (not the physician above referred to), but her "character" had preceded her, and woe to the urchin who as much as glanced at that when the gang pulled all the other bells in the block and laughed at the wrath of the tenants. One luckless chap forgot himself far enough to yank it one night, and immediately an angry cry went up from the gang, "Who pulled dat bell?" "Mickey did," was the answer, and Mickey's howls announced to the amused doctor the next minute that he had been "slugged" and she avenged. This doctor's account of the first formal call of the gang in the block was highly amusing. It called in a body and showed a desire to please that tried the host's nerves not a little. The boys vied with each other in recounting for her entertainment their encounters with the police enemy, and in exhibiting their intimate knowledge of the wickedness of the slums in minutest detail. One, who was scarcely twelve years old, and had lately moved from Bayard Street, knew all the ins and outs of the Chinatown opium dives, and painted them in glowing colors. The doctor listened with half-amused dismay, and when the boys rose to go, told them she was glad they had called. So were they, they said, and they guessed they would call again the next night.

"Oh! Don't come tomorrow," said the doctor, in something of a fright; "come next week!" She was relieved upon hearing the leader of the gang reprove the rest of the fellows for their want of style. He bowed with great precision, and announced that he would call "in about two weeks."

The testimony of these workers agrees with that of most others who reach the girls at an age when they are yet manageable, that the most abiding results follow with them, though they are harder to get at. The boys respond more readily, but also more easily fall from grace. The same good and bad traits are found in both; the same trying superficiality—which merely means that they are raw material; the same readiness to lie as the shortest cut out of a scrape; the same generous helpfulness, characteristic of the poor everywhere. Out of the depth of their bitter poverty I saw the children in the West Fifty-second Street Industrial School, last Thanksgiving, bring for the relief of the aged and helpless and those even poorer than they such gifts as they could—a handful of ground coffee in a paper bag, a couple of Irish potatoes, a little sugar or flour, and joyfully offer to carry them home. It was on such a trip I found little Katie. In her person and work she answered the question sometimes asked, why we hear so much about the boys and so little of the girls; because the home and the shop claim their work much earlier and to a much greater extent, while the boys are turned out to shift for themselves, and because, therefore, their miseries are so much more commonplace, and proportionally uninteresting. It is a woman's lot to suffer in silence. If occasionally she makes herself heard in querulous protest, if injustice long borne gives her tongue a sharper edge than the occasion seems to require, it can at least be said in her favor that her bark is much worse than her bite. The missionary who complains that the wife nags her husband to the point of making the saloon his refuge, or the sister her brother until he flees to the street, bears testimony in the same breath to her readiness to sit up all night to mend the clothes of the scamp she so hotly denounces. Sweetness of temper or of speech is not a distinguishing feature of tenement house life, any more among the children than with their elders. In a party sent out by our committee for a summer vacation on a Jersey farm, last summer, was a little knot of six girls from the Seventh Ward. They had not been gone three days before a letter came from one of them to the mother of one of the others. "Mrs. Reilly," it read, "if you have any sinse you will send for your child." That they would all be murdered was the sense the frightened mother made out of it. The six came home post haste, the youngest in a state of high dudgeon at her sudden translation back to the tenement. The lonesomeness of the farm had frightened the others. She was little more than a baby, and her desire to go back was explained by one of the rescued ones thus: "She sat two mortil hours at the table a stuffin' of herself, till the missus she says, says she, 'Does yer mother lave ye to sit that long at the table, sis?'" The poor thing was where there was enough to eat for once in her life, and she was making the most of her opportunity.

Not rarely does this child of common clay rise to a height of heroism that discovers depths of feeling and character full of unsuspected promise. It was in March a year ago that a midnight fire, started by a fiend in human shape, destroyed a tenement in

Hester Street, killing a number of the tenants. On the fourth floor the firemen found one of these penned in with his little girl and helped them to the window. As they were handing out the child, she broke away from them suddenly and stepped back into the smoke to what seemed certain death. The firemen climbing after, groped around shouting for her to come back. Halfway across the room they came upon her, gasping and nearly smothered, dragging a doll's trunk over the floor.

"I could not leave it," she said, thrusting it at the men as they seized her; "my mother —"

They flung the box angrily through the window. It fell crashing on the sidewalk and, breaking open, revealed no doll or finery, but the deed for her dead mother's grave. Little Bessie had not forgotten her, despite her thirteen years.

Yet Bessie might, likely would, have been found in the front row where anything was going on or to be had, crowding with the best of them and thrusting herself and her claim forward regardless of anything or anybody else. It is a quality in the children which, if not admirable, is at least natural. The poor have to take their turn always, and too often it never comes, or, as in the case of the poor young mother, whom one of our committee found riding aimlessly in a street car with her dying baby, not knowing where to go or what to do, when it is too late. She took mother and child to the dispensary. It was crowded and they had to wait their turn. When it came the baby was dead. It is not to be expected that children who have lived the lawless life of the street should patiently put up with such a prospect. That belongs to the discipline of a life of failure and want. The children know generally what they want and they go for it by the shortest cut. I found that out, whether I had flowers to give or pictures to take. In the latter case they reversed my Hell's Kitchen experience with a vengeance. Their determination to be "took," the moment the camera hove in sight, in the most striking pose they could hastily devise, was always the most formidable bar to success I met. The recollection of one such occasion haunts me yet. They were serving a Thanksgiving dinner free to all comers at a charitable institution in Mulberry Street, and more than a hundred children were in line at the door under the eye of a policeman when I tried to photograph them. Each one of the forlorn host had been hugging his particular place for an hour, shivering in the cold as the line slowly advanced toward the door and the promised dinner, and there had been numberless little spats due to the anxiety of some one farther back to steal a march on a neighbor nearer the goal; but the instant the camera appeared the line broke and a howling mob swarmed about me, up to the very eye of the camera, striking attitudes on the curb, squatting in the mud in alleged picturesque repose, and shoving and pushing in a wild struggle to get into the most prominent position. With immense trouble and labor the policeman and I made a narrow lane through the crowd from the camera to the curb, in the hope that the line might form again. The lane was studded, the moment I turned my back, with dirty faces that were thrust into it from both sides in ludicrous anxiety lest they should be left out, and in the middle of it two frowsy, ill-favored girls, children of ten or twelve, took position, hand in hand, flatly refusing to budge from in front of the camera. Neither jeers nor threats moved them. They stood their ground with a grim persistence that said as plainly as words that they were not going to let this, the supreme opportunity of their lives, pass, cost what it might. In their rags, barefooted, and in that disdainful pose in the midst of a veritable bedlam of shrieks and laughter, they were a most ludicrous spectacle. The boys fought rather shy of them, of one they called "Mag" especially, as it afterward appeared with good reason. A chunk of wood from the outskirts of the crowd that hit Mag on the ear at length precipitated a fight in which the boys struggled ten deep on the pavement, Mag in the middle of the heap, doing her full share. As a last expedient I bethought myself of a dogfight as the means of scattering the mob, and sent around the corner to organize one. Fatal mistake! At the first suggestive bark the crowd broke and ran in a body. Not only the hangers-on, but the hungry line collapsed too in an instant, and the policeman and I were left alone. As an attraction the dogfight outranked the dinner.

This unconquerable vanity, if not turned to use for his good, makes a tough of the lad with more muscle than brains in a perfectly natural way. The newspapers tickle it by recording the exploits of his gang with embellishments that fall in exactly with his tastes. Idleness encourages it. The home exercises no restraint. Parental authority is lost. At a certain age young men of all social grades know a heap more than their fathers, or think they do. The young tough has some apparent reason for thinking that way. He has likely learned to read. The old man has not; he probably never learned anything, not even to speak the language that his son knows without being taught. He thinks him "dead slow," of course, and lays it to his foreign birth. All foreigners are "slow." The father works hard. The boy thinks he knows a better plan. The old man has lost his grip on the lad, if he ever had any. That is the reason why the tough appears in the second generation and disappears in the third. By that time father and son are again on equal terms, whatever those terms may be. The exception to this rule is in the poorest Irish settlements where the manufacture of the tough goes right on, aided by the "inflooence" of the police court on one side and the saloon on the other. Between the two the police fall unwillingly into line. I was in the East Thirty-fifth Street police station one night when an officer came in with two young toughs whom he had arrested in a lumber yard where they were smoking and drinking. They had threatened to kill him and the watchman, and loaded revolvers were taken from them. In spite of this evidence against them, the Justice in the police court discharged them on the following morning with a scowl at the officer, and they were both jeering at him before noon. Naturally he let them alone after that. It was one case of hundreds of like character. The politician, of course, is behind them. Toughs have votes just as they have brickbats and brass knuckles; when the emergency requires, an assortment to suit of the one as of the other.

The story of the tough's career I told in *How the Other Half Lives*, and there is no need of repeating it here. Its end is generally lurid, always dramatic. It is that even when it comes to him "with his boots off," in a peaceful sick bed. In his bravado one can sometimes catch a glimpse of the sturdiest traits in the Celtic nature, burlesqued and caricatured by the tenement. One who had been a cutthroat, bruiser, and prizefighter all his brief life lay dying from consumption in his Fourth Ward tenement not long ago. He had made what he proudly called a stand-up fight against the disease until now the end had come and he had at last to give up.

"Maggie," he said, turning to his wife with eyes growing dim, "Mag! I had an iron heart, but now it is broke. Watch me die!" And Mag told it proudly at the wake as proof that Pat died game.

And the girl that has come thus far with him? Fewer do than one might think. Many more switch off their lovers to some honest work this side of the jail, making decent husbands of them as they are loyal wives, thus proving themselves truly their better halves. But of her who goes his way with him—it is not generally a long way for either—what of her end? Let me tell the story of one that is the story of all. I came across it in the course of my work as a newspaper man a year ago and I repeat it here as I heard it then from those who knew, with only the names changed. The girl is dead, but he is alive and leading an honest life at last, so I am told. The story is that of "Kid" McDuff's girl.

*Their playground a truck*

# 5

# THE STORY OF KID McDUFF'S GIRL

THE BACK ROOM OF THE SALOON on the northwest corner of Pell Street and the Bowery is never cheery on the brightest day. The entrance to the dives of Chinatown yawns just outside, and in the barroom gather the vilest of the wrecks of the Bend and the Sixth Ward slums. But on the morning of which I speak a shadow lay over it even darker than usual. The shadow of death was there. In the corner, propped on one chair, with her feet on another, sat a dead woman. Her glassy eyes looked straight ahead with a stony, unmeaning stare until the policeman who dozed at a table at the other end of the room, suddenly waking up and meeting it, got up with a shudder and covered the face with a handkerchief.

What did they see, those dead eyes? Through its darkened windows what a review was the liberated spirit making of that sin-worn, wasted life, begun in innocence and wasted—there? Whatever their stare meant, the policeman knew little of it and cared less.

"Oh! It is just a stiff," he said, and yawned wearily. There was still half an hour of his watch.

The clinking of glasses and the shuffle of cowhide boots on the sanded floor outside grew louder and was muffled again as the door leading to the bar was opened and shut by a young woman. She lingered doubtfully on the threshold a moment, then walked with unsteady step across the room toward the corner where the corpse sat. The light that struggled in from the gloomy street fell upon her and showed that she trembled, as if with the ague. Yet she was young, not over twenty-five, but on her heavy eyes and sodden features there was the stamp death had just blotted from the other's face with the memory of her sins. Yet, curiously blended with it, not yet smothered wholly, there was something of the child, something that had once known a mother's love and pity.

"Poor Kid," she said, stopping beside the body and sinking heavily in a chair. "He will be sorry, anyhow."

"Who is Kid?" I asked.

"Why, Kid McDuff! You know him? His brother Jim keeps the saloon on — Street. Everybody knows Kid."

"Well, what was she to Kid?" I asked, pointing to the corpse.

"His girl," she said promptly. "An' he stuck to her till he was pulled for the job he didn't do; then he had to let her slide. She stuck to him too, you bet."

"Annie wasn't no more nor thirteen when she was tuk away from home by the Kid," the girl went on, talking as much to herself as to me; the policeman nodded in his chair. "He kep' her the best he could, 'ceptin' when he was sent up on the Island the time the gang went back on him. Then she kinder drifted. But she was all right agin he come back and tuk to keepin' bar for his brother Jim. Then he was pulled for that Bridgeport skin job, and when he went to the pen she went to the bad, and now —"

Here a thought that had been slowly working down through her besotted mind got a grip on her strong enough to hold her attention, and she leaned over and caught me by the sleeve, something almost akin to pity struggling in her bleary eyes.

"Say, young feller," she whispered hoarsely, "don't spring this too hard. She's got two lovely brothers. One of them keeps a daisy saloon up on Eighth Avenue. They're respectable, they are."

Then she went on telling what she knew of Annie Noonan who was sitting dead there before us. It was not much. She was the child of an honest shoemaker who came to this country twenty-two or three years before from his English home, when Annie was a little girl of six or seven. Before she was in her teens she was left fatherless. At the age of thirteen, when she was living in an East Side tenement with her mother, the Kid, then a young tough qualifying with one of the many gangs about the Hook for the penitentiary, crossed her path. Ever after she was his slave, and followed where he led.

The path they trod together was not different from that travelled by hundreds of young men and women today. By way of the low dives and "morgues" with which the East Side abounds, it led him to the Island and her to the street. When he was sent up the first time, his mother died of a broken heart. His father, a well-to-do mechanic in the Seventh Ward, had been spared that misery. He had died before the son was fairly started on his bad career. The family were communicants at the parish church, and efforts without end were made to turn the Kid from his career of wicked folly. His two sisters labored faithfully with him, but without avail. When the Kid came back from the Island to find his mother dead, he did not know his oldest sister. Grief had turned her pretty brown hair a snowy white.

He found his girl a little the worse for rum and late hours than when he left her, but he "took up" with her again. He was loyal at least. This time he tried, too, to be honest. His mother's death had shocked him to the point where his "nerve" gave out.

His brother gave him charge of one of his saloons and the Kid was "at work" keeping bar, with the way to respectability, as it goes on the East Side, open to him, when one of his old pals, who had found him out, turned up with a demand for money. He was a burglar and wanted a hundred dollars to "do up a job" in the country. The Kid refused, and his brother came in during the quarrel that ensued, flew into a rage, and grabbing the thief by the collar, threw him into the street. He went his way shaking his fist and threatening vengeance on both.

It was not long in coming. A jewelry store in Bridgeport was robbed and two burglars were arrested. One of them was the man "Jim" McDuff had thrown out of his saloon. He turned state's evidence and swore that the Kid was in the job too. He was arrested and held in bail of ten thousand dollars. The Kid always maintained that he was innocent. His family believed him, but his past was against him. It was said, too, that back of the arrest was political persecution. His brother the saloonkeeper, who mixed politics with his beer, was the underdog just then in the fight in his ward. The situation was discussed from a practical standpoint in the McDuff household, and it ended with the Kid going up to Bridgeport and pleading guilty to theft to escape the worse charge of burglary. He was sentenced to four years' imprisonment. That was how he got into "the pen."

Annie, after he had been put in jail, went to the dogs on her own account rather faster than when they made a team. For a time she frequented the saloons of the Tenth Ward. When she crossed the Bowery at last she was nearing the end. For a year or two she frequented the disreputable houses in Elizabeth and Hester Streets. She was supposed to have a room in Downing Street, but it was the rarest of all events that she was there.

Two weeks before this morning, Fay Leslie, the girl who sat there telling me her story, met her on the Bowery with a cut and bruised face. She had been beaten in a fight in a Pell Street saloon with Flossie Lowell, one of the habitues of Chinatown. Fay took her to Bellevue Hospital, where she "had a pull with the night watch," she told me, and she was kept there three or four days. When she came out she drifted back to Pell Street and took to drinking again. But she was a sick girl.

The night before she was with Fay in the saloon on the corner, when she complained that she did not feel well. She sat down in a chair and put her feet on another. In that posture she was found dead a little later, when her friend went to see how she was getting on.

"Rum killed her, I suppose," I said, when Fay had ended her story.

"Yes! I suppose it did."

"And you," I ventured, "some day it will kill you too, if you do not look out."

The girl laughed a loud and coarse laugh.

"Me?" she said, "not by a jugful. I've been soaking it fifteen years and I am alive yet."

The dead girl sat there yet, with the cold, staring eyes, when I went my way. Outside the drinking went on with vile oaths. The dead wagon had been sent for, but it had other errands, and had not yet come around to Pell Street.

Thus ended the story of Kid McDuff's girl.

# 6

## THE LITTLE TOILERS

POVERTY AND CHILD LABOR are yokefellows everywhere. Their union is perpetual, indissoluble. The one begets the other. Need sets the child to work when it should have been at school and its labor breeds low wages, thus increasing the need. Solomon said it three thousand years ago, and it has not been said better since: "The destruction of the poor is their poverty."

It is the business of the State to see to it that its interest in the child as a future citizen is not imperilled by the compact. Here in New York we set about this within the memory of the youngest of us. Today we have compulsory education and a factory law prohibiting the employment of young children. All between eight and fourteen years old must go to school at least fourteen weeks in each year. None may labor in factories under the age of fourteen; not under sixteen unless able to read and write simple sentences in English. These are the barriers thrown up against the inroads of ignorance, poverty's threat. They are barriers of paper. We have the laws, but we do not enforce them.

By that I do not mean to say that we make no attempt to enforce them. We do. We catch a few hundred truants each year and send them to reformatories to herd with thieves and vagabonds worse than they, rather illogically, since there is no pretence that there would have been room for them in the schools had they wanted to go there. We set half a dozen factory inspectors to canvass more than twice as many thousand workshops and to catechise the children they find there. Some are turned out and go back the next day to that or some other shop. The great mass that are under age lie and stay. And their lies go on record as evidence that we are advancing, and that child labor is getting to be a thing of the past. That the horrible cruelty of a former day is that the children have better treatment and a better time of it in the shops—often a good enough time to make one feel that they are better off there learning habits of industry than running about the streets, so long as there is no way of *making* them attend school—I believe from what I have seen. That the law has had the effect of greatly diminishing the number of child workers I do not believe. It has had another and worse effect. It has bred wholesale perjury among them and their parents. Already they have become so used to it that it is a matter of sport and a standing joke among them. The child of eleven at home and at night school is fifteen in the factory as a matter of course. Nobody is deceived, but the perjury defeats the purpose of the law.

More than a year ago, in an effort to get at the truth of the matter of children's labor, I submitted to the Board of Health, after consultation with Dr. Felix Adler, who earned the lasting gratitude of the community by his labors on the Tenement House Commission, certain questions to be asked concerning the children by the sanitary police, then about to begin a general census of the tenements. The result was a surprise, and not least to the health officers. In the entire mass of nearly a million and a quarter of tenants [8] only two hundred and forty-nine children under fourteen years of age were found at work in living rooms. To anyone acquainted with the ordinary aspect of tenement house life the statement seemed preposterous, and there are valid reasons for believing that the policemen missed rather more than they found even of those that were confessedly or too evidently under age. They were seeking that which, when found, would furnish proof of law-breaking against the parent or employer, a fact of which these were fully aware. Hence their coming uniformed and in search of children into a house could scarcely fail to give those a holiday who were not big enough to be palmed off as fourteen at least. Nevertheless, upon reflection, it seemed probable that the policemen were nearer the truth than their critics. Their census took no account of the factory in the backyard, but only of the living rooms, and it was made during the day. Most of the little slaves, as of those older in years, were found in the sweater's district on the East Side, where the home work often only fairly begins after the factory has shut down for the day and the stores released their army of child laborers. Had the policemen gone their rounds after dark they would have found a different state of things. Between the sweat shops and the school, which, as I have shown, is made to reach farther down among the poorest in this Jewish quarter than anywhere else in this city, the children were fairly accounted for in the daytime. The record of school attendance in the district shows that forty-seven attended day school for every one who went to night school.

To settle the matter to my own satisfaction I undertook a census of a number of the most crowded houses, in company with a policeman not in uniform. The outcome proved that, as regards those houses at least, it was as I suspected, and I have no doubt they were a fair sample of the rest. In nine tenements that were filled with homeworkers we found five children at work who owned that they were under fourteen. Two were girls nine years of age. Two boys said they were thirteen. We found thirteen who swore that they were of age, proof which the policeman as an uninterested census taker would have respected as a matter of course, even though he believed with me that the children lied. On the other hand, in seven backyard factories we found a total of 63 children, of whom 5 admitted being under age, while of the rest 45 seemed surely so. To the other 13 we gave the benefit of the doubt, but I do not think they deserved it. All the 63 were to my mind certainly under fourteen, judging not only from their size, but from the whole appearance of the children. My subsequent experience confirmed me fully in this belief. Most of them were able to write their names after a fashion. Few spoke English, but that might have been a subterfuge. One of the homeworkers, a marvellously small lad whose arms were black to the shoulder from the dye in the cloth he was sewing, and who said in his broken German, without evincing special interest in the matter, that he had gone to school "e' bische," referred us to his "mother" for a statement as to his age. The "mother," who proved to be the boss' wife, held a brief consultation with her husband and then came forward with a verdict of sixteen. When we laughed rather incredulously the man offered to prove by his marriage certificate that the boy must be sixteen. The effect of this demonstration was rather marred, however, by the inopportune appearance of another tailor, who, ignorant of the crisis, claimed the boy as his. The situation was dramatic. The tailor with the certificate simply shrugged his shoulders and returned to his work, leaving the boy to his fate.

One girl, who could not have been twelve years old, was hard at work at a sewing machine in a Division Street shirt factory when we came in. She got up and ran the moment she saw us, but we caught her in the next room hiding behind a pile of shirts. She said at once that she was fourteen years old but didn't work there. She "just came in." The boss of the shop was lost in astonishment at seeing her when we brought her back. He could not account at all for her presence. There were three boys at work in the room who said "sixteen" without waiting to be asked. Not one of them was fourteen. The habit of saying fourteen or sixteen—the fashion varies with the shops and with the degree of the child's educational acquirements—soon becomes an unconscious one with the boy. He plumps it out without knowing it. While occupied with these investigations I once had my boots blacked by a little shaver, hardly knee-high, on a North River ferryboat. While he was shining away, I suddenly asked him how old he was. "Fourteen, sir!" he replied promptly, without looking up.

In a Hester Street house we found two little girls pulling basting thread. They were both Italians and said that they were nine. In the room in which one of them worked thirteen men and two women were sewing. The child could speak English. She said that she was earning a dollar a week and worked every day from seven in the morning till eight in the evening. This sweat shop was one of the kind that comes under the ban of the new law, passed last winter—that is, if the factory inspector ever finds it. Where the crowds are greatest and the pay poorest, the Italian laborer's wife and child have found their way in since the strikes among the sweater's Jewish slaves, outbidding even these in the fierce strife for bread.

Even the crowding, the feverish haste of the half-naked men and women, and the litter and filth in which they worked, were preferable to the silence and desolation we encountered in one shop up under the roof of a Broome Street tenement. The work there had given out—there had been none these two months, said the gaunt, hard-faced woman who sat eating a crust of dry bread and drinking water from a tin pail at the empty bench. The man sat silent and moody in a corner; he was sick. The room was bare. The only machine left was not worth taking to the pawnshop. Two dirty children, naked but for a torn undershirt apiece, were fishing over the stair rail with a bent pin on an idle thread. An old rag was their bait.

From among a hundred and forty hands on two big lofts in a Suffolk Street factory we picked seventeen boys and ten girls who were patently under fourteen years of age, but who all had certificates, sworn to by their parents, to the effect that they were sixteen. One of them whom we judged to be between nine and ten, and whose teeth confirmed our diagnosis—the second bicuspids in the lower jaw were just coming out—said that he had worked there "by the year." The boss, deeming his case hopeless, explained that he only "made sleeves and went for beer." Two of the smallest girls represented themselves as sisters, respectively sixteen and seventeen, but when we came to inquire which was the oldest, it turned out that she was the sixteen-year one. Several boys scooted as we came up the stairs. When stopped they claimed to be visitors. I was told that this sweater had been arrested once by the factory inspector, but had successfully barricaded himself behind his pile of certificates. I caught the children laughing and making faces at us behind our backs as often as these were brought out anywhere. In an Attorney Street "pants" factory we counted thirteen boys and girls who could not have been of age, and on a top floor in Ludlow Street, among others, two brothers sewing coats, who said that they were thirteen and fourteen, but when told to stand up, looked so ridiculously small as to make even their employer laugh. Neither could read, but the oldest could sign his name and did it thus, from right to left:

*Signature of a young boy working in a sweater [sweat shop]*

It was the full extent of his learning, and all he would probably ever receive.

He was one of many Jewish children we came across who could neither read nor write. Most of them answered that they had never gone to school. They were mostly those of larger growth, bordering on fourteen, whom the charity school managers find it next to impossible to reach, the children of the poorest and most ignorant immigrants, whose work is imperatively needed to make both ends meet at home, the "thousand" the school census failed to account for. To banish them from the shop serves no useful purpose. They are back the next day, if not sooner. One of the factory inspectors told me of how recently he found a little boy in a sweat shop and sent him home. He went up through the house after that and stayed up there quite an hour. On his return it occurred to him to look in to see if the boy was gone. He was back and hard at work, and with him were two other boys of his age who, though they claimed to have come in with dinner for some of the hands, were evidently workers there.

So much for the sweat shops. Jewish, Italian, and Bohemian, the story is the same always. In the children that are growing up, to "vote as would their master's dogs if allowed the right of suffrage," the community reaps its reward in due season for allowing such things to exist. It is a kind of interest in the payment of which there is never default. The physician gets another view of it. "Not long ago," says Dr. Annie S. Daniel, in the last report of the out practice of the Infirmary for Women and Children, "we found in such an apartment five persons making cigars, including the mother. Two children were ill with diphtheria. Both parents attended to the children; they would syringe the nose of each child and, without washing their hands, return to their cigars. We have repeatedly observed the same thing when the work was manufacturing clothing and undergarments, to be bought as well by the rich as the poor. Hand sewed shoes, made for a fashionable Broadway shoe store, were sewed at home by a man in whose family were three children with scarlet fever. And such instances are common. Only death or lack of work closes tenement house manufactories. When reported to the Board of Health, the inspector at once prohibits further manufacture during the continuance of the disease, but his back is scarcely turned before the people return to their work. When we consider that stopping this work means no food and no roof over their heads, the fact that the disease may be carried by their work cannot be expected to impress the people."

And she adds: "Wages have steadily decreased. Among the women who earned the whole or part of the income the finishing of pantaloons was the most common occupation. For this work in 1881 they received ten to fifteen cents per pair; for the same work in 1891 three to five, at the most ten cents per pair. When the women have paid the express charges to and from the factory there is little margin left for profit. The women doing this work claim that wages are reduced because of the influx of Italian women." The rent has not fallen, however, and the need of every member of the family contributing by his or her work to its keep is greater than ever. The average total wages of 160 families whom the doctor personally treated and interrogated during the year was $5.99 per week, while the average rent was $8.62¾. The list included twenty-three different occupations and trades. The maximum wages was $19, earned by three persons in one family; the minimum $1.50, by a woman finishing pantaloons and living in one room for which she paid $4 a month rent! In nearly every instance observed by Dr. Daniel, the children's wages, when there were working children, was the greater share of the family income. A specimen instance is that of a woman with a consumptive husband, who is under her treatment. The wife washes and goes out by the day, when she can get such work to do. The three children, aged eleven, seven, and five years, not counting the baby for a wonder, work at home covering wooden buttons with silk at four cents a gross. The oldest goes to school, but works with the rest evenings and on Saturday and Sunday, when the mother does the finishing. Their combined earnings are from $3 to $6 a week, the children earning two-thirds. The rent is $8 a month.

The doctor's observations throw a bright sidelight upon the economic home conditions that lie at the root of this problem of child labor in the factories. With that I have not done. Taking the factory inspector's report for 1890, the last at that time available, I found that in that year his deputies got around to 2,147 of the 11,000 workshops (the number given in the report) in the Second district, which is that portion of New York south of Twenty-third Street. In other words, they visited less than one-fifth of them all. They found 1,102 boys and 1,954 girls under sixteen at work; 3,485 boys under eighteen, and 12,701 girls under twenty-one, as nearly as I could make the footings. The figures alone are instructive, as showing the preponderance of girls in the shops. The report, speaking of the state as a whole, congratulates the community upon the alleged fact "that the policy of employing very young children in manufactories has been practically abolished." It states that "since the enactment of the law the sentiment among employers has become nearly unanimous in favor of its stringent enforcement," and that it "has had the further important effect of preventing newly arrived non-English speaking foreigners from forcing their children into factories before they learned the language of the country," these being "now compelled to send their children to school, for a time at least, until they can qualify under the law." Further, "the system of requiring sworn certificates, giving the name, date, and place of birth of all children under sixteen years of age ... has resulted in causing parents to be very cautious about making untrue statements of the ages of their children." The deputies "are aware of the various subterfuges which have been tried in order to evade the law and put children at labor before the legal time," and the factory inspector is "happy to say that they are not often imposed upon by such tactics."

Without wading through nearly seventy pages of small print it was not possible to glean from the report how many of the "under sixteen" workers were really under fourteen, or so adjudged. A summary of what has been accomplished since 1886 showed that 1,614 children under fourteen were discharged by the inspector in the Second District in that time, and that 415 were discharged because they could not read or write simple sentences in the English language. The "number of working children who could not read and write English" was in 1890 alone 252, according to the report, or more than one-half of the whole number discharged in the four years, which does not look as if the law had had much effect in that way, at least in New York City. I determined to see for myself what were the facts.

I visited a number of factories, in a few instances accompanied by the deputy factory inspector, more frequently alone. Where it was difficult to gain admission I watched at the door when the

employees were going to or coming from work, finding that on
the whole the better plan, as affording a fairer view of the children
and a better opportunity to judge of their age than when they sat
at their workbenches. I found many shops in which there were
scarcely any children, some from which they had been driven,
so I was informed by the inspectors. But where manufacturers
were willing to employ their labor—and this I believe to be quite
generally the case where children's labor can be made to pay—I
found the age certificate serving as an excellent protection for
the employer, never for the child. I found the law considered as
a good joke by some conscienceless men, who hardly took the
trouble to see that the certificates were filled out properly; loudly
commended by others whom it enabled, at the expense of a little
perjury in which they had no hand, to fill up their shops with
cheap labor, with perfect security to themselves. The bookkeeper
in an establishment of the conscienceless kind told me with glee
how a boy who had been bounced there three times in one year,
upon his return each time had presented a sworn certificate
giving a different age. He was fifteen, sixteen, and seventeen years
old upon the records of the shop, until the inspectors caught him
one day and proved him only thirteen. I found boys at work,
posing as seventeen, who had been so recorded in the same shop
three full years, and were thirteen at most. As seventeen-year
freaks they could have made more money in a dime museum
than at the workbench, only the museum would have required
something more convincing than the certificate that satisfied
the shop. Some of these boys were working at power presses
and doing other work beyond their years. An examination of
their teeth often disproved their stories as to their age. It was not
always possible to make this test, for the children seemed to see
something funny in it, and laughed and giggled so, especially the
girls, as to make it difficult to get a good look. Some of the girls,
generally those with decayed teeth, [9] would pout and refuse
to show them. These were usually American girls, that is to say,
they were born here. The greater number of the child workers
I questioned were foreigners, and our birth returns could have

given no clue to them. The few natives were alert and on the defensive from the moment they divined my purpose. They easily defeated it by giving a false address.

I finally picked out a factory close to my office where Italian girls were employed in large numbers, and made it my business to ascertain the real ages of the children. They seemed to me, going and coming, to average twelve or thirteen years. The year before the factory inspector had reported that nearly a hundred girls "under sixteen" were employed there. She had discharged sixty of them as unable to read or write English. I went to see the manufacturers. They were not disposed to help me and fell back on their certificates—no child was employed by them without one—until I told them that my purpose was not to interfere with their business but to prove that a birth certificate was the only proper warrant for employment of child labor.

"Why," said the manufacturer, in his astonishment forgetting that he had just told me his children were all of age, "my dear sir! would you throw them all out of work?"

It was what I expected. I found out eventually that a number of the children attended the evening classes in the Leonard Street Italian School, and there one rainy night I corralled twenty-three of them, all but one officially certified under oath to be fourteen or sixteen. But for the rain I might have found twice the number. The twenty-three I polled, comparing their sworn age with the entry in the school register, which the teachers knew to be correct. This was the result: one was eleven years old and had worked in the factory a year; one, also eleven, had just been engaged and was going for her certificate that night; three were twelve years old, and had worked in the factory from one month to a year; seven were thirteen, and of them three had worked in the shop two years, the others one; nine were fourteen; one of them had been there three years, four others two years, the rest shorter terms; one was fifteen and had worked in the factory three years; the last and tallest was sixteen and had been employed in the one shop four years. She said with a laugh that she had a "certificate of sixteen" when she first went there. Not one of them all was of legal age when she went to work in the shop, under the warrant of her parents' oath. The majority were not even then legally employed, since of those who had passed fourteen there were several who could not read simple sentences in English intelligibly; yet they had been at work in the factory for months and years. One of the eleven-year workers, who felt insulted somehow, said spitefully that "I needn't bother, there was lots of other girls in the shop younger than she." I have no doubt she was right. I should add that the firm was a highly respectable one, and its members of excellent social standing.

I learned incidentally where the convenient certificates came from, at least those that were current in that school. They were issued, the children said, free of charge, by a benevolent undertaker in the ward. I thought at first that it was a bid for business, or real helpfulness. The neighborhood undertaker is often found figuring suggestively as the nearest friend of the poor in his street, when they are in trouble. But I found out afterward that it was politics combined with business. The undertaker was an Irishman and an active organizer of his district. Unpolitical notaries charged twenty-five cents for each certificate. This one made them out for nothing. All they had to do was to call for them. The girls laughed scornfully at the idea of there being anything wrong in the transaction. Their parents swore in a good cause. They needed the money. The end conveniently justified the means in their case. Besides "they merely had to touch the pen." Evidently, any argument in favor of education could scarcely be expected to have effect upon parents who thus found in their own ignorance a valid defense against an accusing conscience as well as a source of added revenue.

My experience satisfied me that the factory law has had little effect in prohibiting child labor in the factories of New York

City, although it may have had some in stimulating attendance at the night schools. The census figures, when they appear, will be able to throw no valuable light on the subject. The certificate lie naturally obstructs the census as it does the factory law. The one thing that is made perfectly clear by even such limited inquiry as I have been able to make, is that a birth certificate should be substituted for the present sworn warrant, if it is intended to make a serious business of the prohibition. In the piles upon piles of these which I saw, I never came across one copy of the birth registry. There are two obstacles to such a change. One is that our birth returns are at present incomplete; the other, that most of the children are not born here. Concerning the first, the Registrar of Vital Statistics estimates that he is registering nearly or quite a thousand births a month less than actually occur in New York; but even that is a great improvement upon the record of a few years ago. The registered birthrate is increasing year by year, and experience has shown that a determination on the part of the Board of Health to prosecute doctors and midwives who neglect their duty brings it up with a rush many hundreds in a few weeks. A wholesome strictness at the Health Office on this point would in a short time make it a reliable guide for the factory inspector in the enforcement of the law. The other objection is less serious than it appears at first sight. Immigrants might be required to provide birth certificates from their old homes, where their children are sure to be registered under the stringent laws of European governments. But as a matter of fact that would not often be necessary. They all have passports in which the name and ages of their children are set down. The claim that they had purposely registered them as younger to cheapen transportation, which they would be sure to make, need not be considered seriously. One lie is as good and as easy as another.

Another lesson we may learn with advantage from some old-country governments, which we are apt to look down upon as "slow," is to punish the parents for the truancy of their children, whether they are found running in the street or working in a shop when they should have been at school. Greed, the natural child of poverty, often has as much to do with it as real need. In the case of the Italians and the Jewish girls it is the inevitable marriage portion, without which they would stand little chance of getting a husband, that dictates the sacrifice. One little one of twelve in a class in the Leonard Street School, who had been working on coats in a sweat shop nine months, and had become expert enough to earn three dollars a week, told me that she had $200 in bank, and that her sister, also a worker, was as forehanded. Their teacher supported her story. But often a meaner motive than the desire to put money in bank forges the child's fetters. I came across a little girl in an East Side factory who pleaded so pitifully that she had to work, and looked so poor and wan, that I went to her home to see what it was like. It was on the top floor of a towering tenement. The mother, a decent German woman, was sewing at the window, doing her share, while at the table her husband, a big, lazy lout who weighed two hundred pounds if he weighed one, lolled over a game of checkers with another vagabond like himself. A half-empty beer growler stood between them. The contrast between that pitiful child hard at work in the shop, and the big loafer taking his ease, was enough to make anybody lose patience, and I gave him the piece of my mind he so richly deserved. But it rolled off him as water rolls off a duck. He merely ducked his head, shifted his bare feet under the table, and told his crony to go on with the play.

It is only when the child rebels in desperation against such atrocious cruelty and takes to the street as his only refuge, that his tyrant hands him over to the justice so long denied him. Then the school comes as an avenger, not as a friend, to the friendless lad, and it is scarcely to be wondered at if behind his prison bars he fails to make sense of the justice of a world that locks him up and lets his persecutor go free—likely enough applauds him for his public spirit in doing what he did. When the child ceases to be a source of income because he will not work, and has to be supported, at the odd intervals at least when he comes back from the street, the father surrenders him as a truant and incorrigible. A large number of the children that are every year sent to the Juvenile Asylum are admitted in that way. The real animus of it crops out when it is proposed to put the little prisoner in a way of growing up a useful citizen by sending him to a home out of the reach of his grasping relatives. Then follows a struggle for the possession of the child that would make the uninitiated onlooker think a gross outrage was about to be perpetrated on a fond parent. The experienced Superintendent of the Asylum, who has fought many such fights to a successful end, knows better. "In a majority of these cases," he remarks in his report for last year, "the opposition is due, not to any special interest in the child's welfare, but to self-interest, the relative wishing to obtain a situation for the boy in order to get his weekly wages."

Little Susie, whose picture I took while she was pasting linen on tin covers for pocket flasks—one of the hundred odd trades, wholly impossible of classification, one meets with in the tenements of the poor—with hands so deft and swift that even the flash could not catch her moving arm, but lost it altogether, is a type of the tenement house children whose work begins early and ends late. Her shop is her home. Every morning she drags down to her Cherry Street court heavy bundles of the little tin boxes, much too heavy for her twelve years, and when she has finished running errands and earning a few pennies that way, takes her place at the bench and pastes two hundred before it is time for evening school. Then she has earned sixty cents—"more than mother," she says with a smile. "Mother" has been finishing "knee pants" for a sweater, at a cent and a quarter a pair for turning up and hemming the bottom and sewing buttons on; but she cannot make more than two and a half dozen a day, with the baby to look after besides. The husband, a lazy, good-natured Italian, who "does not love work well," in the patient language of the housekeeper, had been out of a job, when I last saw him, three months, and there was no prospect of his getting one again soon, certainly not so long as the agent did not press for the rent long due. That was Susie's doings, too, though he didn't know it. Her sunny smile made everyone and everything, even in that dark alley, gentler, more considerate, when she was around.

*Little Susie at her work*

Of Susie's hundred little companions in the alley—playmates they could scarcely be called—some made artificial flowers, some paper boxes, while the boys earned money at "shinin" or selling newspapers. The smaller girls "minded the baby," so leaving the mother free to work. Most of them did something toward earning the family living, young as they were. The rest did all the mischief. The occupations that claim children's labor in and out of the shop are almost as numberless as the youngsters that swarm in tenement neighborhoods. The poorer the tenements the more of them always. In an evening school class of nineteen boys and nine girls which I polled once I found twelve boys who "shined," five who sold papers, one of thirteen years who by day was the devil in a printing office, and one of twelve who worked in a woodyard. Of the girls, one was thirteen and worked in a paper box factory, two of twelve made paper lanterns, one twelve-year-old girl sewed coats in a sweat shop, and one of the same age minded a pushcart every day. The four smallest girls were ten years old, and of them one worked for a sweater and "finished twenty-five coats yesterday," she said with pride. She looked quite able to do a woman's work. The three others minded the baby at home; one of them found time to help her mother sew coats when baby slept.

*Minding the baby*

I have heard it said that the factory law has resulted in crowding the children under age into the stores, where they find employment as "cash" girls and boys, and have to fear only the truant officer, whose calls are as rare as angels' visits. I do not believe this is true to any great extent. The more general employment of automatic carriers and other mechanical devices for doing the work once done by the children would alone tend to check such a movement, if it existed. The Secretary of the Working Women's Society, who has made a study of the subject, estimates that there are five thousand children under fourteen years so employed all the year round. In the holiday season their number is much larger. Native-born children especially prefer this work, as the more genteel and less laborious than work in the factories. As a matter of fact it is, I think, much the hardest and the more objectionable of the two kinds, and not, as a rule, nearly as well paid. If the factory law does not drive the children from the workshops, it can at least punish the employer who exacts more than ten hours a day of them there, or denies them their legal dinner hour. In the store there is nothing to prevent their being worked fifteen and sixteen hours during the busy season. Few firms allow more than half an hour for lunch, some even less. The children cannot sit down when tired, and their miserable salaries of a dollar and a half or two dollars a week are frequently so reduced by fines for tardiness as to leave them little or nothing. The sanitary surroundings are often most wretched. At best the dust-laden atmosphere of a large store, with the hundreds of feet tramping through it and the many pairs of lungs breathing the air over and over again, is most exhausting to a tender child. An hour spent in going through such a store tires many grown persons more than a whole day's work at their accustomed tasks. These children spend their whole time there at the period when the growth of the body taxes all their strength.

An effort was made last year to extend the prohibition of the factory law to the stores, but it failed. It ought not to fail this winter, but if it is to be coupled with the sworn certificate, it were better to leave things as they are. The five thousand children under age are there now in defiance of one law that requires them to go to school. They lied to get their places. They will not hesitate to lie to keep them. The royal road is provided by the certificate plan. Beneficent undertakers will not be wanting to smooth the way for them.

There is still another kind of employment that absorbs many of the boys and ought to be prohibited with the utmost rigor of the law. I refer to the messenger service of the District Telegraph Companies especially. Anyone can see for himself how old some of these boys are who carry messages about the streets every day; but everybody cannot see the kind of houses they have to go to, the kind of people they meet, or the sort of influences that beset them hourly at an age when they are most easily impressed for good or bad. If that were possible, the line would be drawn against their employment rather at eighteen than at sixteen or fourteen. At present there is none except the fanciful line drawn against truancy, which, to a boy who has learned the tricks of the telegraph messenger, is very elastic indeed.

To send the boys to school and see that they stay there until they have learned enough to at least vote intelligently when they grow up, is the bounden duty of the State—celebrated in theory but neglected in practice. If it did its duty much would have been gained, but even then the real kernel of this question of child labor would remain untouched. The trouble is not so much that the children have to work early as with the sort of work they have to do. It is, all of it, of a kind that leaves them, grown to manhood and womanhood, just where it found them, knowing no more, and therefore less, than when they began, and with the years that should have prepared them for life's work gone in hopeless and profitless drudgery. How large a share of the responsibility for this failure is borne by the senseless and wicked tyranny of so-called organized labor, in denying to our own children a fair chance to learn honest trades, while letting foreign workmen in in shoals to crowd our market under the plea of the "solidarity of labor"—a policy that is in a fair way of losing to labor all the respect due it from our growing youth, I shall not here discuss. The general result was well put by a tireless worker in the cause of improving the condition of the poor, who said to me, "They are down on the scrub level; there you find them and have to put them to such use as you can. They don't know anything else, and that is what makes it so hard to find work for them. Even when they go into a shop to sew, they come out mere machines, able to do only one thing, which is a small part of the whole they do not grasp. And thus, without the slightest training for the responsibilities of life, they marry and transmit their incapacity to another generation that is so much worse to start off with." She spoke of the girls, but what she said fitted the boys just as well. The incapacity of the mother is no greater than the ignorance of the father in the mass of such unions. Ignorance and poverty are the natural heritage of the children.

I have in mind a typical family of that sort which our relief committee wrestled with a whole summer, in Poverty Gap. Suggestive location! The man found his natural level on the island, where we sent him first thing. The woman was decent and willing to work, and the girls young enough to train. But Mrs. Murphy did not get on. "She can't even hold a flat iron in her hand," reported her first employer, indignantly. The children were sent to good places in the country, and repaid the kindness shown them by stealing and lying to cover up their thefts. They were not depraved; they were simply exhibiting the fruit of the only training they had ever received—that of the street. It was like undertaking a job of original creation to try to make anything decent or useful out of them.

I confess I had always laid the blame for this discouraging feature of the problem upon our general industrial development in a more or less vague way—steam, machinery, and all that sort of thing—until the other day I met a man who gave me another view of it altogether. He was a manufacturer of cheap clothing, a very intelligent and successful one at that; a large employer of cheap Hebrew labor and, heaven save the mark!—a Christian. His sincerity was unquestionable. He had no secrets to keep from me. He was in the business to make money, he said with perfect frankness, and one condition of his making money was, as he had had occasion to learn when he was himself a wageworker and a union man, to keep his workmen where they were at his mercy. He had some four hundred hands, all Jewish immigrants, all working for the lowest wages for which he could hire them. Among them all there was not one tailor capable of making a whole garment. His policy was to keep them from learning. He saw to it that each one was kept at just one thing—sleeves, pockets, buttonholes—some small part of one garment, and never learned anything else.

"This I do," he explained, "to prevent them from going on strike with the hope of getting a job anywhere else. They can't.

They don't know enough. Not only do we limit them so that a man who has worked three months in my shop and never held a needle before is just as valuable to me as one I have had five years, but we make the different parts of the suit in different places and keep Christians over the hands as cutters so that they shall have no chance to learn."

Where we stood in his shop, a little boy was stacking some coats for removal. The manufacturer pointed him out. "Now," he said, "this boy is not fourteen years old, as you can see as well as I. His father works here and when the inspector comes I just call him up. He swears that the boy is old enough to work, and there the matter ends. What would you? Is it not better that he should be here than on the street? Bah!" And this successful Christian manufacturer turned upon his heel with a vexed air. It was curious to hear him, before I left, deliver a homily on the "immorality" of the sweat shops, arraigning them severely as "a blot on humanity."

# 7

# THE TRUANTS OF OUR STREETS

O N MY WAY TO THE OFFICE the other day, I came upon three boys sitting on a beer keg in the mouth of a narrow alley intent upon a game of cards. They were dirty and "tough." The bare feet of the smallest lad were nearly black with dried mud. His hair bristled, unrestrained by cap or covering of any kind. They paid no attention to me when I stopped to look at them. It was an hour before noon.

"Why are you not in school?" I asked of the oldest rascal. He might have been thirteen.

"'Cause," he retorted calmly, without taking his eye off his neighbor's cards, "'cause I don't believe in it. Go on, Jim!"

I caught the black-footed one by the collar. "And you," I said, "why don't you go to school? Don't you know you have to?"

The boy thrust one of his bare feet out at me as an argument there was no refuting. "They don't want me; I aint got no shoes." And he took the trick.

I had heard his defense put in a different way to the same purpose more than once on my rounds through the sweat shops. Every now and then some father, whose boy was working under age, would object, "We send the child to school, as the inspector says, and there is no room for him. What shall we do?" He spoke the whole truth, likely enough; the boy only half of it. There was a charity school around the corner from where he sat struggling manfully with his disappointment, where they would have taken him, and fitted him out with shoes in the bargain, if the public school rejected him. If anything worried him, it was probably the fear that I might know of it and drag him around there. I had seen the same thought working in the tailor's mind. Neither had any use for the school; the one that his boy might work, the other that he might loaf and play hookey.

Each had found his own flaw in our compulsory education law and succeeded. The boy was safe in the street because no truant officer had the right to arrest him at sight for loitering there in school hours. His only risk was the chance of that functionary's finding him at home, and he was trying to provide against that. The tailor's defense was valid. With a law requiring—compelling is the word, but the compulsion is on the wrong tack—all children between the ages of eight and fourteen years to go to school at least one-fourth of the year or a little more; with a costly machinery to enforce it, even more costly to the child who falls under the ban as a truant than to the citizens who foot the bills, we should most illogically be compelled to exclude, by force if they insisted, more than fifty thousand of the children, did they all take it into their heads to obey the law. We have neither schools enough nor seats enough in them. As it is, we are spared that embarrassment. They don't obey it.

This is the way the case stands: Computing the school population upon the basis of the Federal Census of 1880 and the State Census of 1892, we had in New York, in the summer of 1891, 351,330 children between five and fourteen years. [10] I select these limits because children are admitted to the public schools under the law at the age of five years, and the statistics of the Board of Education show that the average age of the pupils entering the lowest primary grade is six years and five months. The whole number of different pupils taught in that year was

196,307. [11] The Catholic schools, parochial and select, reported a total of 35,055; the corporate schools (Children's Aid Society's, Orphan Asylums, American Female Guardian Society's, etc.), 23,276; evening schools, 29,165; Nautical School, 111; all other private schools (as estimated by Superintendent of Schools Jasper), 15,000; total, 298,914; any possible omissions in this list being more than made up for by the thousands over fourteen who are included. So that by deducting the number of pupils from the school population as given above, more than 50,000 children between the ages of five and fourteen are shown to have received no schooling whatever last year. As the public schools had seats for only 195,592, while the registered attendance exceeded that number, it follows that there was no room for the fifty thousand had they chosen to apply. In fact, the year before, 3,783 children had been refused admission at the opening of the schools after the summer vacation because there were no seats for them. To be told in the same breath that there were more than twenty thousand unoccupied seats in the schools at that time, is like adding insult to injury. Though vacant and inviting pupils they were worthless, for they were in the wrong schools. Where the crowding of the growing population was greatest and the need of schooling for the children most urgent, every seat was taken. Those who could not travel far from home—the poor never can—in search of an education had to go without.

The Department of Education employs twelve truant officers, who in 1891 "found and returned to school" 2,701 truants. There is a timid sort of pretence that this was "enforcing the compulsory education law," though it is coupled with the statement that at least eight more officers are needed to do it properly, and that they should have power to seize the culprits wherever found. Superintendent Jasper tells me that he thinks there are only about 8,000 children in New York who do not go to school at all. But the Department's own records furnish convincing proof that he is wrong, and that the 50,000 estimate is right. That number is just about one-seventh of the whole number of children between five and fourteen years, as stated above. In January of this year a school census of the Fourth and Fifteenth wards, [12] two widely separated localities, differing greatly as to character of population, gave the following result: Fourth Ward, total number of children between five and fourteen years, 2,016; [13] of whom 297 did not go to school. Fifteenth Ward, total number of children, 2,276; number of non-attendants, 339. In each case the proportion of non-attendants was nearly one-seventh, curiously corroborating the estimate made by me for the whole city.

*"Shooting craps" in the hall of the Newsboys' Lodging House*

Testimony to the same effect is borne by a different set of records, those of the reformatories that receive the truants of the city. The Juvenile Asylum, that takes most of those of the Protestant faith, reports that of 28,745 children of school age committed to its care in thirty-nine years 32 percent could not read when received. The proportion during the last five years was 23 percent. At the Catholic Protectory, of 3,123 boys and girls cared for during the year 1891, 689 were utterly illiterate at the time of their reception and the education of the other 2,434 was classified in various degrees between illiterate and "able to read and write" only. [14] The moral status of these last children may be inferred from the statement that 739 of them possessed no religious instruction at all when admitted. The analysis might be extended, doubtless with the same result as to illiteracy, throughout the institutions that harbor the city's dependent children, to the State Reformatory, where the final product is set down in 75 percent of "grossly ignorant" inmates, in spite of the fact that more than that proportion is recorded as being of "average natural mental capacity." In other words, they could have learned, had they been taught.

How much of this bad showing is due to the system, or the lack of system, of compulsory education, as we know it in New York, I shall not venture to say. In such a system a truant school or home would seem to be a logical necessity. Because a boy does not like to go to school, he is not necessarily bad. It may be the fault of the school and of the teacher as much as of the boy. Indeed, a good many people of sense hold that the boy who has never planned to run away from home or school does not amount to much. At all events, the boy ought not to be classed with thieves and vagabonds. But that is what New York does. It has no truant home. Its method of dealing with the truant is little less than downright savagery. It is thus set forth in a report of a special committee of the Board of Education, made to that body on November 18, 1891. "Under the law the truant agents act upon reports received from the principals of the schools. After exhausting the persuasion that they may be able to exercise to compel the attendance of truant children, and in cases which seem to call for the enforcement of the law, the agent procures the endorsement of the President of the Board of Education and the Superintendent of Schools upon his requisition for a warrant for the arrest of the truant, which warrant, under the provisions of the law, is then issued by a Police Justice. A policeman is then detailed to make the arrest, and when apprehended the truant is brought to the Police Court, where his parents or guardians are obliged to attend. Should it happen that the latter are not present, the boy is put in a cell to await their appearance. It has sometimes happened that a public school boy, whose only offence against the law was his refusal to attend school, has been kept in a cell two or three days with old criminals pending the appearance of his parents or guardians. [15] While we fully realize the importance of enforcing the laws relating to compulsory education, we believe that bringing the boys into associations with criminals in this way and making it necessary for parents to be present under such circumstances, is unjust and improper, and that criminal associations of this kind in connection with the administration of the truancy laws should not be allowed to continue. The Justice may, after hearing the facts, commit the child who, in a majority of cases, is between eight and eleven years old, to one of the institutions designated by law. We do not think that the enforcement of the laws relating to compulsory education should at any time enforce association with criminal classes."

But it does, all the way through. The "institutions designated by law" for the reception of truants are chiefly the Protectory and the Juvenile Asylum. In the thirty-nine years of its existence the latter has harbored 11,636 children committed to it for disobedience and truancy. And this was the company they mingled with there on a common footing: "Unfortunate children," 8,806; young thieves, 3,097; vagrants, 3,173; generally bad boys and girls, 1,390; beggars, 542; children committed for peddling, 51; as witnesses, 50. Of the whole lot barely a hundred, comprised within the last two items, might be supposed to be harmless, though there is no assurance that they were. Of the Protectory children I have already spoken. It will serve further to place them to say that nearly one-third of the 941 received last year were homeless, while fully 35 percent of all the boys suffered when entering from the contagious eye disease that is the scourge of the poorest tenements as of the public institutions that admit their children. I do not here take into account the House of Refuge, though that is also one of the institutions designated by law for the reception of truants, for the reason that only about one-fifth of those admitted to it last year came from New York City. Their number was 55. The rest came from other counties in the state. But even there the percentage of truants to those committed for stealing or other crimes was as 53 to 47.

This is the "system," or one end of it—the one where the waste goes on. The Committee spoken of reported that the city paid in 1890, $63,690 for the maintenance of the truants committed by magistrates, at the rate of $110 for every child, and that two truant schools and a home for incorrigible truants could be established and maintained at less cost, since it would probably not be necessary to send to the home for incorrigibles more than 25 percent of all. It further advised the creation of the special office of Truant Commissioner, to avoid dragging the children into the police courts. In his report for the present year Superintendent Jasper renews in substance these recommendations. But nothing has been done.

The situation is this, then, that a vast horde of fifty thousand children is growing up in this city whom our public school does not and cannot reach; if it reaches them at all it is with the threat of the jail. The mass of them is no doubt to be found in the shops and factories, as I have shown. A large number peddle newspapers or black boots. Still another contingent, much too large, does nothing but idle, in training for the penitentiary. I stopped one of that kind at the corner of Baxter and Grand Streets one day to catechise him. It was in the middle of the afternoon when the schools were in session, but while I purposely detained him with a long talk to give the neighborhood time to turn out, thirteen other lads of his age, all of them under fourteen, gathered to listen to my business with Graccho. When they had become convinced that I was not an officer they frankly owned that they were all playing hookey. All of them lived in the block. How many more of their kind it sheltered I do not know. They were not exactly a nice lot, but not one of them would I have committed to the chance of contact with thieves with a clear conscience. I should have feared especial danger from such contact in their case.

As a matter of fact the record of average attendance (136,413) shows that the public school *per se* reaches little more than a third of all the children. And even those it does not hold long enough to do them the good that was intended. The Superintendent of Schools declares that the average age at which the children leave school is twelve or a little over. It must needs be, then, that very many quit much earlier, and the statement that in New York, as in Chicago, St. Louis, Brooklyn, New Orleans, and other American cities, half or more than half the schoolboys leave school at the age of eleven (the source of the statement is unknown to me) seems credible enough. I am not going to discuss here the value of school education as a preventive of crime. That it is, so far as it goes, a positive influence for good I suppose few thinking people doubt nowadays. Dr. William T. Harris, Federal Commissioner of Education, in an address delivered before the National Prison Association in 1890, stated that an investigation of the returns of seventeen states that kept a record of the educational status of their criminals showed the number of criminals to be eight times as large from the illiterate stratum as from an equal number of the population that could read and write. That census was taken in 1870. Ten years later a canvass of the jails of Michigan, a state that had an illiterate population of less than five percent, showed exactly the same ratio, so that I presume that may safely be accepted.

In view of these facts it does not seem that the showing the public school is making in New York is either creditable or safe. It is not creditable, because the city's wealth grows even faster than its population, [16] and there is no lack of means with which to provide schools enough and the machinery to enforce the law and fill them. Not to enforce it because it would cost a great deal of money is wicked waste and folly. It is not safe, because the school is our chief defense against the tenement and the flood of ignorance with which it would swamp us. Prohibition of child labor without compelling the attendance at school of the freed slaves is a mockery. The children are better off working than idling, any day. The physical objections to the one alternative are vastly outweighed by the moral iniquities of the other.

I have tried to set forth the facts. They carry their own lesson. The then State Superintendent of Education, Andrew Draper, read it aright when, in his report for 1889, he said about the compulsory education law:

"It does not go far enough and is without an executor. It is barren of results.... It may be safely said that no system will be effectual in bringing the unfortunate children of the streets into the schools which at least does not definitely fix the age within which children must attend the schools, which does not determine the period of the year within which all must be there, which does not determine the method for gathering all needed information, which does not provide especial schools for incorrigible cases, which does not punish people charged with the care of children for neglecting their education, and which does not provide the machinery and officials for executing the system."

# 8

## WHAT IT IS THAT MAKES BOYS BAD

I AM REMINDED, in trying to show up the causes that go to make children bad, of the experience of a certain sanitary inspector who was laboring with the proprietor of a seven-cent lodging house to make him whitewash and clean up. The man had reluctantly given in to several of the inspector's demands; but, as they kept piling up, his irritation grew, until at the mention of clean sheets he lost all patience and said, with bitter contempt, "Well! You needn't tink dem's angels!"

They were not—those lodgers of his—they were tramps. Neither are the children of the street angels. If, once in a while, they act more like little devils the opportunities we have afforded them, as I have tried to show, hardly give us the right to reproach them. They are not the kind of opportunities to make angels. And yet, looking the hundreds of boys in the Juvenile Asylum over, all of whom were supposed to be there because they were bad (though, as I had occasion to ascertain, that was a mistake— it was the parents that were bad in some cases), I was struck by the fact that they were anything but a depraved lot. Except as to their clothes and their manners, which were the manners of the street, they did not seem to be very different in looks from a like number of boys in any public school. Fourth of July was just then at hand, and when I asked the official who accompanied me how they proposed to celebrate it, he said that they were in the habit of marching in procession up Eleventh Avenue to Fort George, across to Washington Bridge, and all about the neighborhood, to a grove where speeches were made. Remembering the iron bars and high fences I had seen, I said something about it being unsafe to let a thousand young prisoners go at large in that way. The man looked at me in some bewilderment before he understood.

"Bless you, no!" he said, when my meaning dawned upon him. "If any one of them was to run away that day he would be in eternal disgrace with all the rest. It is a point of honor with them to deserve it when they are trusted. Often we put a boy on duty outside, when he could walk off, if he chose, just as well as not; but he will come in in the evening, as straight as a string, only, perhaps, to twist his bedclothes into a rope that very night and let himself down from a third-story window, at the risk of breaking his neck. Boys will be boys, you know."

But it struck me that boys whose honor could be successfully appealed to in that way were rather the victims than the doers of a grievous wrong, being in that place, no matter if they *had* stolen. It was a case of misdirection, or no direction at all, of their youthful energies. There was one little fellow in the Asylum band who was a living illustration of this. I watched him blow his horn with a supreme effort to be heard above the rest, growing redder and redder in the face, until the perspiration rolled off him in perfect sheets, the veins stood out swollen and blue and it seemed as if he must burst the next minute. He was a tremendous trumpeter. I was glad when it was over, and patted him on the head, telling him that if he put as much vim into all he had to do, as he did into his horn, he would come to something great yet. Then it occurred to me to ask him what he was there for.

"'Cause I was lazy and played hookey," he said, and joined in the laugh his answer raised. The idea of that little body, that fairly throbbed with energy, being sent to prison for laziness was too absurd for anything.

The report that comes from the Western Agency of the

Asylum, through which the boys are placed out on farms, that the proportion of troublesome children is growing larger does not agree with the idea of laziness either, but well enough with the idleness of the street, which is what sends nine-tenths of the boys to the Asylum. Satan finds plenty of mischief for the idle hands of these lads to do. The one great point is to give them something to do—something they can see the end of, yet that will keep them busy right along. The more ignorant the child, the more urgent this rule, the shorter and simpler the lesson must be. Over in the Catholic Protectory, where they get the most ignorant boys, they appreciate this to the extent of encouraging the boys to a game of Sunday baseball rather than see them idle even for the briefest spell. Of the practical wisdom of their course there can be no question.

"I have come to the conclusion," said a well-known educator on a recent occasion, "that much of crime is a question of athletics." From over the sea the Earl of Meath adds his testimony: "Three fourths of the youthful rowdyism of large towns is owing to the stupidity and, I may add, cruelty of the ruling powers in not finding some safety valve for the exuberant energies of the boys and girls of their respective cities." For our neglect to do so in New York we are paying heavily in the maintenance of these costly reform schools. I spoke of the chance for romping and play where the poor children crowd. In a Cherry Street hallway I came across this sign in letters a foot long: "No ball playing, dancing, card playing, and no persons but tenants allowed in the yard." It was a five-story tenement, swarming with children, and there was another just as big across that yard. Out in the street the policeman saw to it that the ball playing at least was stopped, and as for the dancing, that, of course, was bound to collect a crowd, the most heinous offence known to him as a preserver of the peace. How the peace was preserved by such means I saw on the occasion of my discovering that sign. The business that took me down there was a murder in another tenement just like it. A young man, hardly more than a boy, was killed in the course of a midnight "can racket" on the roof, in which half the young people in the block had a hand night after night. It was *their* outlet for the "exuberant energies" of their natures. The safety valve was shut, with the landlord and the policeman holding it down.

It is when the wrong outlet has thus been forced that the right and natural one has to be reopened with an effort as the first condition of reclaiming the boy. The play in him has all run to "toughness," and has first to be restored. "We have no great hope of a boy's reformation," writes Mr. William F. Round, of the Burnham Industrial Farm, to a friend who has shown me his letter, "till he takes an active part and interest in outdoor amusements. Plead with all your might for playgrounds for the city waifs and school children. When the lungs are freely expanded, the blood coursing with a bound through all veins and arteries, the whole mind and body in a state of high emulation in wholesome play, there is no time or place for wicked thought or consequent wicked action and the body is growing every moment more able to help in the battle against temptation when it shall come at other times and places. Next time another transit company asks a franchise make them furnish tickets to the parks and suburbs to all school children on all holidays and Saturdays, the same to be given out in school for regular attendance, as a method of health promotion and a preventive of truancy." Excellent scheme! If we could only make them. It is five years and over now since we made them pass a law at Albany appropriating a million dollars a year for the laying out of small parks in the most crowded tenement districts, in the Mulberry Street Bend for instance, and practically we stand today where we stood then. The Mulberry Street Bend is still there, with no sign of a park or playground other than in the gutter. When I asked, a year ago, why this was so, I was told by the Counsel to the Corporation that it was because "not much interest had been taken" by the previous administration in the matter. Is it likely that a corporation that runs a railroad to make money could be prevailed upon to take more interest in a proposition to make it surrender part of its profits than the city's sworn officers in their bounden duty? Yet let anyone go and see for himself what effect such a park has in a crowded tenement district. Let him look at Tompkins Square Park as it is today and compare the children that skip among the trees and lawns and around the bandstand with those that root in the gutters only a few blocks off. That was the way they looked in Tompkins Square twenty years ago when the square was a sandlot given up to rioting and disorder. The police had their hands full then. I remember being present when they had to take the square by storm more than once, and there is at least one captain on the force today who owes his promotion to the part he took and the injuries he suffered in one of those battles. Today it is as quiet and orderly a neighborhood as any in the city. Not a squeak has been heard about "bread or blood" since those trees were planted and the lawns and flower beds laid out. It is not all the work of the missions, the kindergartens, and Boys' clubs and lodging houses, of which more anon; nor even the larger share. The park did it, exactly as the managers of the Juvenile Asylum appealed to the sense of honor in their prisoners. It appealed with its trees and its grass and its birds to the sense of decency and of beauty, undeveloped but not smothered, in the children, and the whole neighborhood responded. One can go around the whole square that covers two big blocks, nowadays, and not come upon a single fight. I should like to see anyone walk that distance in Mulberry Street without running across half a dozen.

Thus far the street and its idleness as factors in making criminals of the boys. Of the factory I have spoken. Certainly it is to be preferred to the street, if the choice must be between the two. Its offence is that it makes a liar of the boy and keeps him in ignorance, even of a useful trade, thus blazing a wide path for him straight to the prison gate. The school does not come to the rescue; the child must come to the school, and even then is not sure of a welcome. The trades' unions do their worst for the boy by robbing him of the slim chance to learn a trade which the factory left him. Of the tenement I have said enough. Apart from all other considerations and influences, as the destroyer of character and individuality everywhere, it is the wickedest of all the forces that attack the defenseless child. The tenements are increasing in number, and so is "the element that becomes criminal because of lack of individuality and the self-respect that comes with it." [17]

I am always made to think in connection with this subject of a story told me by a bright little woman of her friend's kittens. There was a litter of them in the house and a jealous terrier dog to boot, whose one aim in life was to get rid of its mewing rivals. Out in the garden where the children played there was a sand heap and the terrier's trick was to bury alive in the sand any kitten it caught unawares. The children were constantly rushing to the rescue and unearthing their pets; on the day when my friend was there on a visit they were too late. The first warning of the tragedy in the garden came to the ladies when one of the children rushed in, all red and excited, with bulging eyes. "There," she said, dropping the dead kitten out of her apron before them, "a perfectly good cat spoiled!"

Perfectly good children, as good as any on the Avenue, are spoiled every day by the tenement; only we have not done with them then, as the terrier had with the kitten. There is still posterity to reckon with.

What this question of heredity amounts to, whether in the past or in the future, I do not know. I have not had opportunity enough of observing. No one has that I know of. Those who have had the most disagree in their conclusions, or have come to none. I have known numerous instances of criminality, running apparently in families for generations, but there was always the desperate environment as the unknown factor in the makeup. Whether that bore the greatest share of the blame, or whether the reformation of the criminal to be effective should have begun with his grandfather, I could not tell. Besides, there was always the chance that the great grandfather, or some one still farther back, of whom all trace was lost, might have been a paragon of virtue, even if his descendant was a thief, and so there was no telling just where to begin. In general I am inclined to think with such practical philanthropists as Superintendent Barnard, of the Five Points House of Industry, the Manager of the Children's Aid Society, Superintendent E. Fellows Jenkins, of the Society for the Prevention of Cruelty to Children, and Mr. Israel C. Jones, who for more than thirty years was in charge of the House of Refuge, that the bugbear of heredity is not nearly as formidable as we have half taught ourselves to think. It is rather a question of getting hold of the child early enough before the evil influences surrounding him have got a firm grip on him. Among a mass of evidence quoted in support of this belief, perhaps this instance, related by Superintendent Jones in *The Independent* last March, is as convincing as any:

Thirty years ago there was a depraved family living adjacent to what is now a part of the city of New York. The mother was not only dishonest, but exceedingly intemperate, wholly neglectful of her duties as a mother, and frequently served terms in jail until she finally died. The father was also dissipated and neglectful. It was a miserable existence for the children.

Two of the little boys, in connection with two other boys in the neighborhood, were arrested, tried, and found guilty of entering a house in the daytime and stealing. In course of time both of these boys were indentured. One remained in his place and the other left for another part of the country, where he died. He was a reputable lad.

The first boy, in one way and another, got a few pennies together with which he purchased books. After a time he proposed to his master that he be allowed to present himself for examination as a teacher. The necessary consent was given, he presented himself, and was awarded a "grade A" certificate.

Two years from that time he came to the House of Refuge, as proud as a man could be, and exhibited to me his certificate. He then entered a law office, diligently pursued his studies, and was admitted to the bar. He was made a judge, and is now chief magistrate of the court in the city where he lives.

His sister, a little girl, used to come to the Refuge with her mother, wearing nothing but a thin cloak in very cold weather, almost perishing with the cold. As soon as this young man got on his feet he rescued the little girl. He placed her in a school; she finally graduated from the Normal School, and today holds an excellent position in the schools in the state where she lives.

The records of the three reformatory institutions before mentioned throw their own light upon the question of what makes criminals of the young. At the Elmira Reformatory, of more than five thousand prisoners only a little over one percent were shown to have kept good company prior to their coming there. One and a half percent are put down under this head as "doubtful," while the character of association is recorded for 41.2 percent as "not good," and for 55.9 percent as "positively bad." Three-fourths possessed no culture or only the slightest. As to moral sense, 42.6 percent had absolutely none, 35 percent "possibly some." Only 7.6 percent came from good homes. Of the rest 39.8 percent had homes that are recorded as "fair only," and 52.6 percent downright bad homes; 4.8 percent had pauper, and 76.8 percent poor parents; 38.4 percent of the prisoners had drunken parents, and 13 percent parents of doubtful sobriety. Of more than twenty-two thousand inmates of the Juvenile Asylum in thirty-nine years one-fourth had either a drunken father or mother, or both. At the Protectory the percentage of drunkenness in parents was not quite one-fifth among over three thousand children cared for in the institution last year.

There is never any lack of trashy novels and cheap shows in New York, and the children who earn money selling newspapers or otherwise take to them as ducks do to water. They fall in well with the ways of the street that are showy always, however threadbare may be the cloth. As for that, it is simply the cheap side of our national extravagance.

The cigarette, if not a cause, is at least the mean accessory of half the mischief of the street. And I am not sure it is not a cause too. It is an inexorable creditor that has goaded many a boy to stealing; for cigarettes cost money, and they do not encourage industry. Of course there is a law against the cigarette, or rather against the boy smoking it who is not old enough to work—there is law in plenty, usually, if that would only make people good. It don't in the matter of the cigarette. It helps make the boy bad by adding the relish of law-breaking to his enjoyment of the smoke. Nobody stops him.

The mania for gambling is all but universal. Every street child is a born gambler; he has nothing to lose and all to win. He begins by "shooting craps" in the street and ends by "chucking dice" in the saloon, two names for the same thing, sure to lead to the same goal. By the time he has acquired individual standing in the saloon, his long apprenticeship has left little or nothing for him to learn of the bad it has to teach. Never for his own sake is he turned away with the growler when he comes to have it filled; once in a while for the saloon keeper's, if that worthy suspects in him a decoy and a "job." Just for the sake of the experiment, not because I expected it to develop anything new, I chose at random, while writing this chapter, a saloon in a tenement house district on the East Side and posted a man, whom I could trust implicitly, at the door with orders to count the children under age who went out and in with beer jugs in open defiance of law. Neither he nor I had ever been in or even seen the saloon before. He reported as the result of three and a half hours' watch at noon and in the evening a total of fourteen—ten boys and a girl under ten years of age, and three girls between ten and fourteen years, not counting a little boy who bought a bottle of ginger. It was a cool, damp day; not a thirsty day, or the number would probably have been twice as great. There was not the least concealment about the transaction in any of the fourteen cases. The children were evidently old customers.

The law that failed to save the boy while there was time yet to make a useful citizen of him provides the means of catching him when his training begins to bear fruit that threatens the public peace. Then it is with the same blundering disregard of common sense and common decency that marked his prosecution as a truant that the half grown lad is dragged into a police court and thrust into a prison pen with hardened thieves and criminals to learn the lessons they have to teach him. The one thing New York needs most after a truant home is a special court for the trial of youthful offenders only. I am glad to say that this want seems at last in a way to be supplied. The last Legislature authorized the establishment of such a court, and it may be that even as these pages see the light this blot upon our city is about to be wiped out.

Lastly, but not least, the Church is to blame for deserting the poor in their need. It is an old story that the churches have moved uptown with the wealth and fashion, leaving the poor crowds to find their way to heaven as best they could, and that the crowds have paid them back in their own coin by denying that they, the churches, knew the way at all. The Church has something to answer for; but it is a healthy sign at least that it is accepting the responsibility and professing anxiety to meet it. In much of the best work done among the poor and for the poor it has lately taken the lead, and it is not likely that any more of the churches will desert the downtown field, with the approval of Christian men and women at least.

～

Little enough of the light I promised in the opening chapter has struggled through these pages so far. We have looked upon the dark side of the picture; but there is a brighter. If the battle with ignorance, with misery, and with vice has but just begun, if the army that confronts us is strong, too strong, in numbers still and in malice—the gauntlet has been thrown down, the war waged, and blows struck that tell. They augur victory, for we have cut off the enemy's supplies and turned his flank. As I showed in the case of the immigrant Jews and the Italians, we have captured his recruits. With a firm grip on these, we may hope to win, for the rest of the problem ought to be and *can* be solved. With our own we should be able to settle, if there is any virtue in our school and our system of government. In this, as in all things, the public conscience must be stirred before the community's machinery for securing justice can move. That it has been stirred, profoundly and to useful purpose, the multiplication in our day of charities for attaining the ends the law has failed to reach, gives evidence. Their number is so great that mention can be made here merely of a few of the most important and typical efforts along the line. A register of all those that deal with the children especially, as compiled by the Charity Organization Society, will be found in an appendix to this book. Before we proceed to look at the results achieved through endeavors to stop the waste down at the bottom by private reinforcement of the public school, we will glance briefly at two of the charities that have a plainer purpose—if I may so put it without disparagement to the rest—that look upon the child merely as a child worth saving for its own sake, because it is helpless and poor and wretched. Both of them represent distinct departures in charitable work. Both, to the everlasting credit of our city be it said, had their birth here, and in this generation, and from New York their blessings have been carried to the farthest lands. One is the Society for the Prevention of Cruelty to Children, known far and near now as the Children's Society, whose strong and beneficent plan has been embodied in the structure of law of half the civilized nations of the world. The other, always spoken of as the "Fresh Air Fund," never had law or structural organization of any kind, save the law of love, laid down on the Mount for all time; but the life of that divine command throbs in it and has touched the heart of mankind wherever its story has been told.

9

# LITTLE MARY ELLEN'S LEGACY

O N A THRIVING FARM up in Central New York a happy young wife goes singing about her household work today who once as a helpless, wretched waif in the great city through her very helplessness and misery stirred up a social revolution whose waves beat literally upon the farthest shores. The story of little Mary Ellen moved New York eighteen years ago as it had scarce ever been stirred by news of disaster or distress before. In the simple but eloquent language of the public record it is thus told: "In the summer of 1874 a poor woman lay dying in the last stages of consumption in a miserable little room on the top floor of a big tenement in this city. A Methodist missionary, visiting among the poor, found her there and asked what she could do to soothe her sufferings. 'My time is short,' said the sick woman, 'but I cannot die in peace while the miserable little girl whom they call Mary Ellen is being beaten day and night by her stepmother next door to my room.' She told how the screams of the child were heard at all hours. She was locked in the room, she understood. It had been so for months, while she had been lying ill there. Prompted by the natural instinct of humanity, the missionary sought the aid of the police, but she was told that it was necessary to furnish evidence before an arrest could be made. 'Unless you can prove that an offence has been committed we cannot interfere, and all you know is hearsay.' She next went to several benevolent societies in the city whose object it was to care for children, and asked their interference in behalf of the child. The reply was: 'If the child is legally brought to us, and is a proper subject, we will take it; otherwise we cannot act in the matter.' In turn then she consulted several excellent charitable citizens as to what she should do. They replied: 'It is a dangerous thing to interfere between parent and child, and you might get yourself into trouble if you did so, as parents are proverbially the best guardians of their own children.' Finally, in despair, with the piteous appeals of the dying woman ringing in her ears, she said: 'I will make one more effort to save this child. There is one man in this city who has never turned a deaf ear to the cry of the helpless, and who has spent his life in just this work for the benefit of unoffending animals. I will go to Henry Bergh.'

"She went, and the great friend of the dumb brute found a way. 'The child is an animal,' he said, 'if there is no justice for it as a human being, it shall at least have the rights of the stray cur in the street. It shall not be abused.' And thus was written the first bill of rights for the friendless waif the world over. The appearance of the starved, half naked, and bruised child when it was brought into court wrapped in a horse blanket caused a sensation that stirred the public conscience to its very depths. Complaints poured in upon Mr. Bergh; so many cases of child beating and fiendish cruelty came to light in a little while, so many little savages were hauled forth from their dens of misery, that the community stood aghast. A meeting of citizens was called and an association for the defense of outraged childhood was formed, out of which grew the Society for the Prevention of Cruelty to Children that was formally incorporated in the following year. By that time Mary Ellen was safe in a good home. She never saw her tormentor again. The woman, whose name was Connolly, was not her mother. She steadily refused to tell where she got the child, and the mystery of its descent was never solved. The wretched woman was sent to the Island and forgotten.

John D. Wright, a venerable Quaker merchant, was chosen the first President of the Society. Upon the original call for the first meeting, preserved in the archives of the Society, may still be read a footnote in his handwriting, quaintly amending the date to read, Quaker fashion, "12th mo. 15th 1874." A year later, in his first review of the work that was before the young society, he wrote, "Ample laws have been passed by the legislature of this state for the protection of and prevention of cruelty to little children. The trouble seems to be that it is nobody's business to enforce them. Existing societies have as much, nay more to do than they can attend to in providing for those entrusted to their care. The Society for the Prevention of Cruelty to Children proposes to enforce by lawful means and with energy those laws, not vindictively, not to gain public applause, but to convince those who cruelly ill-treat and shamefully neglect little children that the time has passed when this can be done, in this state at least, with impunity."

The promise has been faithfully kept. The old Quaker is dead, but his work goes on. The good that he did lives after him, and will live forever. The applause of the crowd his Society has not always won; but it has merited the confidence and approval of all right-thinking and right-feeling men. Its aggressive advocacy of defenseless childhood, always and everywhere, is today reflected from the statute books of every state in the American Union, and well-nigh every civilized government abroad, in laws that sprang directly from its fearless crusade.

In theory it had always been the duty of the state to protect the child "in person, and property, and in its opportunity for life, liberty, and happiness," even against a worthless parent; in practice it held to the convenient view that, after all, the parent had the first right to the child and knew what was best for it. The result in many cases was thus described in the tenth annual report of the Society by President Elbridge T. Gerry, who in 1879 had succeeded Mr. Wright and has ever since been so closely identified with its work that it is as often spoken of nowadays as Mr. Gerry's Society as under its corporate name:

"Impecunious parents drove them from their miserable homes at all hours of the day and night to beg and steal. They were trained as acrobats at the risk of life and limb, and beaten cruelly if they failed. They were sent at night to procure liquor for parents too drunk to venture themselves into the streets. They were drilled in juvenile operas and song-and-dance variety business until their voices were cracked, their growth stunted, and their health permanently ruined by exposure and want of rest. Numbers of young Italians were imported by *padroni* under promises of a speedy return, and then sent out on the streets to play on musical instruments, to peddle flowers and small wares to the passersby, and too often as a cover for immorality. Their surroundings were those of vice, profanity, and obscenity. Their only amusements were the dance halls, the cheap theatres and museums, and the saloons. Their acquaintances were those hardened in sin, and both boys and girls soon became adepts in crime, and entered unhesitatingly on the downward path. Beaten and abused at home, treated worse than animals, no other result could be expected. In the prisons, to which sooner or later these unhappy children gravitated, there was no separation of them from hardened criminals. Their previous education in vice rendered them apt scholars in the school of crime, and they ripened into criminals as they advanced in years."

All that has not been changed in the seventeen years that have passed; to remodel depraved human nature has been beyond the power of the Society; but step by step under its prompting the law has been changed and strengthened; step by step life has been breathed into its dead letter, until now it is as able and willing to protect the child against violence or absolute cruelty as the Society is to enforce its protection. There is work enough for it to do yet. I have outlined some in the preceding chapters. In the past year (1891) it investigated 7,695 complaints and rescued 3,683 children from pernicious surroundings, some of them from a worse fate than death. "But let it not be supposed from this," writes the Superintendent, "that crimes of and against children are on the increase. As a matter of fact wrongs to children have been materially lessened in New York by the Society's action and influence during the past seventeen years. Some have entirely disappeared, having been eradicated root and branch from New York life, and an influence for good has been felt by the children themselves, as shown by the great diminution in juvenile delinquency from 1875, when the Society was first organized, to 1891, the figures indicating a decrease of fully fifty percent." [18]

*Case no. 25745 on the Society blotter: Annie Wolff—*
*aged seven years, as she was driven forth by her cruel stepmother, beaten*
*and starved, with her arms tied upon her back, and as she appeared after six*
*months in the Society's care*

Other charitable efforts, working along the same line, contributed their share, perhaps the greater, to the latter result, but the Society's influence upon the environment that shapes the childish mind and character, as well as upon the child itself, is undoubted. It is seen in the hot haste with which a general cleaning up and setting to rights is begun in a block of tenement barracks the moment the "cruelty man" heaves in sight; in the "holy horror" the child beater has of him and his mission, and in the altered attitude of his victim, who not rarely nowadays confronts his tormentor with the threat, "if you do that I will go to the Children's Society," always effective except when drink blinds the wretch to consequences.

The Society had hardly been in existence four years when it came into collision with the padrone and his abominable system of child slavery. These traders in human misery, adventurers of the worst type, made a practice of hiring the children of the poorest peasants in the Neapolitan mountain districts, to serve them begging, singing, and playing in the streets of American cities. The contract was for a term of years at the end of which they were to return the child and pay a fixed sum, a miserable pittance, to the parents for its use, but, practically, the bargain amounted to a sale, except that the money was never paid. The children left their homes never to return. They were shipped from Naples to Marseilles, and made to walk all the way through France, singing, playing, and dancing in the towns and villages through which they passed, to a seaport where they embarked for America. Upon their arrival here they were brought to a rendezvous in some out-of-the-way slum and taken in hand by the padrone, the partner of the one who had hired them abroad. He sent them out to play in the streets by day, singing and dancing in tune to their alleged music, and by night made them perform in the lowest dens in the city. All the money they made the padrone took from them, beating and starving them if they did not bring home enough. None of it ever reached their parents. Under this treatment the boys grew up thieves—the girls worse. The life soon wore them out, and the Potter's Field claimed them before their term of slavery was at an end, according to the contract. In far-off Italy the simple peasants waited anxiously for the return of little Tomaso or Antonia with the coveted American gold. No word ever came of them.

The vile traffic had been broken up in England only to be transferred to America. The Italian government had protested.

Congress had passed an act making it a felony for anyone knowingly to bring into the United States any person inveigled or forcibly kidnapped in any other country, with the intent to hold him here in involuntary service. But these children were not only unable to either speak or understand English, they were compelled, under horrible threats, to tell anyone who asked that the padrone was their father, brother, or other near relative. To get the evidence upon which to proceed against the padrone was a task of exceeding difficulty, but it was finally accomplished by cooperation of the Italian government with the Society's agents in the case of the padrone Ancarola, who, in November, 1879, brought over from Italy seven boy slaves, between nine and thirteen years old, with their outfit of harps and violins. They were seized, and the padrone, who escaped from the steamer, was arrested in a Crosby Street groggery five days later. Before a jury in the United States Court the whole vile scheme was laid bare. One of the boys testified that Ancarola had paid his mother 20 lire (about four dollars) and his uncle 60 lire. For this sum he was to serve the padrone four years. Ancarola was convicted and sent to the penitentiary. The children were returned to their homes.

The news travelled slowly on the other side. For years the padrone's victims kept coming at intervals, but the society's agents were on the watch, and when the last of the kidnappers was sent to prison in 1885 there was an end of the business. The excitement attending the trial and the vigor with which the Society had pushed its pursuit of the rascally padrone drew increased attention to its work. At the end of the following year twenty-four societies had been organized in other states upon its plan, and half the governments of Europe were enacting laws patterned after those of New York State. Today there are a hundred societies for the prevention of cruelty to children in this country, independent of each other but owning the New York Society as their common parent, and nearly twice as many abroad in England, France, Italy, Spain, the West Indies, South America,

Canada, Australia, etc. The old link that bound the dumb brute with the helpless child in a common bond of humane sympathy has never been broken. Many of them include both in their efforts, and all the American societies, whether their care be children or animals, are united in an association for annual conference and cooperation, called the American Humane Association.

In seventeen years the Society has investigated 61,749 complaints of cruelty to children, involving 185,247 children, prosecuted 21,282 offenders, and obtained 20,697 convictions. The children it has saved and released numbered at the end of the year 1891 no less than 32,633. Whenever it has been charged with erring it has been on the side of mercy for the helpless child. It follows its charges into the police courts, seeing to it that, if possible, no record of crime is made against the offending child and that it is placed at once where better environment may help bring out the better side of its nature. It follows them into the institutions to which they are committed through its care, and fights their battles there, if need be, or the battles of their guardians under the law, against the greed of parents that would sacrifice the child's prospects in life for the sake of the few pennies it could earn at home. And it generally wins the fight.

The Society has never received any financial support from the city, but has depended entirely upon private benevolence. Ample means have always been at its disposal. Last year it sheltered, fed, and clothed 1,697 children in its rooms. Most of them were the victims of drunken parents. With the Society they found safe shelter. "Sometimes," Superintendent Jenkins says, "the children cry when they are brought here. They always cry when they go away."

"Lastly," so ran the old Quaker merchant's address in his first annual report, "this Society, so far from interfering with the numerous societies and institutions already existing, is intended to aid them in their noble work. It proposes to labor in the interest of no one religious denomination, and to keep entirely free from political influences of every kind. Its duties toward the children whom it may rescue will be discharged when the future custody of them is decided by the courts of justice." Before the faithful adherence to that plan all factious or sectarian opposition that impedes and obstructs so many other charities has fallen away entirely. Humanity is the religion of the Children's Society. In its Board of Directors are men of all nationalities and of every creed. Its fundamental doctrine is that every rescued child must be given finally into the keeping of those of its own faith who will carry on the work begun in its rescue. Beyond that point the Society does not go. It has once refused the gift of a seaside home lest it become a rival in a field where it would render only friendly counsel and aid.

In the case of the little John Does a doubt arises which the Society settles by passing them on to the best institution available for each particular child, quite irrespective of sect. There are thirteen of them by this time, waifs found in the street by the Society's agents or friends and never claimed by anybody. Though passed on, in the plan of the Society from which it never deviates, to be cared for by others, they are never lost sight of but always considered its special charges, for whom it bears a peculiar responsibility.

Poor little Carmen, of whom I spoke in the chapter about Italian children, was one of the Society's wards. Its footprints may be found all through these pages. To its printed reports, with their array of revolting cruelty and neglect, the reader is referred who would fully understand what a gap in a Christian community it bridges over.

# 10

# THE STORY OF THE FRESH AIR FUND

THE LAST ECHOES OF THE STORM raised by the story of little Mary Ellen had not died in the Pennsylvania hills when a young clergyman in the obscure village of Sherman preached to his congregation one Sunday morning from the text, "Inasmuch as ye did it unto one of these my brethren, even these least, ye did it unto me," a sermon which in its far-reaching effects was to become one of the strongest links in the chain of remorseful human sympathy then being forged in the fires of public indignation. Willard Parsons was a man with a practical mind as well as an open heart. He had lived in the city and had witnessed the suffering of the poor children in the stony streets on the hot summer days. Out there in the country he saw the wild strawberry redden the fields in June only to be trampled down by the cattle, saw, as the summer wore on, the blackberry vines by the wayside groaning under their burden of sweet fruit, unconsidered and going to waste, with this starved host scarce a day's journey away. Starved in body, in mind, and in soul! Not for them was the robin's song *they* scarcely heard; not for them the summer fields or the cool forest shade, the sweet smell of briar and fern. Theirs was poverty and want, and heat and suffering and death—death as the entrance to a life for which the slum had been their only preparation. And such a preparation!

All this the young preacher put in his sermon, and as he saw the love that went out from his own full heart kindling in the eager faces of his listeners, he told them what had been in his mind on many a lonely walk through those fields: that while the flowers and the brook and the trees might not be taken to the great prison pen where the children were, these might be brought out to enjoy them there. There was no reason why it should not be done, even though it had not been before. If they were poor and friendless and starved, yet there had been One even poorer, more friendless than they. They at least had their slum. He had not where to lay his head. Well they might, in receiving the children into their homes, be entertaining angels unawares. "Inasmuch as ye did it unto even the least of these, ye did it unto Me."

The last hymn had been sung and the congregation had gone home, eagerly discussing their pastor's new scheme; but a little company of men and women remained behind in the church to talk it over with the minister. They were plain people. The sermon had shown them a plain duty to be done, and they knew only one way: to do it. The dinner hour found them there yet, planning and talking it over. It was with a light heart that, as a result of their talk, the minister set out for New York the day after with an invitation to the children of the slums to come out in the woods and see how beautiful God had made his world. They were to be the guests of the people of Sherman for a fortnight, and a warm welcome awaited them there. A right royal one they received when, in a few days, the pastor returned, bringing with him nine little waifs, the poorest and the neediest he had found in the tenements to which he went with his offer. They were not such children as the farm folk thereabouts saw every day, but they took them into their homes, and their hearts warmed to them day by day as they saw how much they needed their kindness, how under its influence they grew into bright and happy children like their own; and when, at the end of the two weeks, nine brown-faced laughing boys and girls went back to tell of the wondrous things they had heard and seen, it was only to make room for another little band. Nor has ever a summer passed since that first, which witnessed sixty city urchins made happy at Sherman, that has not seen the hospitable houses of the Pennsylvania village opened to receive holiday parties like those from the slums of the far city.

Thus modestly began the Fresh Air movement that has brought health and happiness to more than a hundred thousand of New York's poor children since, and has spread far and near, not only through our own but to foreign lands, wherever there is poverty to relieve and suffering to soothe. It has literally grown up around the enthusiasm and practical purpose of the one man whose personality pervades it to this day. Willard Parsons preaches now to a larger flock than any church could contain, but the burden of his sermon is ever the same. From the *Tribune* office he issues his appeals each spring, and money comes in abundance to carry on the work in which city and country vie with each other to lend a hand. After that first season at Sherman, a New York newspaper, the *Evening Post*, took the work under its wing and raised the necessary funds until in 1882 it passed into the keeping of its neighbor, the *Tribune*. Ever since it has been known as the Tribune Fresh Air Fund, and year by year has grown in extent and importance until at the end of the year 1891 more than 94,000 children were shown to have been given a two weeks' vacation in the country in the fifteen summers that had passed. The original 60 of 1877 had grown to an army of holidaymakers numbering 13,568 in 1891. By this time the hundred thousand mark has long been passed. The total amount of money expended in sending the children out was $250,633.88, and so well had the great fund been managed that the average cost per child had fallen from $3.12 in the first year to $2.07 in the last. Generalship, indeed, of the highest order was needed at the headquarters of this army. In that summer there was not a day except Sunday when less than seven companies were sent out from the city. The little knot of children that hung timidly to the skirts of the good minister's coat on that memorable first trip to Pennsylvania had been swelled until special trains, once of as many as eighteen cars, were in demand to carry those who came after.

The plan of the Fresh Air Fund is practically unchanged from the day it was first conceived. The neediest and poorest are made welcome. Be they Protestants, Catholics, Jews, or heathen, it matters not if an invitation is waiting. The supply is governed entirely by the demands that come from the country. Sometimes it is a Catholic community that asks for children of that faith, sometimes prosperous Jews, who would bring sunlight and hope even to Ludlow Street; rarely yet Italians seeking their own. The cry of the missionary, from the slums in the hot July days: "How shall we give those babies the breath of air that means life?—no one asks for Italian children," has not yet been answered.

*Summer boarders from Mott Street*

Prejudice dies slowly. When an end has been made of this at last, the Fresh Air Fund will receive a new boom. To my mind there are no more tractable children than the little Italians, none more grateful for kindness; certainly none more in need of it. Against colored children there is no prejudice. Sometimes an invitation comes from Massachusetts or some other New England state for them, and then the missions and schools of Thompson Street give up their children for a gleeful vacation spell. With the first spring days of April a canvass of the country within a radius of five hundred miles of New York has been begun. By the time the local committees send in their returns—so many children wanted in each town or district—the workers from the missions, the King's Daughters' circles, the hospitals, dispensaries, industrial schools, nurseries, kindergartens, and the other gates through which the children's host pours from the tenements, are at work, and the task of getting the little excursionists in shape for their holiday begins.

That is the hardest task of all. Places are found for them readily enough; the money to pay their way is to be had for the asking; but to satisfy the reasonable demand of the country hosts that their little guests shall come clean from their tenement homes costs an effort, how great the workers who go among those homes "with a Bible in one hand and a pair of scissors and a cake of soap in the other" know best. A physician presides over these necessary preliminaries. In the months of July and August he is kept running from church to hospital, from chapel to nursery, inspecting the brigades gathered there and parting the sheep from the goats. With a list of the houses in which the health officers report contagious diseases, he goes through the ranks. Any hailing from such houses—the list is brought up to date every morning—are rejected first. The rest as they pass in review are numbered 1 and 2 on the register. The No. 1's are ready to go at once if under the age limit of twelve years. They are the sheep, and, alas! few in number. Amid wailing and gnashing of teeth the cleansing of the goats is then begun. Heads are clipped and faces "planed off." Sometimes a second and a third inspection still fails to give the child a clean bill of entry. Just what it means is best shown by the following extract from a mission worker's report to Mr. Parsons, last summer, of the condition of her squad of 110, held under marching orders in an uptown chapel:

"All the No. 2's have now been thoroughly oiled, larkspur'd, washed in hot suds, and finally had an application of exterminator. This has all been done in the church to be as sure as possible that they are safe to send away. Ninety have been thus treated." Her experience was typical. Twenty No. 1's in a hundred was the average given by one of the oldest workers in the Fresh Air Service whose field is in the East Side tenements.

But all this is of the past, as are the long braids of many a little girl, sacrificed with tears upon the altar of the coveted holiday, when the procession finally starts for the depot, each happy child carrying a lunch bag, for often the journey is long, though never wearisome to the little ones. Their chaperone—some student, missionary, teacher, or kind man or woman who, for sweet charity's sake, has taken upon him this arduous duty—awaits them and keeps the account of his charges as squad after squad is dropped at the station to which it is consigned. Sometimes the whole party goes in a lump to a common destination, more frequently the joyous freight is delivered, as the journey progresses, in this valley or that village, where wagons are waiting to receive it and carry it home.

Once there, what wondrous things those little eyes behold, whose horizon was limited till that day, likely enough, by the gloom of the filthy court, or the stony street upon which it gave, with the gutter the boundary line between! The daisies by the roadside, with no sign to warn them "off the grass," the birds, the pig in its sty, the cow with its bell—each new marvel is hailed with screams of delight. "Sure, heaven can't be no nicer place than this," said a little child from one of the missions who for the first time saw a whole field of daisies; and her fellow traveller, after watching intently a herd of cows chew the cud asked her host, "Say, mister, do you have to buy gum for all them cows to chew?"

The children sent out by the Fresh Air Fund go as guests always. No penny of it is spent in paying for board. It goes toward paying their way only. Most of the railroad companies charge only one-fourth of the regular fare for the little picnickers up to the maximum of $3.50; beyond that they carry them without increase within the five hundred mile limit. Last year Mr. Parsons' wards were scattered over the country from the White Mountains in the East to Western Pennsylvania, from the lakes to West Virginia. New Hampshire, Massachusetts, Vermont, Connecticut, New York, New Jersey, Pennsylvania, Maryland, and West Virginia were hosts, and Canada entertained one large party. Ohio and North Carolina were on the list of entertainers, but the way was too long for the children. The largest party that went out comprised eleven hundred little summer boarders.

Does any good result to the children? The physical effect may be summed up in Dr. Daniel's terse statement, after many years of practical interest in the work: "I believe the Fresh Air Fund is the best plaster we have for the unjust social condition of the people." She spoke as a doctor, familiar with the appearance of the children when they went out and when they came back. There are not wanting professional opinions showing most remarkable cures to have resulted from even this brief respite from the slum. The explanation is simple: it was the slum that was the real complaint; with it the cause was removed and improvement came with a bound. As to the moral and educational effect, Mr. Parsons thus answers a clergyman who objected that "it will only make the child discontented with the surroundings where God placed him":

"I contend that a great gain has been made if you can only succeed in making the tenement house child thoroughly discontented with his lot. There is some hope then of his getting out of it and rising to a higher plane. The new life he sees in the country, the contact with good people, not at arm's length, but in their homes; not at the dinner, feast, or entertainment given to him while the giver stands by and looks *down* to see how he enjoys it, and remarks on his forlorn appearance; but brought into the family and given a seat at the table, where, as one boy wrote home, 'I can have two pieces of pie if I want, and nobody says nothing if I take three pieces of cake' or, as a little girl reported, where 'We have lots to eat, and so much to eat that we could not tell you how much we get to eat.'

"This is quite a different kind of service, and has resulted in the complete transformation of many a child. It has gone back to its wretchedness, to be sure, but in hundreds of instances about which I have personally known, it has returned with head and heart full of new ways, new ideas of decent living, and has successfully taught the shiftless parents the better way."

The host's side of it is presented by a pastor in northern New York, whose people had entertained a hundred children: "They have left a rich blessing behind them," he wrote, "and they actually gave more than they received. They have touched the hearts of the people and opened the fountains of love, sympathy, and charity. The people have read about the importance of benevolence, and have heard many sermons on the beauty of charity; but these have been quickly forgotten. The children have been an object lesson that will long live in their hearts and minds."

Not least among the blessings of the Fresh Air work has been the drawing closer in a common interest and sympathy of the classes that are drifting farther and farther apart so fast, as wealth and poverty both increase with the growth of our great cities. Each year the invitations to the children have come in greater numbers. Each year the fund has grown larger, and as yet no collector has ever been needed or employed. "I can recall no community," says Mr. Parsons, "where hospitality has been given once, but that some children have been invited back the following years." In at least one instance of which he tells, the farmer's family that nursed a poor consumptive girl back to health and strength did entertain an angel unawares. They were poor themselves in their way, straining every nerve to save enough to pay interest on a mortgage and thus avert the sale of their farm. A wealthy and philanthropic lady, who became interested in the girl after her return from her six weeks' vacation, heard the story of their struggle and saved the farm in the eleventh hour.

What sort of a gap the Fund sometimes bridges over the following instance from its report for 1891 gives a feeble idea of: "Something less than a year ago a boy from this family fell out of an upper-story window and was killed. Later on, a daughter in the same family likewise fell out of a window, sustaining severe injuries, but she is still alive. About this same time a baby came and the father had to quit work and stay at home to see that all was well with the mother. By the time she was well, the father was stricken down with a fever. On his recovery he went to hunt another job. On the first day at work a brick fell off a scaffold and fractured his skull. That night the Tribune Fresh Air Fund came to the rescue and relieved the almost distracted mother by sending four of her children to the country for two weeks. The little ones made so many good friends that the family is now well provided for."

From Mr. Parsons' record of "cases" that have multiplied in fifteen years until they would fill more than one stout volume, this one is taken as a specimen brick:

In the earlier days of the work a bright boy of ten was one of a company invited to Schoharie County, NY. He endeared himself so thoroughly to his entertainers, who "live in a white house with green blinds and Christmas trees all around it," that they asked and received permission to keep the lad permanently. The following is an exact copy of a part of the letter he wrote home after he had been for a few months in his new home:

> DEAR MOTHER: i am still to Mrs. D— and i was so
> Busy that i Could not Write Sooner i drive the horses
> and put up the Cows and clean out the Cow Stable

i am all well i pick stones and i have an apple tree 6 Feet High and i have got a pair of new pants and a new Coat and a pair of Suspenders and Mr. D— is getting a pair of New Boots made for me We killed one pig and one Cow i am going to plow a little piece of land and plant Some Corn. When Mr. D— killed the Cow i helped and Mr. D— had to take the Cow skin to be taned to make leather and Mr. D— gave the man Cow skin for leather to make me Boots i am going to school tomorrow and I want to tell lizzie— pauline— Charlie— Christie— maggie— george and you to all write to me and if they all do when Christmas Comes i will send all of you something nice if my uncle frank comes to see yous you must tell him to write to me i Close my letter

From your oldest son A—.

A year after that time the mother died. Some time afterward an uncle began writing for the lad to come back to the city—he coveted his small earnings. But the little fellow had sense enough to see that he was better off where he was. Finally the uncle went after the boy, and told him his brother was dying in the hospital, and was calling constantly for him. Under such circumstances his foster parents readily gave him permission to return with the uncle for a visit. Before they reached the city the uncle told him he should never go back. He sent him to work at Eleventh Avenue and Twenty-ninth Street, in a workroom situated in the cellar, and his bedroom, like those in most tenement houses, had no outside window. The third day he was sent upstairs on an errand, and as soon as he saw the open door he bolted. He remembered that a car that passed Fourth Street and Avenue C would take him to the People's Line for Albany. He ran with all his might to Fourth Street, and then followed the car tracks till he saw on the large flag "People's Line." He told part of his story to the clerk, and finally added, "I am one of Mr. Parsons' Fresh Air boys and I have got to go to Albany." That settled the matter, and the clerk readily gave him a pass. A gentleman standing by gave him a quarter for his supper. He held on to his appetite as well as his quarter, and in the morning laid his twenty-five cents before the ticket agent at Albany, and called for a ticket to R—, a small place fifty miles distant. He got the ticket. After a few miles' walk from R— he reached his new home safely, and there he proposed to stay. He said he would take to the woods if his uncle came after him again. This happened ten years ago.

About a year ago a letter came from the young fellow. He is now an active Christian, married, and worth property, and expects in a few years to have his farm all paid for.

A hundred benevolent enterprises have clustered about the Fresh Air Fund as the years have passed, patterning after it and accepting help from it to carry out their own plans. Churches provide excursions for their poor children and the Fund pays the way. Vacations for working girls, otherwise out of reach, are made attainable by its intervention. An independent feature is the Tribune Day Excursion that last summer gave nearly thirty thousand poor persons, young and old, a holiday at a beautiful grove on the Hudson, with music and milk to their hearts' desire. The expense was borne by a wealthy citizen of this city, who gave boats, groves, and entertainment free of charge, stipulating only that his name should not be disclosed.

Other cities have followed the example of New York. Boston and Philadelphia have their "Country Week," fashioned after the Fresh Air Fund idea. Chicago, St. Louis, Cincinnati, and other cities clear to San Francisco have sent committees to examine its workings, and deputations have come from Canada, from London and Manchester, where the holiday work is doing untold good and is counted among the most useful of philanthropic efforts. German, Austrian, and Italian cities have fallen into line, and the movement has spread even to the Sandwich Islands. Yet this great work, as far as New York, where it had its origin, is concerned, has never had organization or staff of officers of any sort. Three well-known citizens audit Mr. Parsons' accounts once a year. The rest he manages and always has managed himself. "The constitution and bylaws," he says, drily, "are made and amended from day to day as required, and have yet to be written." The Fresh Air Fund rests firmly upon a stronger foundation than any human law or enactment. Its charter was written in the last commandment that is the sum of all the rest: "That ye love one another."

The method of the Fresh Air Fund was and is its great merit. Its plan, when first presented, was unique. There had been other and successful efforts before that to give the poor in their vile dwellings an outing in the dog days, but they took the form rather of organized charities than of this spontaneous outpouring of goodwill and fellowship between brother and brother: "My house and my home are yours; come and see me!" *The New York Times* had conducted a series of free excursions, and three summers before Mr. Parsons preached his famous sermon, the Children's Aid Society, that had battled for twenty years with the slum for the possession of the child, had established a Health Home down the Bay, to which it welcomed the children from its industrial schools and the sick babies that were gathered in by its visiting physicians. This work has grown steadily in extent and importance with the new interest in the poor and their lives that has characterized our generation. Today the Society conducts a Summer Home at Bath Beach where the girls are given a week's vacation and the boys a day's outing, a cottage for crippled girls, and at Coney Island a Health Home for mothers with sick children. Sick and well, some ten thousand little ones were reached by them last year. The delight of a splash in the "big water" every day is the children's at Bath. Two hundred at a time, the boys plunge in headlong and strike out manfully for the Jersey shore, thirteen miles away; but the recollection of the merry-go-round with the marvellous wooden beasts, the camera obscura, the scups, and the flying machine on shore, not to mention the promised lemonade and cake, makes them turn back before yet they have reached the guard boat where they cease to touch bottom. The girls, less boisterous, but quite as happy, enjoy the sight of the windmill "where they make the wind that makes it so nice and cool," the swings and the dinner, rarely forgetting, at first, after eating as much as they can possibly hold, to hide something away for their next meal, lest the unexampled abundance give out too soon. That it should last a whole week seems to them too unreasonable to risk.

At the Health Home more than eighteen hundred sick babies were cared for last year. They are carried down, pale and fretful, in their mother's arms, and at the end of the week come back running at her side. The effect of the sea air upon a child sick with the summer scourge of the tenements, cholera infantum, is little less than miraculous. Even a ride on a river ferryboat is often enough to put life into the weary little body again. The salt breeze no sooner fans the sunken cheeks than the fretful wail is hushed and the baby slumbers, quietly, restfully, to wake with a laugh and an appetite, on the way to recovery. The change is so sudden that even the mother is often deceived and runs in alarm for the doctor, thinking that the end is at hand.

Scores of such scenes are witnessed daily in the floating hospital of St. John's Guild, the great marine cradle that goes down the Bay every weekday, save Saturday, in July and August, with hundreds upon hundreds of wailing babies and their mothers. Twice a week it is the westsiders' turn; on three days it gathers its cargo along the East River, where crowds with yellow tickets stand anxiously awaiting its arrival. The floating hospital carries its own staff of physicians, including a member of the Health Department's corps of tenement doctors, who is on the lookout for chance contagion. The summer corps is appointed by the Health Board upon the approach of hot weather and begins a systematic canvass of the tenements immediately after the Fourth of July, followed by the King's Daughters' nurses, who take up the doctor's work where he had to leave it. With his prescription pad he carries a bunch of tickets for the Floating Hospital, and the tickets usually give out first. Any illness that is not contagious is the baby's best plea for admission. It never pleads in vain, unless it be well and happy, and even then it is allowed to go along, if there is no other way for the mother to get off with its sick sister. For those who need more than one day's outing, the Guild maintains a seaside hospital, three hours' sail down the bay, on Staten Island, where mother and child may remain without a cent of charge until the rest, the fresh air, and the romp on the beach have given the baby back health and strength. Opposite the hospital, but out at sea where the breeze has free play over the crowded decks, the great hospital barge anchors every day while the hungry hosts are fed and the children given a saltwater bath on board.

*Floating hospital—St. John's Guild c. 1903*
*Source: Library of Congress, United States*

St. John's Guild is not, as some have supposed from its name, a denominational charity. It is absolutely neutral in matters of sect and religion, leaving the Church to take care of the soul while it heals the body of the child. It is so with the Bartholdi Crèche on Randall's Island, in the shadow of the city's Foundling Hospital, that ferries children over the river for a romp on the smooth, green lawns, on presentation of a ticket with the suggestive caution printed on the back that "all persons behaving rudely or taking liberties will be sent back by the first boat." "The Little Mothers" Aid Society follows the same plan in reaching out for the little home worker whose work never ends, the girl upon whom falls the burden and responsibility of caring for the perennial baby when scarcely more than a baby herself, often even the cooking and all the rest of the housework so that the mother may have her own hands free to help earn the family living. These little slaves the Society drums up, "hires" the baby attended in a nursery if need be, and carries the little mother off for a day in the woods up at Pelham Bay Park where the Park Commissioners have set a house on the beach apart for their use in the summer months. There was much opposition to this plan at first among the East Side Jews, whose children needed the outing more sorely than any other class; but when a few of the more venturesome had come back well-fed, in clean clothes, whereas they went out in rags, and reported that they had escaped baptism, the sentiment of Ludlow Street underwent a change, and so persistent were the raids made upon the Society's chaperones after that that they had to take another route for a while, lest their resources should be swamped in a single trip. The United Hebrew Charities, like many other relief societies with a special field, provide semi-weekly excursions for the poorest of their own people, and maintain a seaside sanitarium for the sick children.

There is no lack of fresh air charities nowadays. Their number is increasing year by year and so is their helpfulness, though it has come to a pass where it is necessary to exercise some care to prevent them from lapping over, as Sunday School Christmas trees have been known to do, and opening the way for mischief. There can be no doubt that their civilizing influence is great. It could hardly be otherwise, with the same lessons of cleanliness and decency enforced year after year. The testimony is that there is an improvement; the children come better "groomed" for inspection. The lesson has reached the mother and the home. The subtler lesson of the flowers, the fields, the sky, and the sea, and of the kindness that asked no reward, has not been lost either. One very striking fact this charity has brought out that is most hopeful. It emphasizes the difference I pointed out between the material we have here to work upon in these children and that which is the despair of philanthropists abroad, in England for instance. We are told of children there who, coming from their alleys into the field, "are able to feel no touch of kinship between themselves and Mother Nature" [19] when brought into her very presence. Not so with ours. They may "guess" that the sea is salt because it is full of codfish; may insist that the potatoes are homemade "cause I seen the garding"; both of which were actual opinions expressed by the Bath Beach summer boarders; but the interest, the sympathy, the hearty appreciation of it, is there always, the most encouraging symptom of all. Down in the worst little ruffian's soul there is, after all, a tender spot not yet preempted by the slum. And Mother Nature touches it at once. They are chums on the minute.

# 11

# THE KINDERGARTENS AND NURSERIES

IF THE INFLUENCE of an annual cleaning up is thus distinctly traced in the lives of the children, what must be the effect of the daily teaching of the kindergarten, in which soap is always the moral agent that leads all the rest? I have before me the inventory of purchases for a single school of this kind that was started a year ago in a third loft of a Suffolk Street tenement. It included several boxes of soap and soap dishes, 200 feet of rope, 10 beanbags, 24 tops, 200 marbles, a box of chalk, a baseball outfit for indoor use, a supply of tiddledywinks and "sliced animals," and 20 clay pipes. The pipes were not for lessons in smoking, but to smooth the way for a closer acquaintance with the soap by the friendly intervention of the soap bubble. There were other games and no end of colored paper to cut up, the dear delight of childhood, but made in the hands and under the eyes of the teacher to train eye and hand while gently but firmly cementing the friendship ushered in by the gorgeous bubble. No wonder, with such a stock, a mother complained that she had to whip her Jimmie to keep him home.

Without a doubt the kindergarten is one of the longest steps forward that has yet been taken in the race with poverty; for in gathering in the children it is gradually, but surely, conquering also the street with its power for mischief. There is only one force that, to my mind, exerts an even stronger influence upon the boys' lives especially; I mean the club, of which I shall speak presently. But that comes at a later stage. The kindergarten begins at the very beginning, and in the best of all ways, with the children's play. What it does, counts at both ends on that tack. Very soon it makes itself felt in the street and in what goes on there, as anyone can see for himself by observing the children's play in a tenement neighborhood where there is a kindergarten and again where there is none, while by imperceptibly turning the play into work that teaches habits of observation and of industry that stick, it builds a strong barrier against the doctrine of the slum that the world owes one a living, which lies in ambush for the lad on every grog-shop corner. And all corners in the tenement districts are grog-shop corners. Beyond all other considerations, beyond its now admitted function as the right beginning of all education, whether of rich or poor, its war upon the street stands to me as the true office of the kindergarten in a city like New York, with a tenement house population of a million and a quarter souls. [20] The street itself owns it, with virtual surrender. Hostile as its normal attitude is to every new agency of reform, the best with the worst, I have yet to hear of the first instance in which a kindergarten has been molested by the toughest neighborhood, or has started a single dead cat on a postmortem career of window smashing, whether it sprang from Christian, Jewish, or heathen humanity. There is scarce a mission or a boy's club in the city that can say as much.

The kindergarten is no longer an experiment in New York. Probably as many as a hundred are today in operation, or will be when the recently expressed purpose of the Board of Education to make the kindergarten a part of the public school system has been fully carried out. The Children's Aid Society alone conducts a dozen in connection with its industrial schools, and the New York Kindergarten Association nine, if its intention of opening two new schools by the time this book is in the printer's hands is realized. There is no theology, though there is a heap of religion in most of them. Protestants, Catholics, Jews, Theosophists, and Ethical Culturists, if I may so call them, men of one or of various opinions, or of none, concerning the hereafter, alike make use of the kindergarten as a means of reaching and saving the shipwrecked of the present. Sometimes the Sunday School is made to serve as a feeder for the kindergarten, or the kindergarten for the Sunday School. Sometimes the wisdom that wrests success from doubt and perplexity is expressed in the fundamental resolution that the kindergarten "shall not be a Sunday School." The system is the same in all cases with very little change. "We have tried it and seen it tried with various kinks and variations," said one of the old managers of the Children's Aid Society to me, "but after all there is only one way, the way of the great kindergartner who said, 'We learn by doing.'"

A clean face is the ticket of admission to the kindergarten. A clean or whole frock is wisely not insisted upon too firmly at the start; torn or dirty clothes are not so easily mended as a smudged face, but the kindergarten reaches that too in the end, and by the same road as the Fresh Air scrubbing—the home. Once he is let in, the child is in for a general good time that has little of school or visible discipline to frighten him. He joins in the ring for the familiar games, delighted to find that the teacher knows them too, and can be "It" and his "fair lady" in her turn. He does not notice the little changes the game has undergone, the kindergarten touch here and there that lifts it out of the mud; but the street does presently, when the new version is transferred to it, and is the better for it. After the game there are a hundred things for him to do that do not seem like work in the least. Between threading colored beads, cutting and folding pink and green papers in all sorts of odd ways, as boats and butterflies and fancy baskets; moulding, pasting, drawing, weaving and blowing soap bubbles when all the rest has ceased to hold his attention, the day slips by like a beautiful dream, and he flatly refuses to believe that it is gone when the tenement home claims him again. Not infrequently he goes home howling, to be found the next morning waiting at the door an hour before the teacher comes. Little Jimmie's mother says that he gets up at six o'clock to go to the Fifty-first Street kindergarten, and that she has to whip him to make him wait until nine.

The hours pass with happy play that slowly but surely moulds head, hand, and heart together. The utmost freedom is allowed, but it stops short of the license of the street. Its law of violence is replaced by the law of love. The child learns to govern himself. Not at once; I observed two or three black eyes during a tour of a half-score kindergartens, last June, that showed that the street yielded its reign reluctantly. During my visit to the East Sixty-third Street school I became interested in a little fellow who was its special pet and the ward of the alumnae of the Normal College, who through the New York Kindergarten Association had established and maintained the school. Johnny was a sweet little fellow, one of eight children from a wretched tenement home down the street into which the kindergartner had found her way. The youngest of the eight was a baby that was getting so big and heavy that it half killed the mother to drag it around when she went out working, and the father, with a consideration for her that was generously tempered with laziness, was considering the advisability of staying home to take care of it himself, "so as to give her a show." There was a refinement of look and manner, if not of dress, about little Johnny after he was washed clean, that made the tenement setting seem entirely too plebeian for him, and his rescuers had high hopes of his future. I regret to say that I saw the pet, before I left, deliberately knock the smallest baby in the school down, and when he was banished from the ring in consequence and condemned to take his howling playmate over in the corner and show her pictures until he repented, take an unworthy revenge by pinching her surreptitiously until she howled louder. Worse than that, when the baby had finally been comforted with a headless but squeaking toy sheep, he secretly pulled the insides and the baa out of the lambkin through its broken neck, when no one was looking. I was told that Johnny was believed to have the making of a diplomat in his little five-year-old body, and I think it very likely—of a politician anyway.

While this was going on, another boy, twice as large as Johnny, had been temporarily exiled from the ring for clumsiness. It was even more hopelessly constitutional, to all appearances, than Johnny's Machiavellian cunning. In the game he had persistently stumbled over his own feet. Made to take a seat at the long table, he fell off his chair twice in one minute from sheer embarrassment. In luminous contrast to his awkwardness was the desperate agility of a little Irishman I had just left in another kindergarten. Each time he was told to take his seat, which was about every ten seconds, he would perform the feat with great readiness by climbing over the back of the chair as a dog climbs over a fence, to the consternation of the teacher, whose reproachful "O Alexander!" he disarmed with a cheerful "I'm all right, Miss Brown," and an offer to shake hands.

Let it not be inferred from this that the kindergarten is the home of disorder. Just the reverse. Order and prompt obedience are the cardinal virtues taught there, but taught in such a way as to make the lesson seem all fun and play to the child. It sticks all the better. It is the province of the kindergarten to rediscover, as it were, the natural feelings the tenement had smothered. But for its appeal, the love of the beautiful might slumber in those children forever. In their homes there is nothing to call it into life. The ideal of the street is caricature, burlesque, if nothing worse. Under the gentle training of the kindergartner the slumbering instinct blossoms forth in a hundred different ways, from the day the little one first learns the difference between green and red by stringing colored beads for a necklace "for teacher," until later on he is taught to make really pretty things of pasteboard and chips to take home for papa and mamma to keep. And they do keep them, proud of the child—who would not?—and their influence is felt where mayhap there was darkness and dirt only before. So the kindergarten reaches directly into the home, too, and thither follows the teacher, if she is the right kind, with encouragement and advice that is not lost either. No door is barred against her who comes in the children's name. In the truest and best sense she is a missionary to the poor.

Nearly all the kindergartens in this city are crowded. Many have scores of applicants upon the register whom they cannot receive. There are no truants among their pupils. All of the New York Kindergarten Association's schools are crowded, and new are added as fast as the necessary funds are contributed. The Association was organized in the fall of 1889 with the avowed purpose of engrafting the kindergarten upon the public school system of the city, through persistent agitation. There had been no official recognition of it up till that time. The Normal School kindergarten was an experiment not countenanced by the School Board. The Association has now accomplished its purpose, but its work, far from being ended, has but just begun. It is doubtful if all the kindergartens in the city, including those now in the public schools, accommodate much more than five or six thousand children, if that number. The last sanitary census showed that there were 160,708 children under five years old in the tenements. At least half of these are old enough to be in a kindergarten, and ought to be, seeing how little schooling they will get after they outgrow it. That leaves in round numbers 75,000 children yet to be so provided for in New York's tenements. There is no danger that the kindergarten will become too "common" in this city for a while yet. As an adjunct to the public school in preparing the young minds for more serious tasks, it is admitted by teachers to be most valuable. But its greatest success is as a jail deliverer. "The more kindergartens the fewer prisons" is a saying the truth of which the generation that comes after us will be better able to grasp than we.

The kindergarten is the city's best truant officer. Not only has it no truants itself, but it ferrets out a lot who are truants from necessity, not from choice, and delivers them over to the public school. There are lots of children who are kept at home because someone has to mind the baby while father and mother earn the bread for the little mouths. The kindergarten steps in and releases these little prisoners. If the baby is old enough to hop around with the rest, the kindergarten takes it. If it can only crawl and coo, there is the nursery annex. Sometimes it is an independent concern. Almost every church or charity that comes into direct touch with the poor has nowadays its nursery where poor mothers may leave their children to be cared for while they are out working. Relief more practical could not be devised. A small fee, usually five cents, is charged as a rule for each baby. Pairs come cheaper, and three go for ten cents at the nursery in the Wilson mission. Over 50,000 babies were registered there last year, which meant, if not 5,000 separate children, at least 5,000 days' work and wages to poor mothers in dire need of both, and a good, clean, healthy start for the infants, a better than the tenement could have given them. To keep them busy, when the rocking horse and the picture book have lost their charm, the kindergarten grows naturally out of the nursery, where that was the beginning, just as the nursery stepped in to supplement the kindergarten where that had the lead. The two go hand in hand. The soap cure is even more potent in the nursery than in the kindergarten, as a silent rebuke to the mother, who rarely fails to take the hint. At the Five Points House of Industry the children who come in for the day receive a general scrubbing twice a week, and the whole neighborhood has a cleaner look after it. The establishment has come to be known among the ragamuffins of Paradise Park as "the school where dey washes 'em." Its value as a moral agent may be judged from the statements of the Superintendent that some of the children "cried at the sight of a washtub," as if it were some new and hideous instrument of torture for their oppression.

Private benevolence in this, as in all measures for the relief of the poor, has been a long way ahead of public action; properly so, though it has seemed sometimes that we might as a body make a little more haste and try to catch up. It has lately, by the establishment of children's playgrounds in certain tenement districts, west and east, provided a kind of open-air kindergarten that has hit the street in a vital spot. These playgrounds do not take the place of the small parks which the city has neglected to provide, but they show what a boon these will be some day. There are at present, as far as I know, three of them, not counting the backyard "beaches" and "Coney Islands," that have made the practical missionaries of the College Settlement, the King's Daughters' Tenement Chapter, and like helpers of the poor, solid with their little friends. One of them, the largest, is in Ninety-second Street, on the East Side, another at the foot of West Fiftieth Street, and still another in West Twenty-eighth Street, between Tenth and Eleventh Avenues, the block long since well named Poverty Gap. Two, three, or half a dozen vacant lots, borrowed or leased of the owner, have been levelled out, a few loads of sand dumped in them for the children to dig in; scups, swings, and seesaws, built of rough timber; a hydrant in the corner; little wheelbarrows, toy spades and pails to go round, and the outfit is complete. Two at least of the three are supported each by a single generous woman, who pays the salaries of a man janitor and of two women "teachers" who join in the children's play, strike up "America" and the "Star Spangled Banner" when they tire of "Sally in our Alley" and "Ta-ra-ra-boom-de-ay," and by generally taking a hand in what goes on manage to steer it into safe and mannerly ways.

More than two hundred children were digging, swinging, seesawing, and cavorting about the Poverty Gap playground when I looked in on a hot Saturday afternoon last July. Long files of eager girls, whose shrill voices used to make the echoes of the Gap ring with angry clamor, awaited their turn at the scups, quiet as mice and without an ill word when they trod upon each other's toes. The street that used to swarm with mischievous imps was as quiet as a church. The policeman on the beat stood swinging his club idly in the gate. It was within sight of this spot that the Alley Gang beat one of his comrades half to death for telling them to go home and let decent people pass; the same gang which afterward murdered young Healey for the offence of being a decent, hardworking lad, who was trying to support his aged father and mother by his work. The Healeys lived in one of the rear houses that stood where the children now skip at their play, and the murder was done on his doorstep. The next morning I found the gang camping on a vacant floor in the adjoining den, as if nothing had happened. The tenants knew the toughs were there, but were afraid of betraying them. All that was only a couple of years ago; but a marvellous transformation had been wrought in the Gap. The toughs were gone, with the old tenements that harbored them. Poverty Gap itself was gone. A decent flat had taken the place of the shanty across the street where a longshoreman kicked his wife to death in drunken rage. And this playground, with its swarms of happy children who a year ago would have pelted the stranger with mud from behind the nearest truck—that was the greatest change of all. The retiring toughs have dubbed it "Holy Terror Park" in memory of what it was, not of what it is. Poverty Park the policeman called it, with more reason. It was not exactly an attractive place. A single stunted ailanthus tree struggled over the fence of the adjoining yard, the one green spot between ugly and ragged brick walls. The "sand" was as yet all mud and dirt, and the dust the many little feet kicked up was smothering. But the children thought it lovely, and lovely it was for Poverty Gap, if not for Fifth Avenue.

I came back to my office to find a letter there from a rich man who lives on the Avenue, offering to make another Poverty Park for the tenement house children of another street, if he had to buy the lots. I told him the story of Poverty Gap and bade him go and see for himself if he could spend his money to better purpose. There are no playgrounds yet below Fourteenth Street and room and need for fifty. The Alley and the Avenue could not meet on a plane that argues better for the understanding between the two that has been too long and needlessly delayed.

# 12

# THE INDUSTRIAL SCHOOLS

T HAT "DIRT IS A DISEASE," and their mission to cure it,
was the new gospel which the managers of the Children's
Aid Society carried to the slums a generation ago. In practice
they have not departed from their profession. Their pill is the
industrial school, their plaster a western farm and a living chance
in exchange for the tenement and the city slum. The wonder cures
they have wrought by such simple treatment have been many. In
the executive chair of a sovereign state sits today a young man
who remembers with gratitude and pride the day they took him
in hand and, of the material the street would have moulded
into a tough, made an honorable man and a governor. And
from among the men whose careers of usefulness began in the
Society's schools, and who today, as teachers, ministers, lawyers,
and editors, are conspicuous ornaments of the communities,
far and near, in which they have made their homes, he would
have no difficulty in choosing a cabinet that would do credit and
honor to his government. Prouder monument could be erected
to no man's memory than this record at the grave of the late
Charles Loring Brace, the founder of the Children's Aid Society.

The industrial school plants itself squarely in the gap between
the tenement and the public school. If it does not fill it, it at least
spreads itself over as much of it as it can, and in that position
demonstrates that this land of lost or missing opportunities is
not the barren ground once supposed, but of all soil the most
fruitful, if properly tilled. Wherever the greatest and the poorest

crowds are, there also is the industrial school.

*Charles Loring Brace, founder of the Children's Aid Society*

The Children's Aid Society maintains twenty-one in seventeen of the city's twenty-four wards, not counting twelve evening schools, five of which are in the Society's lodging houses. It is not alone in the field. The American Female Guardian Society conducts twelve such day schools, and individual efforts in the same direction are not wanting. The two societies' schools last year reached a total enrolment of nearly fifteen thousand children, and an average attendance of almost half that number. Slum children, all of them. Only such are sought and admitted. The purpose of the schools, in the language of the last report of the Children's Aid Society, whose work, still carried on with the aggressive enthusiasm that characterized its founder, may well be taken as typical and representative in this field, "is to receive and educate children who cannot be accepted by the public schools, either by reason of their ragged and dirty condition, or owing to the fact that they can attend but part of the time, because they are obliged to sell papers or to stay at home to help their parents. The children at our schools belong to the lowest and poorest class of people in the city." They are children, therefore, who to a very large extent speak another language at home than the one they come to the school to learn, and often have to work their way in by pantomime. It is encouraging to know that these schools are almost always crowded to their utmost capacity.

A census of the Society's twenty-one day schools, that was taken last April, showed that they contained that day 5,132 pupils, of whom 198 were kindergarten children under five years of age, 2,347 between five and seven, and 2,587 between eight and fourteen years of age. Considerably more than ten percent— the exact number was 571—did not understand questions put to them in English. They were there waiting to "catch on," silent but attentive observers of what was going on, until such time as they should be ready to take a hand in it themselves. Divided according to nativity, 2,082 of the children were found to be of foreign birth. They hailed from 22 different countries; 3,050 were born in this country, but they were able to show only 1,009 native parents out of 6,991 whose pedigrees could be obtained. The other 5,176 were foreign born, and only 810 of them claimed English as their mother tongue. This was the showing the chief nationalities made in the census:

| Born In | Children | Parents |
|---------|----------|---------|
| United States | 3050 | 1009 |
| Italy | 1066 | 2354 |
| Germany | 460 | 1819 |
| Bohemia | 198 | 720 |
| Ireland | 98 | 583 |

At that time the Jewish children were crowding into the Monroe Street and some other schools, at a rate that promised to put them in complete possession before long. Upon this lowest level, as upon every other where they come into competition with the children of Christian parents, they distanced them easily, taking all the prizes that were to be had for regular attendance, proficiency in studies, and good conduct generally. Generally these prizes consisted of shoes or much needed clothing. Often, as in the Monroe Street School, the bitter poverty of the homes that gave up the children to the school because there they would receive the one square meal of the day, made a loaf of bread the most acceptable reward, and the teachers gladly took advantage of it as the means of forging another link in the chain to bind home and school, parents, children, and teachers, firmly together.

This "square meal" is a chief element in the educational plan of most of the schools, because very often it is the one hot meal the little ones receive—not infrequently, as I have said, the only one of the day that is worthy of the name. It is not an elaborate or expensive affair, though substantial and plentiful. At the West Side Industrial School, on Seventh Avenue, where one day, not long ago, I watched a file of youngsters crowding into the dining room with glistening eyes and happy faces, the cost of the dinners averaged 2½ cents last year. In a specimen month they served there 4,080 meals and compared this showing gleefully with the record of the old School in Twenty-ninth Street, nine years before. The largest number of dinners served there in any one month, was 2,666. It is perhaps a somewhat novel way of measuring the progress of a school: by the amount of eating done on the premises. But it is a very practical one, as the teachers have found out. Yet it is not used as a bait. Care is taken that only those are fed who would otherwise go without their dinner, and it is served only in winter, when the need of "something warm" is imperative. In the West Side School, as in most of the others, the dinners are furnished by some one or more practical philanthropists, whose pockets as well as their hearts are in the work. The schools themselves, like the Society's lodging houses for homeless children, stand as lasting monuments to a Christian charity that asks no other reward than the consciousness of having done good where the need was great. Sometimes the very name of the generous giver is unknown to all the world save the men who built as he or she directed. The benefactor is quite as often a devoted woman as a rich and charitable man, who hides his munificence under a modesty unsuspected by a community that applauds and envies his shrewd and successful business ventures, but never hears of the investment that paid him and it best of all.

According to its location, the school is distinctively Italian, Bohemian, Hebrew or mixed; the German, Irish, and colored children coming in under this head, and mingling usually without the least friction. The Leonard Street School and the West Side Italian School in Sullivan Street are devoted wholly to the little swarthy Southerners. In the Leonard Street School alone there were between five and six hundred Italian children on the register last year; but in the Beach Street School, and in the Astor Memorial School in Mott Street they are fast crowding the Irish element, that used to possess the land, to the wall. So, in Monroe Street and East Broadway are the Jewish children. Neither the teachers nor the Society's managers are in any danger of falling into sleepy routine ways. The conditions with which they have to deal are constantly changing; new problems are given them to solve before the old are fairly worked out, old prejudices to be forgotten or worked over into a new and helpful interest. And they do it bravely, and are more than repaid for their devotion by the real influence they find themselves exerting upon the young lives which had never before felt the touch of genuine humane sympathy, or been awakened to the knowledge that somebody cared for them outside of their own dark slum.

All the children are not as tractable as the Russian Jews or the Italians. The little Irishman, brimful of mischief is, like his father, in the school and in the street, "ag'in' the government" on general principles, though in a jovial way that often makes it hard to sit in judgment on his tricks with serious mien. He feels, too, that to a certain extent he has the sympathy of his father in his unregenerate state, and is the more to be commended if he subdues the old Adam in himself and allows the instruction to proceed. The hardest of them all to deal with, until he has been won over as a friend and ally, is perhaps the Bohemian child. He inherits, with some of his father's obstinacy, all of his hardships, his bitter poverty and grinding work. School to him is merely a change of tasks in an unceasing round that leaves no room for play. If he lingers on the way home to take a hand in a stolen game of ball, the mother is speedily on his track. Her instruction to the teacher is not to let the child stay "a minute after three o'clock." He is wanted at home to roll cigars or strip tobacco leaves for his father, while the mother gets the evening meal ready. The Bohemian has his own cause for the reserve that keeps him a stranger in a strange land after living half his life among us; his reception has not been altogether hospitable, and it is not only his hard language and his sullen moods that are to blame. All the better he knows the value of the privilege that is offered his child, and will "drive him to school with sticks" if need be; an introduction that might be held to account for a good deal of reasonable reluctance, even hostility to the school, in the pupil. The teacher has only to threaten the intractable ones with being sent home to bring them round. And yet, it is not that they are often cruelly treated there. On the contrary, the Bohemian is an exceptionally tender and loving father, perhaps because his whole life is lived with his family at home, in the tenement that is his shop and his world. He simply proposes that his child shall enjoy the advantages that are denied him—denied partly perhaps because of his refusal to accept them, but still from his point of view denied. And he takes a short cut to that goal by sending the child to school. The result is that the old Bohemian disappears in the first generation born upon our soil. His temper remains to some extent, it is true. He still has his surly streaks, refuses to sing or recite in school when the teacher or something else does not suit him, and can never be driven where yet he is easily led; but as he graduates into the public school and is thrown more into contact with the children of more lighthearted nationalities, he grows into that which his father would have long since become, had he not got a wrong start: a loyal American, proud of his country, and a useful citizen.

In the school in East Seventy-third Street, of which I am thinking, there was last winter, besides the day school of some four hundred pupils, an evening class of big factory girls, most of them women grown, that vividly illustrated the difficulties that beset teaching in the Bohemian quarter. It had been got together with much difficulty by the principal and one of the officers of the Society, who gave up his nights and his own home life to the work of instructing the school. On the night when it opened, he was annoyed by a smell of tobacco in the hallways and took the janitor to task for smoking in the building. The man denied the charge, and Mr. H— went hunting through the house for the offender with growing indignation, as he found the teachers in the classrooms sneezing and sniffing the air to locate the source of the infliction. It was not until later in the evening, when the sneezing fit took him too as he was bending over a group of the girls to examine their slates, that he discovered it to be a feature of the new enterprise. The perfume was part of the school. Without it, it could not go on. The girls were all cigar makers; so were their parents at home. The shop and the tenement were organized on the tobacco plan, and the school must needs adopt it with what patience it could, if its business were to proceed.

It did, and got on fairly well until a reporter found his way into it and roused the resentment of the girls by some inconsiderate, if well-meant, criticisms of their ways. The rebellion he caused was quelled with difficulty by Mr. H—, who reestablished his influence over them at this point and gained their confidence by going to live among them in the schoolhouse with his family. Still the sullen moods, the nightly ructions. The girls were as ready to fight as to write, in their fits of angry spite, until my friend was almost ready to declare with the angry Irishman, that he would have peace in the house if he had to whip all hands to get it.

Christmas was at hand with its message of peace and goodwill, but the school was more than usually unruly, when one night, in despair, he started to read a story to them to lay the storm. It was Hans Christian Andersen's story of the little girl who sold matches and lighted her way to mother and heaven with them as she sat lonely and starved, freezing to death in the street on New Year's Eve. As match after match went out with the pictures of home, of warmth, and brightness it had shown the child, and her trembling fingers fumbled eagerly with the bunch to call them back, a breathless hush fell upon the class, and when the story was ended, and Mr. H— looked up with misty eyes, he found the whole class in tears. The picture of friendless poverty, more bitterly desolate than any even they had known, had gone to their hearts and melted them. The crisis was passed and peace restored.

A crisis of another kind came later, when the pupils' "young men" got into the habit of coming to see the girls home. They waited outside until school was dismissed, and night after night Mr. H— found a ball in progress on the sidewalk when the girls should long have been home. The mothers complained and the success of the class was imperilled. Their passion for dancing was not to be overcome. They would give up the school first. Mr. H— thought the matter out and took a long step—a perilous one. He started a dancing class, and on certain nights in the week taught the girls the lanciers instead of writing and spelling. Simultaneously he wrote to every mother that the school was not to be blamed if the girls were not home at ten minutes after nine o'clock; it was dismissed at 8.55 sharp every night. The thing took tremendously. The class filled right up, complaints ceased, and everything was lovely, when examination day approached with the annual visit of friends and patrons. My friend awaited its coming with fear and trembling. There was no telling what the committee might say to the innovation. The educational plan of the Society is most liberal, but the lanciers was a step even the broadest of its pedagogues had not yet ventured upon. The evil day came at last, and, full of forebodings, Mr. H— had the girls soothe their guests with cakes and lemonade of their own brewing, until they were in a most amiable mood. Then, when they expected the reading to begin, with a sinking heart he bade them dance. The visitors stared in momentary amazement, but at the sight of the happy faces in the quadrilles, and the enthusiasm of the girls, they caught the spirit of the thing and applauded to the echo. The dancing class was a success, and so has the school been ever since.

As far as I know, this is the only instance in which the quadrille has been made one of the regular English branches taught in the industrial schools. But cake and lemonade have more than once smoothed the way to a hearty acceptance of the three R's with their useful concomitants, as taught there. One of the excellent features of the system is the "kitchen garden," for the little ones, a kind of play housekeeping that covers the whole range of housework, and the cooking class for the larger girls that gives many of them a taste for housekeeping which helps to overcome their prejudice against domestic service, and so to solve one of the most perplexing questions of the day—no less serious to the children of the poor than to the wives of the rich, if they only knew or would believe it. It is the custom of the wise teachers, when the class has become proficient, to invite the mothers to a luncheon gotten up by their children. "I never," reports the teacher of the Eighteenth Ward Industrial School after such a session, "saw women so thoroughly interested." And it was not only the mother who was thus won over in the pride over her daughter's achievement. It was the home itself that was invaded with influences that had been strangers to it heretofore. For the mother learned something she would not be apt to forget, by seeing her child do intelligently and economically what she had herself done ignorantly and wastefully before. Poverty and waste go always hand in hand. The girls are taught, with the doing of a thing, enough also of the chemistry of cooking to enable them to understand the "why" of it. The influence of that sort

of teaching in the tenement of the poor no man can measure.
I am well persuaded that half of the drunkenness that makes
so many homes miserable is at least encouraged, if not directly
caused, by the mismanagement and bad cooking at home. All
the wife and mother knows about housekeeping she has picked
up in the tenement since she was married, among those who
never knew how to cook a decent meal or set a clean table; while
the saloonkeeper hires the best cook he can get for money, and
serves his hot lunch free to her husband in a tidy and cheerful
room, where no tired women—tired of the trials and squabbles
of the day—no cross looks, and no dirty, fighting children come
to spoil his appetite and his hour of rest.

Here, as everywhere, it is the personal influence of the
teacher that counts for most in dealing with the child. It follows
it into the home, and often through life to the second and third
generation, smoothing the way of trouble and sorrow and
hardship with counsel and aid in a hundred ways. "Sometimes,"
says one of the teachers, who has seen the children of her first
pupils go from her school into their own homes to take up the
battle of life, "sometimes a teacher, while conducting a class, is
also fashioning, from some soft white material, a shroud for some
little one whose parents can provide none themselves. When a
child dies of a disease that is not contagious, its classmates gather
around the coffin and sing in German or English, 'I am Jesus'
little lamb.' Sometimes the children's hymn and the Lord's Prayer
are the only service." Her life work has been among the poorest
Germans on the East Side. "Among our young men," she reports,
"I know of only three who have become drunkards, and many
are stanch temperance men. I have never known of one of our
girls drinking to excess. I have looked carefully over our records,
and can truly say that, so far as I can learn, not one girl who
remained with us until over seventeen lived a life of shame."

What teaching meant to this woman the statement that
follows gives an idea of: "Shrove Tuesday evening is a time when

all Germans plan for a frolic; they call it 'Fastnacht.' Twenty years ago I gave the young people of the evening school a party on that evening, and at the suggestion of one of the girls decided to have a reunion every year at that time. So each year our married girls and boys, and those still unmarried, who have grown beyond us in other ways, come 'home.' We sing the old songs, talk over old times, play games, drink coffee and eat doughnuts, and always end the evening with 'Auld Lang Syne.' Last spring, two of the young men stood at the stairway and counted the guests as they went to the supper room: they reported over four hundred. Letters came from Boston, Chicago, Philadelphia, Washington, Texas, Idaho, and Wyoming from those who would gladly have been with us. All who live within a radius of fifty miles try to be here."

"Among our grown girls," she adds, "we have teachers, governesses, dressmakers, milliners, trained nurses, machine operators, hand sewers, embroiderers, designers for embroidering, servants in families, saleswomen, bookkeepers, typewriters, candy packers, bric-à-brac packers, banknote printers, silk winders, button makers, box makers, hairdressers, and fur sewers. Among our boys are bookkeepers, workers in stained glass, painters, printers, lithographers, salesmen in wholesale houses, as well as in many of our largest retail stores, typewriters, stenographers, commission merchants, farmers, electricians, ship carpenters, foremen in factories, grocers, carpet designers, silver engravers, metal burnishers, carpenters, masons, carpet weavers, plumbers, stone workers, cigar makers, and cigar packers. Only one of our boys, so far as we can learn, ever sold liquor, and he has given it up."

Not a few of these, without a doubt, got the first inkling of their trade in the class where they learned to read. The curriculum of the industrial schools is comprehensive. The nationality of the pupils makes little or no difference in it. The start, as often as is necessary, is made with an object lesson—

soap and water being the elements, and the child the object. As in the kindergarten, the alphabet comes second on the list. Then follow lessons in sewing, cooking, darning, mat weaving, pasting, and dressmaking for the girls, and in carpentry, wood carving, drawing, printing, and like practical "branches" for the boys, not a few of whom develop surprising cleverness at this or that kind of work. The system is continually expanding. There are schools yet that have not the necessary facilities for classes in manual training, but as the importance of the subject is getting to be more clearly understood, and interest in the subject grows, new "shops" are being constantly opened and other occupations found for the children. Even where the school quarters are most pinched and inadequate, a shift is made to give the children work to do that will teach them habits of industry and precision as the all-important lesson to be learned there. In some of the industrial schools the boys learn to cook with the girls, and in the West Side Italian School an attempt to teach them to patch and sew buttons on their own jackets resulted last year in their making their own shirts, and making them well, too. Perhaps the possession of the shirt as a reward for making it acted as a stimulus. The teacher thought so, and she was probably right, for more than one of them had never owned a whole shirt before, let alone a clean one. A heap can be done with the children by appealing to their proper pride—much more than many might think, judging hastily from their rags. Call it vanity—if it is a kind of vanity that can be made a stepping-stone to the rescue of the child, it is worth laying hold of. It was distinct evidence that civilization and the nineteenth century had invaded Lewis Street, when a class of Hungarian boys in the American Female Guardian Society's school in that thoroughfare earned the name of the "necktie class" by adopting that article of apparel in a body. None of them had ever known collar or necktie before.

It is the practice to let the girls have what garments they make, from material, old or new, furnished by the school, and thus a good many of the pupils in the industrial schools are supplied with decent clothing. In the winter especially, some of them need it sadly. In the Italian school of which I just spoke, one of the teachers found a little girl of six years crying softly in her seat on a bitter cold day. She had just come in from the street. In answer to the question what ailed her, she sobbed out, "I'se so cold." And no wonder. Beside a worn old undergarment, all the clothing upon her shivering little body was a thin calico dress. The soles were worn off her shoes, and toes and heels stuck out. It seemed a marvel that she had come through the snow and ice as she had, without having her feet frozen.

Naturally the teacher would follow such a child into her home and there endeavor to clinch the efforts begun for its reclamation in the school. It is the very core and kernel of the Society's purpose not to let go of the children of whom once it has laid hold, and to this end it employs its own physicians to treat those who are sick, and to canvass the poorest tenements in the summer months, on the plan pursued by the Health Department. Last year these doctors, ten in number, treated 1,578 sick children and 174 mothers. Into every sickroom and many wretched hovels, daily bouquets of sweet flowers found their way too, visible tokens of a sympathy and love in the world beyond—seemingly so far beyond the poverty and misery of the slum—that had thought and care even for such as they. Perhaps in the final reckoning these flowers, that came from friends far and near, will have a story to tell that will outweigh all the rest. It may be an "impracticable notion," as I have sometimes been told by hardheaded men of business; but it is not always the hard head that scores in work among the poor. The language of the heart is a tongue that is understood in the poorest tenements where the English speech is scarcely comprehended and rated little above the hovels in which the immigrants are receiving their first lessons in the dignity of American citizenship.

Very lately a unique exercise has been added to the course in these schools, that lays hold of the very marrow of the problem with which they deal. It is called "saluting the flag," and originated with Colonel George T. Balch, of the Board of Education, who conceived the idea of instilling patriotism into the little future citizens of the Republic in doses to suit their childish minds. To talk about the Union, of which most of them had but the vaguest notion, or of the duty of the citizen, of which they had no notion at all, was nonsense. In the flag it was all found embodied in a central idea which they could grasp. In the morning the star-spangled banner was brought into the school, and the children were taught to salute it with patriotic words. Then the best scholar of the day before was called out of the ranks, and it was given to him or her to keep for the day. The thing took at once and was a tremendous success.

Then was evolved the plan of letting the children decide for themselves whether or not they would so salute the flag as a voluntary offering, while incidentally instructing them in the duties of the voter at a time when voting was the one topic of general interest. Ballot boxes were set up in the schools on the day before the last general election (1891). The children had been furnished with ballots for and against the flag the week before, and told to take them home to their parents and talk it over with them, a very apt reminder to those who were naturalized citizens of their own duties, then pressing. On the face of the ballot was the question to be decided: "Shall the school salute the Nation's flag every day at the morning exercises?" with a Yes and a No, to be crossed out as the voter wished. On its back was printed a Voter's A, B, C, in large plain type, easy to read:

This country in which I live, and which is my country, is called a REPUBLIC. In a Republic, *the people govern.* The people who govern are called *citizens.* I am one of the people and a *little citizen.*

The way the citizens govern is, either by voting for the person whom they want to represent them, or who will say what the people want him to say—or by voting *for* that thing they would like to do, or *against* that thing which they do not want to do.

The Citizen who votes is called a *voter* or an *elector*, and the right of voting is called the *suffrage*. The voter puts on a piece of paper what he wants. The piece of paper is called a *Ballot*. THIS PIECE OF PAPER IS MY BALLOT.

The right of a Citizen to vote; the right to say what the citizen thinks is best for himself and all the rest of the people; the right to say who shall govern us and make laws for us, is A GREAT PRIVILEGE, A SACRED TRUST, A VERY GREAT RESPONSIBILITY, which I must learn to exercise conscientiously, and to the best of my knowledge and ability, as a little Citizen of this great AMERICAN REPUBLIC.

On Monday the children cast their votes in the Society's twenty-one industrial schools, with all the solemnity of a regular election and with as much of its simple machinery as was practicable. Eighty-two percent of the whole number of enrolled scholars turned out for the occasion, and of the 4,306 votes cast, 88, not quite two percent, voted against the flag. Some of these, probably the majority, voted No under a misapprehension, but there were a few exceptions. One little Irishman, in the Mott Street school, came without his ballot. "The old man tored it up," he reported. In the East Seventy-third Street school five Bohemians of tender years set themselves down as opposed to the scheme of making Americans of them. Only one, a little girl, gave her reason. She brought her own flag to school: "I vote for that," she said, sturdily, and the teacher wisely recorded her vote and let her keep the banner.

I happened to witness the election in the Beach Street school, where the children are nearly all Italians. The minority elements were, however, represented on the Board of Election Inspectors by a colored girl and a little Irish miss, who did not seem in the least abashed by the fact that they were nearly the only representatives of their people in the school. The tremendous show of dignity with which they took their seats at the poll was most impressive.

*Board of Election Inspectors in the Beach Street School*

As a lesson in practical politics, the occasion had its own humor. It was clear that the Negress was most impressed with the solemnity of the occasion, and the Irish girl with its practical opportunities. The Italian's disposition to grin and frolic, even in her new and solemn character, betrayed the ease with which she would, were it real politics, become the game of her Celtic colleague. When it was all over they canvassed the vote with all the solemnity befitting the occasion, signed together a certificate stating the result, and handed it over to the principal sealed in a manner to defeat any attempt at fraud. Then the school sang Santa Lucia, a sweet Neapolitan ballad. It was amusing to hear the colored girl and the half-dozen little Irish children sing right along with the rest the Italian words, of which they did not understand one. They had learned them from hearing them sung by the others, and rolled them out just as loudly, if not as sweetly, as they.

The first patriotic election in the Fifth Ward Industrial School was held on historic ground. The house it occupies was John Ericsson's until his death, and there he planned nearly all his great inventions, among them one that helped save the flag for which the children voted that day. The children have lived faithfully up to their pledge. Every morning sees the flag carried to the principal's desk and all the little ones, rising at the stroke of the bell, say with one voice: "We turn to our flag as the sunflower turns to the sun!" One bell, and every brown right fist is raised to the brow, as in military salute: "We give our heads!" Another stroke, and the grimy little hands are laid on as many hearts: "and our hearts!" Then with a shout that can be heard around the corner: "— to our country! One country, one language, one flag!" No one can hear it and doubt that the children mean every word and will not be apt to forget that lesson soon.

*First patriotic election in the Beach Street Industrial School—*
*parlor in John Ericsson's old house*

The industrial school has found a way of dealing with even the truants, of whom it gets more than its share, and the success of it is suggestive. As stated by the teacher in the West Eighteenth Street school who found it out, it is very simple: "I tell them, if they want to play truant to come to me and I will excuse them for the day, and give them a note so that if the truant officer sees them it will be all right." She adds that "only one boy ever availed himself of that privilege." The other boys with few exceptions became interested, as one would expect, and came to school regularly. It was the old story of the boys in the Juvenile Asylum who could be trusted to do guard duty in the grounds when put upon their honor, but the moment they were locked up for the night risked their necks to escape by climbing out of the third-story windows.

But when it has cheated the street and made of the truant a steady scholar, the work of the industrial school is not all done. Next, it hands him over to the Public School, clothed and in his right mind, if his time to go to work has not yet come. Last year the thirty-three industrial schools of the Children's Aid Society and the American Female Guardian Society thus dismissed nearly eleven hundred children who, but for their intervention, might never have reached that goal. That their charity had not been allowed to corrupt the children may be inferred from the statement that, with an average daily attendance of 4,348 in the Children's Aid Society's Schools, 1,729 children were depositors in the School Savings Banks to the aggregate amount of about $800—a very large sum for them—and this in the face of the fact, recorded on the school register, that 938 of the lot came from homes where drunkenness and poverty went hand in hand. It is not in the plan of the industrial school to make paupers, but to develop to the utmost the kernel of self-help that is the one useful legacy of the street. The child's individuality is preserved at any cost. Even the clothes that are given to the poorest in exchange for their rags are of different cut and color, made so with this one end in view. The distressing "institution look" is wholly absent from these schools, and one of the great stumbling blocks of charity administered at wholesale is thus avoided.

The night schools are for the boys and girls already enlisted in the treadmill, and who must pick up what learning they can in their off hours. Together with the day schools they footed up a total enrolment of nearly ten thousand children whom this Society reached in 1891. Upon the basis of the average daily attendance, the cost of their education to the community, which supported the charity, was $24.53 for each child. The cost of sheltering, feeding, and teaching 11,770 boys and girls in the Society's six lodging houses was $32.76 for each; the expense of sending 2,825 children to farm homes $9.96 for each. The average cost per year for each prisoner in the Tombs is $107.75, and for every child maintained in an asylum, or in the poorhouse, nearly $140. [21]

"One of our great difficulties," says the Secretary of the Children's Aid Society, in a recent statement of the Society's aims and purposes, echoing an old grievance, "is with the large boys of the city. There seems to be no place for them in the world as it is. They have grown up in it without any training but that in street trades. The trades unions have kept them from being apprenticed. They are soon too large for street occupations, and are unable to compete with the small boys. They are too old for our lodging houses. We know not what to do with them. Some succeed well on Western farms, but they are usually disliked by their employers because they change places soon; and their occasional offences and disposition to move about have given us more trouble in the West than any other one thing. Very few people are willing to bear with them, even though a little patience will sometimes bring out excellent qualities in them." They are the boys for whom the street and the saloon have use that shall speedily fashion of their "excellent qualities" a lash to sting the community's purse, if not its conscience, with the memory of its neglect. As 107.75 is to 24.53, or 140 to 9.96, so will be the smart of it compared with the burden of patience that would have turned the scales the other way, to put the matter in a light where the hardheaded man of business can see it without an effort.

There is at least one man of that kind in New York who has seen and understood it to some purpose. His name is Richard T. Auchmuty, and he is by profession an architect. In that capacity he has had opportunity enough of observing how the virtual exclusion of the New York boy from the trades worked to his harm, and he started for his relief an industrial school that deserves to be ranked among the great benefactions of our day, even more for its power to set people to thinking than for the direct benefit it confers upon the boy, great as that is. Once it comes to be thoroughly understood that a chance to learn his father's honest trade is denied the New York boy by a foreign conspiracy, because he is an American lad and cannot be trusted to do its bidding, it is inconceivable that an end should not be put in quick order to this astounding abuse. This thing is exactly what is being done in New York now by the consent of its citizens, who without a protest read in the newspapers that a trades union, one of the largest and strongest in the building trades, has decreed that for two years from a fixed date no apprentice shall be admitted to that trade in New York—decreed, with the consent and connivance of subservient employers, that so many lads who might have become useful mechanics shall grow up tramps and loafers; decreed that a system of robbery of the American mechanic shall go on by which it has come to pass that out of twenty-three millions of dollars paid in a year to the building trades in this city barely six millions are grudgingly accorded the native worker. There is no decree to exclude the mechanic from abroad. He may come and go—and go he does, in shoals, to his home across the sea at the end of each season, with its profits—under the scheme of international comradeship that excludes only the American workman and his boy. I have talked with some of the most intelligent of the labor leaders, men well known all over the land, to find out if there were any defense to be made for this that I was not aware of, but have got nothing but evasion and sophistries about the "protection of labor" for my answer. A protection, indeed, that has nearly resulted already in the practical extinction of the American mechanic, the best and cleverest in the world, in America's chief city, at the bidding of the Walking Delegate.

Even to Colonel Auchmuty's Industrial School this persecution has been extended in a persistent attempt for years to taboo its graduates. In spite of it, the New York Trade Schools open their twelfth season this winter with six hundred scholars and more, in place of the thirty who sat in the first class eleven years ago. The community's better sense is coming to the rescue, and the opposition to the school is wearing off. In the spring as many hundred young plasterers, printers, tailors, plumbers, stonecutters, bricklayers, carpenters, and blacksmiths will go forth capable mechanics, and with their self-respect unimpaired by the associations of the shop and the saloon under the old apprentice system. In this one respect the trades union may have done them a service it did not intend. Colonel Auchmuty's school has demonstrated what it amounts to by furnishing from among its young men the bricklayers for more than as many handsome buildings in New York as there were pupils in its first class. When a committee of master builders came on from Philadelphia to see what their work was like, the report it brought back was that it looked as if the builders had put their hearts in it, and a trade school was forthwith established in that city. Of that, too, Colonel Auchmuty paid the way from the start.

His wealth has kept the New York school above water since it was started; but this winter a benevolent millionaire, Mr. J. Pierpont Morgan, for whom wealth has other and greater responsibilities than that of ministering to his own comfort, has endowed it with half a million dollars, and Mrs. Auchmuty has added a hundred thousand with the land on First Avenue between Sixty-seventh and Sixty-eighth Streets upon which the school stands, so that it starts out with an endowment sufficient to insure its future. The charges for tuition in the day and evening classes have never been much more than nominal, but these may now, perhaps, be reduced even further to allow the "excellent qualities" of the big boys, of whom the reformer despairs, to be put to their proper use without robbing them of the best of all, their self-respect. Then the gage will have been thrown to the street in good earnest, and the Walking Delegate's day will be nearly spent.

# 13

# THE BOYS' CLUBS

B UT IT IS BY THE BOYS' CLUB that the street is hardest hit. In the fight for the lad it is that which knocks out the "gang," and with its own weapon—the weapon of organization. That this has seemed heretofore so little understood, even by some who have wielded the weapon valiantly, is to me the strongest argument for the University Settlement plan, which sends those who would be of service to the poor out to live among them, to study their ways and their needs. Very soon they discover why the gang has such a grip on the boy. It is because it responds to a real need of his nature. The distinguishing characteristic of the American city boy is his genius for organization. Whether it be in the air, in the soil, or in an aptitude for self-government that springs naturally from the street, where every little heathen is a law unto himself—one of them surely, for the children of foreigners, who never learn to speak the language in which their sons vote, exhibit it, if anything, more plainly than the native-born—he has it, undeniably. Unbridled, allowed to run riot, it results in the gang. Thwarted, it defeats all attempts to manage the boy. Accepted as a friend, an ally, it is the indispensable key to his nature in all efforts to reclaim him *en bloc*. Individuals may require different methods of treatment. To the boys as a class the club is the passkey.

There are many boys' clubs in New York now, and room for more. Some have had great success; a few have failed. I venture the guess that the real failure in a good many instances—most of them perhaps—was the failure to trust the boys to rule themselves. I say *rule*. Rule there must be; boss rule at that. That is the kind their fathers own, the fashion of the slums. It is a case of rule or ruin, order or anarchy. To let the boys have full swing would merely be to invite the street in to take charge of the house, and only trouble would come of it. But the boss must be a benevolent and very politic despot. The boy must have a fair chance. To enlist him heart and soul, the opportunity must be given him to show that he can rule himself. And he will show it. He must be allowed to choose his own leaders. His freedom of speech must not be abridged in debate by any rule but that of parliamentary law. Ten to one he will not abuse it, but will enforce that rule and submit to it as scrupulously as the most punctilious of his elders. Let him be sure that his right to self-government will not be interfered with, and he will voluntarily give up the street and his gang. Three boys' clubs had been started by the ladies of the College Settlement, on the principle of noninterference within the few and simple rules of the house. The boys wrote their own laws and maintained order with success. The street looked on, observant. To the policeman it had opposed secret hostility or open war. But a social order with the policeman eliminated was something worthy of approval. Its offer of surrender was brought in form by a committee representing the "Pleasure Club" in the toughest block of the neighborhood. "We will change and have your kind of a club," was its message. Thus the fourth boys' club of the Settlement was launched.

They have not all had so peaceful a beginning. Storm and stress of weather have ushered in most of them. Each new one has cost something for window glass, and the mud of the neighborhood has had its inning before it was forced to abdicate in favor of the club. It was so with the first that was started, fourteen years ago, in Tompkins Square, that was then pretty much all mud and given over to anarchy and disorder. In fact, it was the mud that started the club. It flew so thick about the Wilson Mission, and bespattered those who went out and in so freely that on a particularly boisterous night the good missionary's wife decided that something must be done. She did not send for a policeman. She had tried that before, but the relief he brought lasted only while he was in sight. She went out and confronted the mob herself. When it had yelled itself hoarse at her, she sweetly asked it in to have some coffee and cakes. The mob stared, breathless. Coffee and cakes for stones and mud! This was the Gospel in a shape that was new and bewildering to Tompkins Square. The boys took counsel among themselves. Visions of a big policeman behind the door troubled the timid; but the more courageous were in favor of taking chances. When they had sidled through the open door and no yell of distress had betrayed treason within, the rest followed to find the coffee and the cakes a solid and reassuring fact. No awkward questions were asked about the broken windows, and the boys came out voting the "missionary people" trumps, with a tinge of remorse, let us hope, for the reception they had given them. There was no more mudslinging after that, but the boys fell naturally into neighborly ways with the house and its occupants, and the proposition to be allowed to come in and "play games," came from them when the occasional misunderstandings with the policeman on the post made the street a ticklish playground. They were let in, and when certain good people heard of what was going on in Tompkins Square, they sent down chairs and tables and games, so that they might be made to feel at home. Thus kindness conquered the street, and that winter was founded the first boys' club here or, for aught I know, anywhere. It is still the Boys' Club of St. Mark's Place, and has grown more popular with the boys as the years have passed. The record of last winter's doings over there show no less than 2,757 boys on its roll of membership. The total attendance for the year was 42,118, and the nightly average 218 boys, everyone of whom, but for the coffee and cakes of that memorable night, might have been in the streets slinging mud.

These doings include, nowadays, more than amusements and games. They made the beginning, and they are yet the means of bringing the boys in. Once there, as many as choose may join classes in writing, in bookkeeping, singing, and modelling; those who come merely for fun can have all they want, on condition that they pay their respects to the washroom and keep within the bounds of the house. This they do with the aid of the Superintendent and his assistants, who are chosen from among the bigger boys and manage to preserve order marvellously well with very little show of authority, all considered. The present Superintendent, Mr. Tyrrell, still nurses the memory of a pair of black eyes he achieved in the management of a "tough" club in Macdougal Street, where the boys came with "billies" and pistols in their hip pockets and taught him the secret of club management in their own way. He puts it briefly this way: "It is just a question of who is to be boss." That settled, things run smoothly enough if the right party is on top.

In justice to the Tompkins Square boys, it should be said that the question with them once for all was decided by the missionary's coffee and cakes. If there was ever a passing disposition to forget it, "Pop's" blighting eye helped the club to recall it in no time. Pop was the doorkeeper, and a cripple, with a single mind. His one conscious purpose in life was to keep order in the club, and he was blessed beyond most mortals in attaining his ambition, if blessed in nothing else. Under different auspices Pop might have been a rare bruiser, for, cripple that he was, he was as strong as he was determined. Under the humanizing influences that had conquered Tompkins Square he became one of the jewels of the Boys' Club. If a round in the boxing room threatened to wind up in a "slugging match," if luck had gone against a boy at the game of "pot cheese" until he felt that he must avenge his defeat by thumping his adversary, or burst—Pop's stern glance transfixed the offender and pointed him to the street, silent and meek, all the fight taken out of him on the spot. The boys liked him for all that, perhaps just because they were a little afraid of him, and when Pop died last summer, at the age of twenty-two, after ten years of faithful attendance upon the basement door in St.

Mark's Place, many an honest sob was gulped down at his funeral behind a dirty and tattered cap. It is not the style for boys to cry in Tompkins Square, but it *is* the style to honor the memory of a dead friend, and the Square never saw such a funeral as poor Pop's. The boys chipped in and bought a gorgeous floral pillow for his coffin. So soft a pillow Pop never knew in life.

Many a little account in the club's penny savings bank was wiped out to do Pop that last good turn; but the Superintendent cashed all demands without a remonstrance. It is not often the money is drawn with so lofty a purpose. Most of the depositors earn a few pennies selling newspapers or doing errands. Their accounts are seldom large. In the aggregate they make up quite a little sum, however. On a certain night last June, when I was there, the bank contained almost a hundred dollars, in deposits ranging from ten cents up to nearly five dollars. That week the Superintendent had cashed sixteen books; the smallest had eleven cents to the credit of its owner, who had been greatly taken with a mouth organ and had withdrawn his capital to buy it. Another had been saving up for a pair of boots. There were a few capitalists in the club, who, when they got a dollar and a half or two dollars together, transferred them to the Bowery Bank, where they kept an account. It was easy to predict a successful business career for these; not so with the general run, who were anything but steady depositors, though the Superintendent gave them the credit that "very few drew out their money till they had fifty cents in bank."

If the club has developed no great financiers, it has at least brought out one latent genius in a young sculptor who has graduated from the modelling class into an art museum, and was at last accounts preparing to go abroad and spend his accumulated savings in the pursuit of further knowledge. A short time before the visit of which I speak, a sudden crisis had made the old class in "First Aid to the Injured" come out strong under difficulties. A man had fallen down the basement stairs into the clubroom, in an epileptic fit. It was three years since the boys had been taught how to manage till the doctor came, in case of accident, but they rose to the emergency with a jump. One unbuttoned the man's collar, another slapped his hands, while a third yelled for a dollar to put between his teeth. It had not occurred to the young surgeon who taught the boys the first principles of his profession that dollars are rather scarcer about Tompkins Square than on the Avenue, and this oversight came near upsetting the good done by the rest of his teaching. There was no dollar, not even a quarter, in the crowd, and the man lay gritting his teeth until one of the rescuers, less literal but more practical than the rest, suggested a pencil or a pocketknife and broke the spell.

The mass of the boys come in nightly just to have a good time, and they have it. They play at Parcheesi and messenger boy with an ardor that leaves them no time to care what visitors come and go. Like street boys everywhere, they have a special fondness for games that admit the dice as an element. Gambling is in the very air of the street, and is encouraged in a hundred hidden ways the police rarely discover. Small candy stores and grocery backrooms harbor policy shops, lotteries, and regular gambling hells, where the boys are taught how to buck the tiger on a penny scale. In the club games the dice are robbed of their power for evil. It is the environment here again that makes the difference. It has made a vast difference in the boy who once stalked in, hat on the back of his head, and grimy fists in his breeches' pockets until Pop's stony eye caught his. Now he hangs up his hat upon entering, and goes to the washroom without waiting to be asked by the Superintendent if there is no soap and water where he comes from. Then he gets the game or the book he wants, surrendering his card as a check upon him until it is returned. It is a precaution intended to identify the borrower in case of any damage being done to the club's property. Such a thing as theft of book or game is not known. In his business meetings the boy debates a point of order with the skill and persistence of a trained politician. The aptitude for politics sticks out all over him; but he has some lessons of that trade to learn yet, to his harm. He has not mastered the trick of betraying a friend. Any member of his club, the Superintendent feels sure, would stand up for him and take a thrashing, if need be, should he be found in trouble on his "beat." The "beats" that converge at St. Mark's Place and Avenue A cover a good deal of ground. The lads come from a mile around to the Boys' Club. Occasionally "the gang" calls in a body. One evening it is the Thirteenth Street gang, the next the Eighth Street gang, and again a detachment from Avenue A. By the firstcomers it is sometimes possible to foretell the particular complexion of the *clientèle* of the night; but the business character of the gang is left outside on the sidewalk. Within it is amiability itself, and gradually the rough corners are rubbed off, old quarrels made up, feuds forgotten in the new companionship; the gang is merged in the club, the victory over the street won.

*Boys' Club reading room*

At Christmas and at odd seasons, when the necessary talent can be secured, entertainments are given in the clubroom. Sometimes the boys themselves furnish the entertainment, and then there is never a lack of critics in the audience. There never is, for that matter. Mr. Evert Jansen Wendell, who has been one of the boys' best friends, tells some amusing things about his experience at such gatherings. Ice cream is always intensely popular as a side issue. Some of the boys never fail to wrap a piece up in paper, or put it in the pocket without wrapping, to take home to the baby sister or brother. Only one, to Mr. Wendell's knowledge, ever refused ice cream at an entertainment, and he explained, by way of apology, that he had had the colic all day and his mother had told him "she'd lick him if he took any." For a dignified missionary, who in telling the boys about the spread of the Gospel in the Far East, proposed to illustrate heathen customs by arraying himself in native costumes, brought along for the purpose, it must have been embarrassing to a degree to be cautioned by the audience to "keep his shirt on." But his mishap was as nothing to what befell a young lady, the daughter of a wealthy and distinguished financier, who with infinite trouble had persuaded her father to assist at a certain festive occasion in her favorite club. He was an amateur with the magic lantern, the boys' dear delight, and took it down to amuse them. Mr. Wendell tells what followed:

The show was progressing famously, and the daughter was beaming with pride, when one of the boys suddenly beckoned to her, and pointing to the distinguished financier remarked:

"What der yer call dat bloke?"

"Whom do you mean?" asked the proud daughter, in a tone of much surprise, being quite unaccustomed to hearing the distinguished financier described as a "bloke."

"I mean dat bloke over dere, settin' off dem picturs!" replied the boy.

"What do you desire to know about him?" inquired the proud daughter, with freezing dignity.

"I want ter know what yer call one of them fellers dat sets off picturs?" persisted the boy.

"That gentleman," said the proud daughter, in her most impressive tone, "is my father."

"Well!" said the boy, surveying her with supreme contempt, "don't yer know yer own father's trade?"

The Boys' Club has had many followers. Some aim at teaching the lads trades; others content themselves with trying to mend their manners, while weaning them from the street and its coarse ways. Still others keep the moral improvement in view as the immediate object, as it is the ultimate end. Some follow the precedent of the Boys' Club in charging nothing for admission; other club organizers, like the managers of the College Settlement, have found the weekly fee as necessary as home rule to encourage self-help and self-respect in the boy, and to bring out the best that is in him. Most of them have libraries suited to the children. The College Settlement has a very excellent one of more than a thousand volumes, which is in constant use. The managers report that the boys clamor for history and science, popularly presented, as boys do everywhere, while the girls mainly read fiction. The success of different plans demonstrates the futility of some pet theories on this phase of social economics at least, in the present state of knowledge on the subject. The Boys' Club in St. Mark's Place, for instance, is kept entirely free from religious influence of any sort, and their experience has led many of its friends to believe that success is possible only in that way. Probably in that particular case it might not have been possible on anything like such a scale in any other way. The mud of Tompkins Square testified loudly enough to that. On the other hand, the managers of some very successful and active boys' clubs that have sprouted under Church influence and with a strong Sunday-school bias, maintain with conviction that theirs is the true and only plan. One holds that only in leaving religion out is there hope of success; the other, that there can be none without letting it in and keeping it ever in the foreground. Each sees only half the truth. It is not the profession, or lack of profession, of a principle, but the principle itself that is the condition of success—the real sympathy and interest in the children that bids them come and be welcome, that seeks to understand their needs and help them for their own sake, a religion that "beats preaching" among the poor any day. It is a question of men and of hearts, not of faith. And the poorer the children, the more friendless and forsaken, the more readily do they respond to approaches in that spirit. The testimony of a teacher in the Poverty Gap playground, who went up town to take charge of one where the children were better dressed and correspondingly "stuck up," was that in all their rags and dirt the little toughs of the Gap were much the more approachable and more promising to work with.

Naturally the Church might be expected to have found this out and to be turning the knowledge to use. And it is so. All sects are reaching now for the children in a healthy rivalry, in which the old cry about empty pews is being smothered and forgotten. Of the twenty-six boys' clubs that are down in the Charity Organization Society's directory, nineteen are under church roofs or patronage, and of the remaining seven I know two at least to have been founded by churches. The proportion is more than preserved, I think, in the larger number not registered there, as in all the philanthropic work of many kinds that is now going on among the children. The Roman Catholics never lost sight of the fact that the little ones were the life of the Church, which the Protestants have had, in a measure, to rediscover. Their grip upon the children was never relaxed. The parochial school has enabled them to maintain it without need of recourse to the social shifts the Protestants are adopting to regain lost prestige. Nevertheless, they have not let lie unused the best grappling hook by which the boy might be caught and held. Their schools and churches abound with clubs and societies, organized upon a plan of absolute home rule, under the spiritual directorship of the parish priest. Among

Protestant denominations the Episcopal Church especially shows this evidence of a strong life stirring within it. The Boys' Clubs of Calvary Parish, of St. George's, and of many other churches, are powerful moral agents in their own neighborhoods. Everywhere some strong sympathetic personality is found to be the centre and the life of the work. It may be that the pastor himself is the moving force; or he has the faculty of stirring it in others. His young men are at work in the parish. It is a hopeful sign to find young men, to whom the sacrifice meant the loss of much that makes life beautiful, giving their time and services freely to the poor night schools and rough boys' clubs—hopeful alike for the Church, for the boys, and for their teachers. The women have had the missionary work of the Church, as well as the pews, long enough to themselves. I am not speaking now of the college-bred men and women, who in their University Settlements pursue the plan that has proven so beneficent in England, but of another class, young business men, bank clerks, and professional men—sometimes of large means and of high social standing—whom night after night I have found thus unostentatiously working among the children with more patience than I could muster, and with the genuine love for their work that overcame all obstacles. They were not always going the errand of a church there, but that they were doing the work of the Church there could be no doubt, and doing it in a way to make it once more a living issue among the poor.

The rector of old St. George's, which under his pastorate has grown from a forgotten temple with empty pews to be one of the strong factors in life on the crowded East Side, with Sunday congregations the great building can hardly contain, roughly outlines his plans for work among the children this way, which with variations of detail is the plan of all the churches:

"Get as many of the very little children as possible into our kindergartens, and there let them have the advantage of Christian kindergarten training, before they are old enough to go to the public schools. Keep touch of those same children and get them into the infant departments of the Sunday school. Then take the little fellows from these, and see that in one or two nights in the week we reach them in our boys' clubs; and then, when they are fourteen years old, they are eligible for admission to our battalion. There, by drills, exercises, etc., we hold them till they can enter our Men's Club."

The Sunday school commands the approach to the club, but does not obstruct it. It stands at the door and takes the tickets. Anyone may enter, but through that door only. Once he has passed in, he is his own master. The church is content with claiming only his Sundays when the club is not in session. The experience at St. George's on the home-rule question has been eminently characteristic. The boys could not be made to take a live interest in the club except on condition that they must run it themselves. That point yielded, they promptly boomed it to high-water mark. At present they elect their officers twice a year, to give them full swing, and one set is no sooner installed than wire-pulling begins for the next election. Once, when some trouble in the Athletic Club caused the clergy to take it in hand and appoint a president of their own choice, the membership fell off so rapidly that it was on the point of collapse when the tide was turned by a bold stroke. The managers announced a free election. The boys returned with a rush, put opposition tickets in the field, and amid intense enthusiasm over three hundred and fifty out of a total of four hundred votes were cast. The club was saved. It has been popular ever since.

The payment of monthly dues was found at St. George's to be equally essential to success. "The boys know that they have to pay," said the young clergyman, who quietly superintends their doings; "if they didn't, it wouldn't be a right club." So they pay their pennies and enjoy the independence of it. The result has been a transformation in which the entire neighborhood rejoices. "Four years ago," said their friend, the clergyman, "these same boys stoned us and carried on like the toughs they were. Now we have got here a lot of young gentlemen and loyal friends." Every weekday night the Parish House in East Sixteenth Street resounds with their merriment; on Saturday, with the roll of drums and crash of martial music. Then the Battalion Club meets for drill under the instruction of a former officer in the United States Army. In their natty uniforms the lads are good to look upon, and thoroughly enjoy the exercises, as any boy of spirit would.

The Little Boys' Club languished somewhat for want of a definite programme until the happy idea of a series of talks on elementary chemistry and physics was hit upon. An eminently practical turn was given to the talks by taking the boys to the gashouse, for instance, when gas was up for discussion; to the shipyard, when boat-building was the topic; to the waterworks, when it was water; and to see the great dynamos at work, when they were grappling with the subject of electricity. Afterward the boys were made to tell in writing what they had seen, and some of them told it surprisingly well, showing that they had made excellent use of their eyes and their brains. There is a limit, unfortunately, to the range of subjects that can be illustrated to advantage in that way; the managers had come to the end of their tether, and were puzzling over the question what to do next, when a friend of the club gave it several thousand dollars with which to fit up a manual training school. Since then it has been in clover. A house was hired in East Eleventh Street and transformed into a carpenter shop, and preparations to open it were in progress when these pages were sent to the printer. The club then had over two hundred members. It will probably have twice as many before the winter is over.

The carpenter shop of the Avenue C Working Boys' Club has been a distinct success for several seasons. The work done by the boys after a few months' instruction compares often well with that of the majority of apprentices who have been years learning the trade in the regular way. The shop is fitted out with benches and all the necessary tools.

*Carpenter shop in the Avenue C Working Boys' Club*

A class in typesetting vies with the young carpenters in excellence of workmanship and devotion to business. The printers have ambitious designs upon the reading public. They intend to start a monthly "organ" of their club, an experiment that was tried once but frustrated by a change of base from Twenty-first Street to the present quarters at No. 650 East Fourteenth Street. The club grew up under the eaves of St. George's Church eight years ago, and was known by the name of the St. George's Boys' Club after it had been forced to move away to make room for the erection of the Parish House. Some of the boys work in the daytime at the trades which they are taught at the club in the evening, and the instruction thus received has helped them to earn better salaries in many cases. One of the managers keeps a bank account for those who can save money and want to invest it, and more than one of them has a snug little sum to his credit. There are fifty boys in each class, and always plenty waiting for vacancies to occur. The best pupils receive medals at the end of the year, and once every summer the managers, who are young men of position and character, take them out in the country for an outing, and are boys with them in their games and in their delight over the new sights they see there.

Mr. Wendell tells of one of these trips down to see "Buffalo Bill" on Staten Island. There was a big crowd of excursionists on the boat going down, and the captain took a fatherly interest in the boys, who were gathered together in the bow of the boat, quiet as lambs. The return trip was not so peaceful, though the captain good-naturedly delayed the boat beyond the starting time for fear some of "our boys" would get left, as indeed proved to be the fate of several. But by the time this was discovered it was no longer a source of regret to him. The Indians and the bucking broncos had made the boys restless. They stood around the brass band, and one of them attempted to relieve his pent-up feelings by sticking a button into the big trombone, with the effect of nearly strangling the stout gentleman who was playing on it. The enraged musician made a wild dive for the boy, who dodged around the smokestack and caught up a chair to defend himself with. In a moment a first-class riot was in progress, chairs flying, the band men swearing, and the boys yelling like Comanches. When quiet had been finally restored, the boys banished to the afterdeck, and the button fished out of the trombone, the perspiring captain swore with a round oath that he "wouldn't take those d—d boys down to Staten Island again for ten dollars a head."

The trade-school feature of the Working Boys' Club may soon be reproduced in the Calvary Parish Boys' Club in East Twenty-third Street. They have already a useful typesetting class there, and they have that which their neighbors in Fourteenth Street have yet to get: their own handsome building, bought for the club by wealthy members of Calvary Church, in which it had its birth four years ago. More than that, they have a gymnasium that is the chief attraction of all that neighborhood, particularly the boxing gloves in it.

*Bout with gloves in the Boys' Club of Calvary Parish*

There were some serious doubts about these, and long and grave discussion before they were added to the general outfit. The street was rather too partial to fisticuffs, it was thought, and there were too many outstanding grudges among the boys to make their introduction safe. However, another view prevailed and the choice proved to be a wise one. The gloves are popular—very, and under the firm management of the experienced superintendent, who knows where to draw the safe line, the boys work off their superabundant spirits and sundry other little accounts very successfully in their nightly bouts. The feeling of fellowship and neighborly interest thus encouraged has even led to the establishment of a mutual benefit fund, through which the boys help each other in sickness or distress, and which they manage themselves, electing their own officers.

For anyone who knows the boys of the East Side it is not hard to understand that the Calvary Parish Boys' Club has registered more than twenty-eight thousand callers since it was opened, only four years ago. It has four hundred enrolled members, who pay monthly dues of ten cents, so that they may feel that the club is theirs by right, not by charity. Though church and temperance stood at the cradle of the club—it was organized at a meeting of the Calvary branch of the Church Temperance Society—there is no preaching to the boys. The only sermons they hear at the club are the sermons of brotherly love and kindness, which the cheerful rooms, the games, the books, and the gymnasium— even the boxing gloves—preach to them every night, and which the contrast of it all with the street, that was their all only a little while ago, is not apt to let them forget.

A small sign, with the words "Wayside Boys' Club," hung for a while over the Third Avenue door of the Bible House. Two years ago it was taken down; the club had been merged in the Boys' Club of Grace Mission, in East Thirteenth Street. The members were all little fellows. They were soon made aware that they had fallen among strangers who, boylike, proposed to investigate them and to test their prowess before letting them in on equal terms. Within a week, says Mr. Wendell, this note came to their patroness in the Bible House:

> DEAR MRS. —:
>
> Would you please come and see to our Wayside Boys' Club; that the first time it was open it was very nice, and after that near every boy in that neighborhood came walking in. And if you would be so kind to come and put them out it would be a great pleasure to us.
>
> Mrs. —, the club is not nice any more, and when we want to go home, the boys would wait for us outside, and hit you.
>
> Mrs. —, since them boys are in the club we don't have any games to play with, and if we do play with the games, they come over to us and take it off us.

And by so doing please oblige,

—, *President*   —, *Vice President*   —, *Treasurer*
—, *Secretary*   —, *Floor Manager.*

Please excuse the writing. I was in haste.

—, *Treasurer.*

The appeal had its effect. The Wayside boys were rescued and there has been quiet in Thirteenth Street since. They have got a new house now, and are looking hopefully forward to the day when "near every boy in that neighborhood," shall "come walking in" upon an errand of peace.

Most of the clubs close in the summer months, when it has heretofore been supposed that few of the boys would attend. The experience of the Boys' Club in St. Mark's Place, which this past summer was kept open a full month later than usual and experienced no such collapse, although the park across the street might be supposed to be an extra attraction on warm evenings, suggests that there is some mistake about this which it would be worthwhile to find out. The street is no less dangerous to the boy in summer because it is more crowded. The Free Reading Room for boys in West Fourteenth Street is open all the year round, and though the attendance in summer decreases one-half, yet the rooms are never empty.

The wish expressed by the President of the Society for the Prevention of Cruelty to Children, in a public utterance a year ago, that there might be a boys' club for every ward in the city, has been more than fulfilled. There are more boys' clubs nowadays than there are wards, though I am not sure that they are so distributed that each has one. There are some wards in which twenty might not come amiss. A directory of the local gangs, which might be obtained by consultation with the corner grocers and with the policeman on the beat after a "scrap" with the boys, would be a good guide to the right spots and also in the choice of managers. Something over a year ago a club was opened in Bleecker Street that forthwith took on the character of a poultice upon a rather turbulent neighborhood. In the second week more than a hundred boys crowded to its meetings. It "drew" entirely too well. When I looked for it this fall, it was gone—"Thank goodness!" said the owner of the tenement, a little woman who kept a shop across the street, with a sigh of relief that spoke volumes. Yet she had no more definite complaint to make than what might be inferred from the emphasis she put on the words "them boys!" A friend of the club, or of some of the boys belonging to it, whom I hunted up, interpreted the sigh and the emphasis. The boys got the upper hand, he said. They had just then made a fresh start under another roof and with a new manager.

Such experiences have not been uncommon and, as it often happens when inquiry is pursued in the right spirit, the mistakes they buoyed have been the greatest successes of the cause. There has been enough of the other kind too. Any club manager can tell of cases, lots of them, in which the club has been the stepping-stone of the boy to a useful career. In some cases the boys, having outgrown their club, have carried on the work unaided and organized young men's societies on a plane of indoor respectability that has raised an effectual barrier against the gang and its clubroom, the saloon. These things show what a hold the idea has upon the boy and how much more might be made of it. So far, private benevolence has had the field to itself, properly so; but there is a way in which the municipality might help without departing from safe moorings, so it seems to me. Why not lend such schools or classrooms as are not used at night to boys' clubs that can show a responsible management, for their meetings? In England the Recreative Evening Schools Association has accomplished something very like this by simply demonstrating its justice and usefulness. "Its object," says Robert Archey Woods, in his work on English social movements, "is to carry on through voluntary workers evening classes in the board schools, combining instruction and recreation for boys and girls who have passed through the elementary required course. Its plan includes also the use of the schools for social clubs, and the use of school playgrounds for gymnastics and outdoor games. This simple programme, as carried out, has shown how much may be accomplished through means which are close at hand. There are in London three hundred and forty-five such classes, combining manual training with entertainment, and their average attendance is ten thousand. Schools of the same kind are carried on in a hundred other places outside of London. Beside their immediate success under private efforts, these schools are bringing Parliament to see the importance of their object. Of late the Government has been assuming the care of recreative evening classes, little by little, and it looks as if ultimately all the work of the Evening Schools Association would be undertaken by the school boards." I am not advocating the surrender of the boys' club to our New York School Board. I am afraid it would gain little by it and lose too much. But they might be trusted as landlords, if not as managers. The rent is always the heaviest item in the expense account of a boys' club, for the lads must have room. If cramped, they will boil over and make trouble. If this item were eliminated, the cause might experience a boom that would more than repay the community for the wear and tear of the schoolrooms, by a reduction in the outlay for jails and police courts. There would be another advantage in the introduction of the school to the boy in the *rôle* of a friend, which might speed the work of the truant officer. I cannot see any serious objection to such a proposition. I have no doubt there are school trustees who can see a whole string of them; but I should not be surprised if they all came to this, that the schools are not for any such purpose. To this it would be a sufficient answer that the schools belong to the people.

Another suggestion came home to me with force while watching the drill of the Battalion Club at St. George's one night recently. It has long been the favorite idea of a friend and neighbor of mine, who is an old army officer and has seen service in the field, that a summer camp for boys from the city tenements could be established somewhere in the mountains at a safe distance from tempting orchards, where an army of them might be drilled with immense profit to themselves and to everybody. He will have it that they could be managed as easily as an equal number of men, with the right sort of organization and officers, and as in his business he runs along smoothly with four or five hundred girls under his command, I am bound to defer to his judgment, however much my own may rebel, particularly as he would be acting out my own convictions, after all, in his wholesale way. In any event the experiment might be tried with a regiment if not with an army, and it would be a very interesting one. The boys would have lots of chance for wholesome play as well as drill, and would get no end of fun out of it. The possible hardships of camping out would have no existence for them. As for any lasting good to come of it, outside of physical benefits, I think the discipline alone, with what it stands for, would cover that. In the reform schools, where they have military drill, they have found it their most useful ally in dealing with the worst and wildest class of the boys. It is the bump of organization that is touched again there. Resistance ceases of itself and the boys fall into line. Too much can be made of discipline, of course. The body may be drilled until it is a mere machine and the real boy is dead. But that has nothing to do with such an experiment as I spoke of. That is the concern of reform schools, and I do not think they are in any danger of overdoing it.

I spoke of managing the girls. It is just the same with them. I have had the "gang" in mind as the alternative of the club, and therefore have dealt so far only with their brothers. Girls do not go in gangs, thank goodness, at least not yet in New York. They flock, until the boys scatter them and drive them off one by one. But the same instinct of self-government is in them. They take just as kindly to the club. The Neighborhood Guild, the College Settlement, and various church and philanthropic societies, carry on such clubs with great success. The girls sew, darn stockings, cook, make their own dresses, and run their own meetings with spirit when the boys are made to keep their profaning hands off. On occasion they develop the same rugged independence with an extra feminine touch to it, that is, a mixture of dash and spite. I recall the experience of a band of early philanthropists, who, a score of years ago or more, bought the Big Flat in the Sixth Ward and fitted it up as a boardinghouse for working girls. They filled it without any trouble, though with a rather better grade of boarders than they had expected. No sooner were the girls in possession than they promptly organized and "resolved" that the management should make no rules for the house without first submitting them to their body for approval. Philanthropy chose the least pointed horn of the dilemma, and retired from the field. The Big Flat, from a model boardinghouse became a very bad tenement, and the boarders' club dissolved, to the loss and injury of a posterity that was distinctly poorer and duller, no less for the want of the club than for the possession of the tenement.

The boys' club was born of the struggle of the community with the street, as a measure of self-defense. It has proven a useful war club too, but its conquests have been the conquests of peace. It has been the kernel of success in many a philanthropic undertaking, secular and religious alike. In the plan of the Free Reading Room for Working Boys, of which I made mention, it is used as a battering ram in an attack upon the saloon. The Free Reading Room was organized some nine or ten years ago by the Loyal Legion Temperance Society. It has been popular with lads of all ages from the very start, not least on account of the club or clubs which they were encouraged to found—literary societies they call them there. The Superintendent found them helpful, too, as a means of interesting the boys, by debate and otherwise, in the cause of temperance which he had at heart. The first thing a boys' club casts about for after the offices have been manned and the bylaws made hard and fast, is a cause. One of young boys, that had been in existence a month or less at the College

Settlement, almost took the ladies' breath away by announcing one day that it had decided to expel any boy who smoked or got drunk. The Free Reading Room gives ample opportunity for the exercise of this spirit of convert zeal, when it manifests itself. The average nightly attendance last year was seventy-one, and a good deal larger than that in winter. The boys came from as far south as Houston Street, nearly a mile below, and from Forty-second Street, a mile and half to the north, in all kinds of weather.

The doors of the reading room stand wide open on Sunday as on weekday nights. With singing, and talks on serious or religious subjects in a vein the boys can follow, they try to give to the proceedings a Sabbath turn of which the impression may abide with them. The regular Sunday School exercises have, I am told by the Superintendent, been abandoned, and the present less formal, but more effective, programme substituted. One has need of being wiser than the serpent if he would build effectually in this field among the poor of many races and faiths that swarm in New York's tenements, and he must make his foundation very broad. The great thing for the boys is that the room is not closed against them on the very night in all the week when they need it most. I think we are coming at last to understand what a trap we have been digging for the young in our great cities, when we thought to save them from temptation, by shutting every door but that of the church against them on the day when the devil was busiest finding mischief for their idle hands to do, while narrowing that down to the size of a wicket gate with our creeds and confessions. The poor bury their dead on Sunday to save the loss of a day's pay. Poverty has given over their one day of rest to their sorrows. Is it likely that any attempt to rob it of its few harmless joys should win them over? It is the shadow of bigotry and intolerance falling across it that has turned healthy play into rioting and moral ruin. Open the museums, the libraries, and the clubs on Sunday, and the church that draws the bolt will find the tide of reawakened interest that will set in strong enough to fill its own pews, too, to overflowing.

# 14

## THE OUTCAST AND THE HOMELESS

UNDER THE HEADING "Just one of God's Children," one of the morning newspapers told the story last winter of a newsboy at the Brooklyn Bridge, who fell in a fit with his bundle of papers under his arm, and was carried into the waiting room by the bridge police. They sent for an ambulance, but before it came the boy was out selling papers again. The reporters asked the little dark-eyed newswoman at the bridge entrance which boy it was.

"Little Maher it was," she answered.

"Who takes care of him?"

"Oh! No one but God," said she, "and he is too busy with other folks to give him much attention."

Little Maher was the representative of a class that is happily growing smaller year by year in our city. It is altogether likely that a little inquiry into his case could have placed the responsibility for his forlorn condition considerably nearer home, upon someone who preferred giving Providence the job to taking the trouble himself. There are homeless children in New York. It is certain that we shall always have our full share. Yet it is equally certain that society is coming out ahead in its struggle with this problem. In ten years, during which New York added to her population one-fourth, the homelessness of our streets, taking the returns of the Children's Aid Society's lodging houses as the gauge, instead of increasing proportionally, has decreased nearly one-fifth; and of the Topsy element, it may be set down as a fact, there is an end.

*Homeless boys sleeping on the stairs*

If we were able to argue from this a corresponding improvement in the general lot of the poor, we should be on the high road to the millennium. But it is not so. The showing is due mainly to the perfection of organized charitable effort, that proceeds nowadays upon the sensible principle of putting out a fire, viz., that it must be headed off, not run down, and therefore concerns itself chiefly about the children. We are yet a long, a very long way from a safe port. The menace of the Submerged Tenth has not been blotted from the register of the Potter's Field, and though the "twenty thousand poor children who would not have known it was Christmas," but for public notice to that effect, be a benevolent fiction, there are plenty whose brief lives have had little enough of the embodiment of Christmas cheer and goodwill in them to make the name seem like a bitter mockery. Yet, when all is said, this much remains, that we are steering the right course. Against the drift and the headwinds of an unparalleled immigration that has literally drained the pauperism of Europe into our city for two generations, against the false currents and the undertow of the tenement in our social life, we are making headway at last.

Every homeless child rescued from the street is a knot made, a man or a woman saved, not for this day only, but for all time. What if there be a thousand left? There is one less. What that one more on the wrong side of the account might have meant will never be known till the final reckoning. The records of jails and brothels and poorhouses, for a hundred years to come, might but have begun the tale.

When, in 1849, the Chief of Police reported that in eleven wards there were 2,955 vagrants and dissolute children under fifteen years of age, the boys all thieves and the girls embryo prostitutes, and that ten percent of the entire child population of school age in the city were vagrants, there was no Children's Aid Society to plead their cause. There *was* a reformatory and that winter the American Female Guardian Society was incorporated, "to prevent vice and moral degradation," but Mr. Brace had not yet found his lifework and little Mary Ellen had not been born. The story of the legacy her sufferings left to the world of children I have briefly told, and in the chapter on Industrials Schools some of the momentous results of Mr. Brace's devotion have been set forth. The story is not ended; it never will be, while poverty and want exist in this great city. His greatest work was among the homeless and the outcast. In the thirty-nine years during which he was the life and soul of the Children's Aid Society it found safe country homes for 84,318 [22] poor city children. And the work goes on. Very nearly already, the army thus started on the road to usefulness and independence equals in numbers the whole body of children that, four years before it took up its march, yielded its Lost Tenth, as the Chief of Police bore witness, to the prisons and perdition.

This great mass of children—did they all come from the

street? Not all of them. Not even the larger number. But they would have got there, all of them, had not the Society blocked the way. That is how the race of Topsies has been exterminated in New York. That in this, of all fields, prevention is the true cure, and that a farmer's home is better for the city child that has none than a prison or the best-managed public institution, are the simple lessons it has taught and enforced by example that has carried conviction at last. The conviction came slowly and by degrees. The degrees were not always creditable to sordid human nature that had put forth no hand to keep the child from the gutter, and in the effort to rescue it now saw only its selfish opportunity. There are people yet at this day, whose offers to accept "a strong and handsome girl of sixteen or so with sweet temper," as a cheap substitute for a paid servant—"an angel with mighty strong arms," as one of the officers of the Society indignantly put it once—show that the selfish stage has not been quite passed. Such offers are rejected with the emphatic answer: "We bring the children out because they need you, not because you need them." The Society farms out no girls of sixteen with strong arms. For them it finds ways of earning an honest living at such wages as their labor commands, homes in the West, if they wish it, where good husbands, not hard masters, are waiting for them. But, ordinarily, its effort is to bend the twig at a much tenderer age. And in this effort it is assisted by the growth of a strong humane sentiment in the West, that takes less account of the return the child can make in work for his keep, and more of the child itself. Time was when few children but those who were able to help about the farm could be sure of a welcome. Nowadays babies are in demand. Of all the children sent West in the last two years, 14 percent were under five years, 43.6 percent over five and under ten years, 36.8 percent over ten and under fifteen, and only 5.3 percent over fifteen years of age. The average age of children sent to Western homes in 1891 by the Children's Aid Society was nine years and forty days, and in 1892 nine years and eight months, or an average of nine years, four months, and twenty days for the two years.

It finds them in a hundred ways—in poverty-stricken homes, on the Island, in its industrial schools, in the street. Often they are brought to its office by parents who are unable to take care of them. Provided they are young enough, no questions are asked. It is not at the child's past, but at its future, that these men look. That it comes from among bad people is the best reason in the world why it should be put among those that are good. That is the one care of the Society. Its faith that the child, so placed, will respond and rise to their level, is unshaken after these many years. Its experience has knocked the bugbear of heredity all to flinders.

So that this one condition may be fulfilled, a constant missionary work of an exceedingly practical and businesslike character goes on in the Western farming communities, where there is more to eat than there are mouths to fill, and where a man's children are yet his wealth. When interest has been stirred in a community to the point of arousing demands for the homeless children, the best men in the place—the judge, the pastor, the local editor, and their peers—are prevailed upon to form a local committee that passes upon all applications, and judges of the responsibility and worthiness of the applicants. In this way a sense of responsibility is cultivated that is the best protection for the child in future years, should he need any, which he very rarely does. On a day set by the committee the agent arrives from New York with his little troop. Each child has been comfortably and neatly dressed in a new suit, and carries in his little bundle a Bible as a parting gift from the Society. The committee is on hand to receive them. So usually are half the mothers of the town, who divide the children among themselves and take them home to be cared for until the next day. If there are any babies in the lot, it is always hard work to make them give them up the next morning, and sometimes the company that gathers in the morning at the town hall, for inspection and apportionment among the farmers, has been unexpectedly depleted overnight. From twenty and thirty miles around, the bighearted farmers come in their wagons to attend the show and to negotiate with the committee. The negotiations are rarely prolonged. Each picks out his child, sometimes two, often more than one the same child. The committee umpires between them. They all know each other, and the agent's knowledge of each child, gained on the way out and perhaps through previous acquaintance, helps to make the best choice. There is no ceremony of adoption. That is left to days to come, when the child and the new home have learned to know each other, and to the watchful care of the local committee. To any questions concerning faith or previous condition that may be asked, the Society's answer is always the same. In substance it is this:

"We do not know. Here is the child. Take him and make a good Baptist, or Methodist, or Christian of any sect of him! That is your privilege and his gain. The fewer questions you ask the better. Let his past be behind him and the future his to work out. Love him for himself." [23]

And in the spirit in which the advice is given it is usually accepted. Night falls upon a joyous band returning home over the quiet country roads, the little stranger snugly stowed among his new friends, one of them already, with home and life before him.

And does the event justify the high hopes of that home journey? Almost always in the end, if the child was young enough when it was sent out. Sometimes a change has to be made. Oftener the change is of name, in the adoption that follows. Some of the boys get restless as they grow up, and "run about a good deal," to the anguish of the committee. A few are reported as having "gone to the bad." But even these commonly come out all right at last. One of them, of whom mention is made in the Society's thirty-fifth annual report, turned up after long years as Mayor of his town and a member of the legislature. "We can think," wrote Mr. Brace before his death, "of little Five Points thieves who are now ministers of the gospel or honest farmers; vagrants and street children who are men in professional life; and women who, as teachers or wives of good citizens, are everywhere respected; the children of outcasts or unfortunates whose inherited tendencies have been met by the new environment, and who are industrious and decent members of society." Only by their losing themselves does the Society lose sight of them. Two or three times a year the agent goes to see them all. In the big ledgers in St. Mark's Place each child who has been placed out has a page to himself on which all his doings are recorded, as he is heard of year by year. There are twenty-nine of these canvas-bound ledgers now, and the stories they have to tell would help anyone, who thinks he has lost faith in poor human nature, to pick it up with the vow never to let go of it again. I open one of them at random, and copy the page—page 289 of ledger No. 23. It tells the story of an English boy, one of four who were picked up down at Castle Garden twelve years ago. His mother was dead, and he had not seen his father for five years before he came here, a stowaway. He did not care, he said, where they sent him, so long as it was not back to England:

> June 15, 1880. James S—, aged fourteen years, English; orphan; goes West with J. P. Brace.
>
> Placed with J. R—, Neosha Rapids, Kan. January 26, 1880, James writes that he gets along pleasantly; wrote to him; twenty-sixth annual report sent August 4th. July 14, 1880, Mr. and Mrs. R— write that James is impudent and tries them greatly. Wrote to him August 17, 1880; wrote again October 15th. October 21, 1880, Mr. R— writes that they could not possibly get along with James and placed him with Mr. G. H—, about five miles from his house. Mr. H— is a good man and has a handsome property. Wrote to James March 8, 1881. May 1, 1883, has left his place and has engaged to work for Mr. H—, of Hartford. James seems to be a pretty wild boy, and the probability is he will turn out badly; is very profane and has a violent temper. April 17, 1887,

Mrs. Lyman Fry writes James was crushed to death in Kansas City, where he was employed as brakeman on a freight train.

October 16, 1889.—The above is a mistake. James calls today at the office and says that after I saw him he turned over a new leaf, and has made a pretty good character for himself. Has worked steadily and has many friends in Emporia. Has been here three days and wants to look up his friends. Is grateful for having been sent West.

So James came out right after all, and all his sins are forgiven. He was a fair sample of those who have troubled the Society's managers most, occasionally brought undeserved reproach upon them, but in the end given them the sweet joy of knowing that their faith and trust were not put to shame. Many pages in the ledgers shine with testimony to that. I shall mention but a single case, the one to which I alluded in the introduction to the story of the industrial schools. Andrew H. Burke was taken by the Society's agents from the nursery at Randall's Island, thirty-three years ago, with a number of other boys, and sent out to Nobleville, IN. They heard from him in St. Mark's Place as joining the Sons of Temperance, then as going to the war, a drummer boy; next of his going to college with a determination "to be somebody in the world." He carried his point. That boy is now the Governor of North Dakota. Last winter he wrote to his kind friends, full of loyalty and gratitude, this message for the poor children of New York:

To the boys now under your charge please convey my best wishes, and that I hope that their pathways in life will be those of morality, of honor, of health, and industry. With these four attributes as a guidance and incentive, I can bespeak for them an honorable and happy and successful life. The goal is for them as well as for the rich man's son. They must learn to labor and to wait, for 'all things come to him who waits.' Many times will the road be rugged, winding, and long, and the sky overcast with ominous clouds. Still, it will not do to fall by the wayside and give up. If one does, the battle of life will be lost.

Tell the boys I am proud to have had as humble a beginning in life as they, and that I believe it has been my salvation. I hope my success in life, if it can be so termed, will be an incentive to them to struggle for a respectable recognition among their fellow men. In this country family name cuts but little figure. It is the character of the man that wins recognition, hence I would urge them to build carefully and consistently for the future.

The bigger boys do not always give so good an account of themselves. I have already spoken of the difficulty besetting the Society's efforts to deal with that end of the problem. The street in their case has had the first inning, and the battle is hard, often doubtful. Sometimes it is lost. These are rarely sent West, early consignments of them having stirred up a good deal of trouble there. They go South, where they seem to have more patience with them. "The people there," said an old agent of the Society to me, with an enthusiasm that was fairly contagious, "are the most generous, kindhearted people in the world. And they are more easy going. If a boy turns out badly, steals and runs away perhaps, a letter comes, asking not for retaliation or upbraiding us for letting him come, but hoping that he will do better, expressing sorrow and concern, and ending usually with the bighearted request that we send them another in his place." And another comes, and, ten to one, does better. What lad is there whose wayward spirit such kindness would not conquer in the end? [24]

These bigger boys come usually out of the Society's lodging houses for homeless children. Of these I spoke so fully in the account of the Street Arab in *How the Other Half Lives*, that I shall not here enter into any detailed description of them. There are six, one for girls in East Twelfth Street, lately moved from St. Mark's Place, and five for boys. The oldest and best known of these is the Newsboys' Lodging House in Duane Street, now called the Brace Memorial Lodging House for Boys. The others are the East Side house in East Broadway, the Tompkins Square house, the West Side house at Seventh Avenue and Thirty-second Street, and the lodging house at Forty-fourth Street and Second Avenue. A list of the builders' names emphasizes what I said a while ago about the unostentatious charity of rich New Yorkers. I have never seen them published anywhere except in the Society's reports, but they make good and instructive reading, and here they are in the order in which I gave the houses they built, beginning with the one on East Broadway: Miss Catharine L. Wolfe, Mrs. Robert L. Stuart, John Jacob Astor, Morris K. Jesup. The girls' home in East Twelfth Street, just completed, was built as a memorial to Miss Elizabeth Davenport Wheeler by her family, and is to be known as the Elizabeth Home. The list might be greatly extended by including the twenty-one industrial schools, which are in fact links in the same great chain; but that is not to the present purpose, and probably I should not be thanked for doing it. I have already transgressed enough. The wealth that seeks its responsibilities among the outcast children in this city, is of the kind that prefers that it should remain unidentified and unheralded to the world in connection with its benefactions.

It is in these lodging houses that one may study the homelessness that mocks the miles of brick walls which enclose New York's tenements, but not its homes. Only with special opportunities is it nowadays possible to study it anywhere else in New York. One may still hunt up by night waifs who make their beds in alleys and cellars and abandoned sheds. This last winter two stable fires that broke out in the middle of the night routed out little colonies of boys, who slept in the hay and probably set it on fire. But one no longer stumbles over homeless waifs in the street gutters. One has to hunt for them and to know where. The "cruelty man" knows and hunts them so assiduously that the game is getting scarcer every day. The doors of the lodging houses stand open day and night, offering shelter upon terms no cold or hungry lad would reject: six cents for breakfast and supper, six for a clean bed. They are not pauper barracks, and he is expected to pay; but he can have trust if his pockets are empty, as they probably are, and even a bootblack's kit or an armful of papers to start him in business, if need be. The only conditions are that he shall wash and not swear, and attend evening school when his work is done. It is not possible today that an outcast child should long remain supperless and without shelter in New York, unless he prefers to take his chances with the rats of the gutter. Such children there are, but they are no longer often met. The winter's cold drives even them to cover and to accept the terms they rejected in more hospitable seasons. Even the "dock rat" is human.

It seems a marvel that he is, sometimes, when one hears the story of what drove him to the street. Drunkenness and brutality at home helped the tenement do it, half the time. It drove his sister out to a life of shame, too, as likely as not. I have talked with a good many of the boys, trying to find out, and heard some yarns and some stories that were true. In seven cases out of ten, of those who had homes to go to, it was that, when we got down to hard pan. A drunken father or mother made the street preferable to the house, and to the street they went. [25] In other cases death, perhaps, had broken up the family and thrown the boys upon the world. That was the story of one of the boys I tried to photograph at a quiet game of "craps" in the hallway of the Duane Street Lodging House—James Brady. Father and mother had both died two months after they came here from Ireland, and he went forth from the tenement alone and without a friend, but not without courage. He just walked on until he stumbled on the lodging house, and fell into a job of selling papers. James, at the age of sixteen, was being initiated into the mysteries of the alphabet in the evening school. He was not sure that he liked it. The German boy who took a hand in the game, and who made his grub and bed money, when he was lucky, by picking up junk, had just such a career. The third, the bootblack, gave his reasons briefly for running away from his Philadelphia home: "Me muther wuz all the time hittin' me when I cum in the house, so I cum away." So did a German boy I met there, if for a slightly different reason. He was fresh from over the sea, and had not yet learned a word of English. In his own tongue he told why he came. His father sent him to a gymnasium, but the Latin was "zu schwer" for him, and "der Herr Papa sagt heraus!" He was evidently a boy of good family, but slow. His father could have taken no better course, certainly, to cure him of that defect, if he did not mind the danger of it.

There are always some whom nobody owns. Boys who come from a distance perhaps, and are cast up in our streets with all the other drift that sets toward the city's maelstrom. But the great mass were born of the maelstrom and ground by it into what they are. Of fourteen lads rounded up by the officers of the Society for the Prevention of Cruelty to Children one night this past summer, in the alleys and byways down about the printing offices, where they have their run, two were from Brooklyn, one a runaway from a good home in White Plains, and the rest from the tenements of New York. Only one was really without home or friends. That was perhaps an unusually—I was going to say good showing; but I do not know that it can be called a good showing that ten boys who had homes to go to should prefer to sleep out in the street. The boy who has none would have no other choice until someone picked him up and took him in. The record of the 84,318 children that have been sent to Western homes in thirty-nine years show that 17,383 of them had both parents living, and therefore presumably homes, such as they were; 5,892 only the father, and 11,954 the mother, living; 39,406 had neither father nor mother. The rest either did not know, or did not tell. That again includes an earlier period when the streets were full of vagrants without home ties, so that the statement, as applied to today, errs on the other side. The truth lies between the two extremes. Four-fifths, perhaps, are outcasts, the rest homeless waifs.

The great mass, for instance, of the newsboys who cry their "extrees" in the streets by day, and whom one meets in the Duane Street Lodging House or in Theatre Alley and about the post office by night, are children with homes who thus contribute to the family earnings, and sleep out, if they do, because they have either not sold their papers or gambled away the money at "craps," and are afraid to go home. It was for such a reason little Giuseppe Margalto and his chum made their bed in the ventilating chute at the post office on the night General Sherman died, and were caught by the fire that broke out in the mail room toward midnight. Giuseppe was burned to death; the other escaped to bring the news to the dark Crosby Street alley in which he had lived. Giuseppe did not die his cruel death in vain. A much stricter watch has been kept since upon the boys, and they are no longer allowed to sleep in many places to which they formerly had access.

A bed in the street, in an odd box or corner, is good enough for the ragamuffin who thinks the latitude of his tenement unhealthy, when the weather is warm. It is cooler there, too, and it costs nothing, if one can keep out of the reach of the policeman. It is no new experience to the boy. Half the tenement population, men, women, and children, sleep out of doors, in streets and yards, on the roof, or on the fire escape, from May to October. In winter the boys can curl themselves up on the steam pipes in the newspaper offices that open their doors after midnight on secret purpose to let them in. When these fail, there is still the lodging house as a last resort. To the lad whom ill-treatment or misfortune drove to the street it is always a friend. To the chronic vagrant it has several drawbacks: the school, the wash, the enforced tax for the supper and the bed, that cuts down the allowance for "craps," his all-absorbing passion, and finally the occasional inconvenient habit of mothers and fathers to come looking there for their missing boys. The police send them there, and sometimes they take the trouble to call when the boys have gone to bed, taking them at what they consider a mean disadvantage. However, most of them do not trouble themselves to that extent. They let the strap hang idle till the boy comes back, if he ever does.

*2 AM in the delivery room of the Sun newspaper*

Last February Harry Quill, aged fifteen, disappeared from the tenement No. 45 Washington Street, and though he was not heard of again for many weeks, his people never bothered the police. Not until his dead body was fished up from the air shaft at the bottom of which it had lain two whole months, was his disappearance explained. But the full explanation came only the other day, in September, when one of his playmates was arrested for throwing him down and confessed to doing it. Harry was drunk, he said, and attacked him on the roof with a knife. In the struggle he threw him into the air shaft. Fifteen years old, and fighting drunk! The mere statement sheds a stronger light on the sources of child vagabondage in our city than I could do, were I to fill the rest of my book with an enumeration of them.

However, it is a good deal oftener the father who gets drunk than the boy. Not all, nor even a majority, of the boys one meets at the lodging houses are of that stamp. If they were, they would not be there long. They have their faults, and the code of morals proclaimed by the little newsboys, for instance, is not always in absolute harmony with that generally adopted by civilized society. But even they have virtues quite as conspicuous. They are honest after their fashion, and tremendously impartial in a fight. They are bound to see fair play, if they all have to take a hand. It generally ends that way. A good many of them—the great majority in all the other lodging houses but that in Duane Street—work steadily in shops and factories, making their home there because it is the best they have, and because there they are among friends they know. Two little brothers, John and Willie, attracted my attention in the Newsboys' Lodging House by the sturdy way in which they held together, back to back, against the world, as it were. Willie was thirteen and John eleven years old. Their story was simple and soon told. Their mother died, and their father, who worked in a gashouse, broke up the household, unable to maintain it. The boys went out to shift for themselves, while he made his home in a Bowery lodging house. The oldest of the brothers was then earning three dollars a week in a factory; the younger was selling newspapers, and making out. The day I first saw him he came in from his route early—it was raining hard—to get dry trousers out for his brother against the time he should be home from the factory. There was no doubt the two would hew their way through the world together. The right stuff was in them, as in the two other lads, also brothers, I found in the Tompkins Square Lodging House. Their parents had both died, leaving them to care for a palsied sister and a little brother. They sent the little one to school, and went to work for the sister. Their combined earnings at the shop were just enough to support her and one of the brothers who stayed with her. The other went to the lodging house, where he could live for eighteen cents a day, turning the rest of his earnings into the family fund. With this view of these homeless lads, the one who goes much among them is not surprised to hear of their clubbing together, as they did in the Seventh Avenue Lodging House, to fit out a little ragamuffin, who was brought in shivering from the street, with a suit of clothes. There was not one in the crowd that chipped in who had a whole coat to his back.

*Night school in the West Side Lodging House—*
*Edward, the little pedlar, caught napping*

It was in this lodging house I first saw Buffalo. He was presented to me the night I took the picture of my little vegetable-peddling friend, Edward, asleep on the front bench in evening school. Edward was nine years old and an orphan, but hard at work every day earning his own living by shouting from a pedlar's cart. He could not be made to sit for his picture, and I took him at a disadvantage—in a double sense, for he had not made his toilet; it was in the days of the threatened water famine, and the boys had been warned not to waste water in washing, an injunction they cheerfully obeyed. I was anxious not to have the boy disturbed, so the spelling class went right on while I set up the camera. It was an original class, original in its answers as in its looks. This was what I heard while I focused on poor Eddie:

The teacher: "Cheat! Spell cheat."

Boy spells correctly. Teacher: "Right! What is it to cheat?"

Boy: "To skin one, like Tommy—"

The teacher cut the explanation short, and ordering up

another boy, bade him spell "nerve." He did it. "What is nerve?" demanded the teacher; "what does it mean?"

"Cheek! don't you know," said the boy, and at that moment I caught Buffalo blacking my sleeping pedlar's face with ink, just in time to prevent his waking him up. Then it was that I heard the disturber's story. He *was* a character, and no mistake. He had run away from Buffalo, whence his name, "beating" his way down on the trains, until he reached New York. He "shined" around until he got so desperately hard up that he had to sell his kit. Just about then he was discovered by an artist, who paid him to sit for him in his awful rags with his tousled hair that had not known the restraint of a cap for months. "Oh! It was a daisy job," sighed Buffalo, at the recollection. He had only to sit still and crack jokes. Alas! Buffalo's first effort at righteousness upset him. He had been taught in the lodging house that to be clean was the first requisite of a gentleman, and on his first payday he went bravely, eschewing "craps," and bought himself a new coat and had his hair cut. When, beaming with pride, he presented himself at the studio in his new character, the artist turned him out as no longer of any use to him. I am afraid that Buffalo's ambition to be "like folks," received a shock by this mysterious misfortune, that spoiled his career. A few days after that he was caught by a policeman in the street, at his old game of "craps." The officer took him to the police court and arraigned him as a hardened offender. To the judge's question if he had any home, he said frankly yes! in Buffalo, but he had run away from it.

"Now, if I let you go, will you go right back?" asked the magistrate, looking over the desk at the youthful prisoner. Buffalo took off his tattered cap and stood up on the footrail so that he could reach across the desk with his hand.

"Put it there, jedge!" he said. "I'll go. Square and honest, I will."

And he went. I never heard of him again.

The evening classes are a sort of latchkey to knowledge for belated travellers on the road. They make good use of it, if they are late, as instanced in the class in history in the Duane Street Lodging House, which the younger boys irreverently speak of as "The Soup-House Gang."

*"Soup-House Gang" in class, Duane Street Newsboys' Lodging House*

I found it surprisingly proficient, if it was in its shirtsleeves, and there were at least a couple of pupils in it who promised to make their mark. All of its members are working lads, and not a few of them are capitalists in a small but very promising way. There is a savings bank attached to each lodging house, with the superintendent as president and cashier at once. No less than $5,197 was deposited by the 11,435 boys who found shelter in them in 1891. They were not all depositors, of course. In the Duane Street Lodging House, out of 7,614 newsboys who were registered, 1,108 developed the instinct of saving, or were able to lay by something. Their little pile at the end of the year held the respectable sum of $3,162.39. [26] It is safe to say that the interest of the Soup-House Gang in it was proportionate to its other achievements. In the West Side Lodging House, where nearly a thousand boys were taken in during the year, 54 patronized the bank and saved up $360.11. I found a little newsboy there who sells papers in the Grand Central Depot, and whose bankbook showed deposits of $200. Some day that boy, for all he has a "tough" father and mother who made him prefer the lodging house as a home at the age of nine years, will be running the news business on the road as the capable "boss" of any number of lads of his present age. He neglects no opportunity to learn what the house has to offer, if he can get to the school in time. On the whole, the teachers report the boys as slow at their books, and no wonder. A glimpse of little Eddie, in from the cart after his day's work and dropping asleep on the bench from sheer weariness, more than excuses him, I think. Eddie may have a chance now to learn something better than peddling apples. They have lately added to the nightly instruction there, I am told, the feature of manual training in the shape of a printing office, to which the boys have taken amazingly and which promises great things.

There was one pupil in that evening class, at whose door the charge of being "slow" could not be laid, indifferent though his scholarship was in anything but the tricks of the street. He was the most hopeless young scamp I ever knew, and withal so aggravatingly funny that it was impossible not to laugh, no matter how much one felt like scolding. He lived by "shinin'" and kept his kit in a saloon to save his dragging it home every night. When I last saw him he was in disgrace, for not showing up at the school four successive nights. He explained that the policeman who "collared" him "fur fightin'" was to blame. It was the third time he had been locked up for that offence. When he found out that I wanted to know his history, he set about helping me with a readiness to oblige that was very promising. Did he have any home? Oh, yes, he had.

"Well, where do you live?" I asked.

"Here!" said Tommy, promptly, with just a suspicion of a wink at the other boys who were gathered about watching the examination. He had no father; didn't know where his mother was.

"Is she any relation to you!" put in one of the boys, gravely. Tommy disdained the question. It turned out that his mother had been after him repeatedly and that he was an incorrigible runaway. She had at last given him up for good. While his picture was being "took," one of the lads reported that she was at the door again, and Tommy broke and ran. He returned just when they closed the doors of the house for the night, with the report that "the old woman was a fake."

The crippled boys' brush shop is a feature of the lodging house in East Forty-fourth Street. It is the *bête noire* of the Society, partly on account of the difficulty of making it go without too great an outlay, partly on account of the boys themselves. They are of all the city's outcasts the most unfortunate and the hardest to manage. Their misfortune has soured their temper, and as a rule they are troublesome and headstrong. No wonder. There seems to be no room for a poor crippled lad in New York. There are plenty of institutions that are after the well and able-bodied, but for the cripples the only chance is to shrivel and die in the Randall's Island Asylum. No one wants them. The brush shop pays them wages that enables them to make their way, and the boys turn out enough brushes, if a market could only be found for them. It is a curious and saddening fact that the competition that robs it of its market comes from the prisons, to block the doors of which the Society expends all its energies—the prisons of other states than our own at that. The managers have a good word to say for the trades unions, which have been very kind to them, they say, in this matter of brushes, trying to help the boys, but without much success. The shop is able to employ only a small fraction of the number it might benefit, were it able to dispose of its wares readily. Despite their misfortunes the cripples manage to pick up and enjoy the good things they find in their path as they hobble through life. Last year they challenged the other crippled boys in the hospital on Randall's Island to a champion game of baseball, and beat them on their crutches with a score of 42 to 31. The game was played on the hospital lawn, before an enthusiastic crowd of wrecks, young and old, and must have been a sight to see.

A worse snag than the competition of the prisons is struck by the Society in the cheap Bowery lodging houses—"hotels" they are called—that attract the homeless boys with their greater promise of freedom. There are no troublesome rules to obey there, no hours to keep, and very little to pay. An ordinance of the Health Department, which exercises jurisdiction over those houses, prohibits the admission of boys under sixteen years old, but the prohibition is easily evaded, and many slip in to encounter there the worst of all company for such as they. The lowest of these houses, that are also the cheapest and therefore the ones the boys patronize, are the nightly rendezvous of thieves and, as the police have more than once pointed out, murderers as well. There should be a much stricter supervision over them— supervision by the police as well as by the health officers—and the age limit should be put at eighteen years instead of sixteen. There is this much to be said for the lodging houses, however, that it is a ticklish subject to approach until the city as a municipality has swept before its own door. They at least offer a bed, such as it is, and shelter after their fashion. The hospitality the city offers to its homeless poor in the police station lodging rooms is one of the scandals of a civilized age. The moral degradation of an enforced stay in these dens is immeasurable. To say that they are the resort of tramps and "bums" who know and deserve nothing better, is begging the question. It is true of the majority, but that very fact consigns the helpless minority, too poor to pay and too proud to beg, to a fate worse than death. I myself picked from the mass of festering human filth in a police station lodging room, one night last winter, six young lads, not one of whom was over eighteen, and who for one reason or another had been stranded there that night. They were not ruffians either, but boys who to all appearances had come from good homes, the memory of which might not efface the lessons learned that night in a lifetime. The scandal has been denounced over and over again by grand juries, by the Police Commissioners, and by philanthropists who know of the facts, and efforts without end have been made to get the city authorities to substitute some decent system of municipal hospitality for this unutterable disgrace, as other cities have done, but they have all been wrecked by political jobbery or official apathy.

A thing to be profoundly thankful for is the practical elimination of the girl vagrant from our social life. Ten years ago, Broadway from Fourteenth Street up was crowded with little girls who, under the pretence of peddling flowers and newspapers, pandered to the worst immorality. They went in regular gangs, captained and employed by a few conscienceless old harpies, who took the wages of their infamy and paid them with blows and curses if they fell short of their greed. The police and the officers of the Society for the Prevention of Cruelty to Children put an end to this traffic after a long fight, sending the old wretches to jail and some of their victims to the reformatories. One of the gangs that were broken up had a rendezvous in a stable in Thirtieth Street, near Broadway. The girls had latchkeys and went out and in at all hours of the night. Today the flower girl of tender years is scarcely ever met with in New York. Even the newsgirl has disappeared almost entirely and left the field to the boys. Those who are not at work at home or in the shop have been gathered in by the agencies for their rescue, that have multiplied with the growth of the conviction that girl vagrancy is so much more corrosive than boy vagabondism, as it adds sexual immorality to the other dangers of the street. In 1881 the society's lodging house in St. Mark's Place sheltered 1,287 girls. Their number has gone down since, as the census has gone up, until last year it had fallen to 335, and even these were no longer vagrants, but wayward daughters brought by their parents to be trained to obedience and industry. In the same period, during which the city's population increased more than one-fourth, the increase being very largely made up of just the material to feed its homelessness, the register of the boys' lodging houses showed a reduction from 13,155 to 11,435.

In the introductory chapter I pointed out, as a result of the efforts made in behalf of the children in the past generation, not only by the Children's Aid Society, but by many kindred organizations, that the commitments of girls and women for vagrancy fell off between the years 1860 and 1890 from 5,880 to 1,980, or from 1 in every 138½ persons to 1 in every 780 of a population that had more than doubled in the interval, while the commitments of petty girl thieves fell between 1865 and 1890 from 1 in 743 to 1 in 7,500. Illustrated by diagram this last statement looks this way, the year 1869 being substituted as the starting point; it had almost exactly the same number of commitments as 1865. The year is at the top, and its record of commitments of petty girl thieves at the bottom. The tendency is steadily downward, it will be seen, and downward here is the safe course [see Chart A].

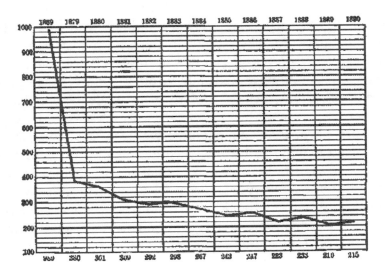

*Chart A*

The police court arraignments for what is known as juvenile delinquency, which is, in short, all the mischief that is not crime under the code, make the following showing, starting with the year 1875, the upper line representing the boys and the lower the girls [see Chart B].

Taking, finally, the commitments of girls under twenty for all causes, in thirteen years, we have this showing [see chart C, end of chapter].

These diagrams would be more satisfactory if they always meant exactly what they seem to show. The trouble is that they share in the general inapplicability to the purposes of scientific research of all public reports in this city (save those of the Health Department, which is fortunate in possessing a responsible expert statistician in Dr. Roger S. Tracy) by reason of lack of uniformity or otherwise. When one gets down to the bottom of a slump like that between the years 1888 and 1889, in the last diagram, one is as likely to find a negligent police clerk or some accidental change of classification there as an economic fact. Something like this last is, I believe, hidden in this particular one. The figures for 1891 maintain the point reached in 1887 and in 1890. However, the important thing is that the decrease has gone on more or less steadily through good years and bad since the children's societies took the field, while the population has increased as never before. Had these forms of disorder even held their own, the slope should have been steadily upward, not downward. In this there is encouragement, surely. There is enough left to battle with. The six lodging houses sheltered in the last twelve years 149,994 children, 8,820 of them girls. We are not near the end yet. The problem is a great one, but the efforts on foot to solve it are great and growing. It has been a forty years' fight with poverty and ignorance and crime, and it is only just begun. But the first blow is half the battle, it is said, and it has been struck in New York, and struck to win.

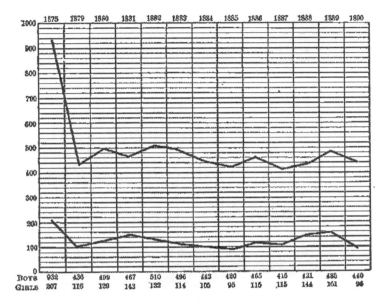

| | 1875 | 1879 | 1880 | 1881 | 1882 | 1883 | 1884 | 1885 | 1886 | 1887 | 1888 | 1889 | 1890 |
|---|---|---|---|---|---|---|---|---|---|---|---|---|---|
| BOYS | 932 | 436 | 409 | 467 | 510 | 496 | 443 | 420 | 465 | 416 | 431 | 485 | 440 |
| GIRLS | 207 | 116 | 129 | 143 | 132 | 114 | 105 | 95 | 116 | 115 | 144 | 161 | 96 |

*Chart  B*

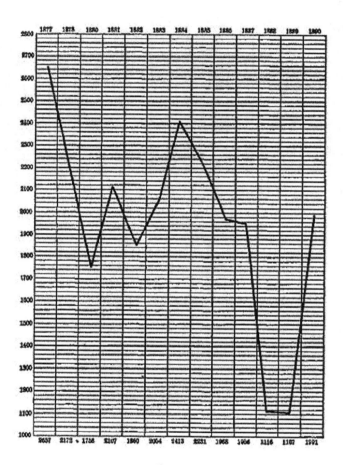

*Chart C*

# 15

# PUTTING A PREMIUM ON PAUPERISM

IN SPITE OF ALL THIS LABOR and effort, in the face of the fact that half of the miseries of society are at last acknowledged to be due to the sundering of the home tie in childhood, and that therefore the remedy lies in restoring it, where that can be done, as early as possible, we have in New York a city of mighty institutions, marshalling a standing army of nearly or quite sixteen thousand children, year in and year out. [27] Homes they are sometimes called; but too many of them are not homes in the saving sense. Those are, that are merely halfway houses to the ultimate family home that shall restore to the child what it has lost. Failing in that, they become public tenements, with most of the bad features of the tenement left out, but the worst retained: the smothering of the tenant's individuality. He is saved from becoming a tough to become an automaton.

It is money scattered without judgment—not poverty—that makes the pauper. It is money scattered without judgment—not poverty—that marshals the greater part of this army. Money backed up by pharisaical sectarianism. Where two such powerful factors combine, politics is never far in the rear, though modestly invisible to the naked eye. To this irresponsible combination— conspiracy it might be called without stretching the point far— the care of the defenseless child that comes upon the public for support has been handed over without check or control of any sort. Worse, a premium has been put upon his coming, upon child desertion in our community. What are the causes of this?

They have been stated often and urgently enough by those whose great experience gave weight to their arguments. Clothed in legal phrase, they may be found summed up in the law of 1875, which ordains that a dependent child shall be committed to an institution controlled by persons of the same religious faith as its parents, when that can be done, and that the county shall pay the child's board. It was a tremendous bid for child pauperism, and poverty, ignorance, and greed were not slow to respond. Under this so-called "religious clause," the number of children thrown upon the county, in New York City alone, was swelled, between 1875 and 1890, from 9,363 to 16,358, this statement including only the twenty-nine institutions that can demand or do receive public money toward their support. Some of them, that have come into existence since it was passed, were directly created by the law. It was natural that this should be so, "because it provided exactly the care which parents desired for their children, that of persons of their own religious faith, and supplied ample means for the children's support; while, although the funds were to be derived from public sources, yet since the institutions were to be managed by private persons, the stigma which fortunately attaches to *public* relief was removed. Thus every incentive to parents to place their children upon the public for support was created by the provisions of the law, and every deterrent was removed; for the law demanded nothing from the parent in return for the support of the child, and did not deprive him of any of his rights over the child, although relieving him of every duty toward it." [28] But New York City went a step further, by having special laws passed securing a stated income from the money raised by local taxation to nine of its largest institutions. This is where the trail of the politician might perhaps be traced with an effort. The amount drawn by the nine in 1890 was nearly a million dollars, while the total so expended footed up in that year over sixteen hundred thousand dollars. New York City today supports one dependent child to each one hundred of its population, and the tax levied, directly and indirectly, for the purpose is about a dollar a head for every man, woman, and child in the city. The State in 1888 supported one child to every 251 of its population. The State of California, which had also gone into the wholesale charity business, supported one dependent child to every 290 of its population, while Michigan, which had gone out of it, taking her children out of the poorhouses and sending them to a State public school, with the proviso that thenceforth parents surrendering their children to be public charges should lose all rights over or to their custody, services, or earnings, had only 1 to every 10,000 of its people. [29]

That proviso cut the matter to the quick. The law declared the school to be a "temporary home for dependent children, where they shall be detained only until they can be placed in family homes." That is a very different thing from the institution that, with its handsome buildings, its lawns, and its gravelled walks, looks to the poor parent like a grand boarding school where his child can be kept, free of charge to him, and taught on terms that seem alluringly like the privileges enjoyed by the rich, until it shall be old enough to earn wages and help toward the family support; very different from the plan of sending the boy to the asylum to be managed, the moment parental authority fails at home. To what extent these things are done in New York may be inferred from the statement of the Superintendent of the Juvenile Asylum, which contains an average of a thousand children, that three-fourths of the inmates could not be sent to free homes in the West because their relatives would not consent to their going. [30] It was only last summer that my attention was attracted, while on a visit to this Juvenile Asylum, to a fine looking little fellow who seemed much above the average of the class in which I found him. On inquiring as to the causes that had brought him to that place, I was shocked to find that he was the son of a public official, well-known to me, whose income from the city's treasury was sufficient not only to provide for the support of his family, but to enable him to gratify somewhat expensive private tastes as well. The boy had been there two years, during which time the Asylum had drawn for his account from the public funds about

$240, at the per capita rate of $110 for each inmate and his share of the school money. His father, when I asked him why the boy was there, told me that it was because he would insist upon paying unauthorized visits to his grandmother in the country. There was no evidence that he was otherwise unmanageable. Seeing my surprise, he put the question, as if that covered the ground: "Well, now! Where would you put him in a better place?" It was a handsome compliment to the Asylum, which as a reform school it perhaps deserved; but it struck me, all the same, that he could hardly have put him in a worse place, on all accounts.

I do not know how many such cases there were in the Asylum then. I hope not many. But it is certain that our public institutions are full of children who have parents amply able, but unwilling, to support them. From time to time enough such cases crop out to show how common the practice is. Reference to cases 59,703, 59,851, and 60,497 in the report of the Society for the Prevention of Cruelty to Children (1892), will discover some striking instances that were ferreted out by the Society's officers. All of the offenders were in thriving business. One of them kept a store in Newark—in another state—and was not even a resident of the city. He merely "honored it with the privilege of paying his children's boarding school expenses in the institution." They were all Italians. These people seem to consider that it is their right to thus feed at the public crib. Perhaps it is the first quickening of the seed of municipal politics that sprouts so energetically among them in the slums, under the teaching of their Irish patrons.

When Mrs. Lowell inspected the New York City institutions in 1889, she found "that of 20,384 individual children sheltered in them, 4,139 had been that year returned to parents or friends, that is, to the persons who had given them up to be paupers; that there were only 1,776 orphans among them, and 4,987 half orphans, of whom 2,247 had living fathers, who presumably ought to have been made to support their children themselves." Three years later, the imperfect returns to a circular inquiry sent out by the State Board of Charities, showed that of 18,556 children in institutions in this state, 3,671, or less than twenty percent, were orphans. The rest then had, or should have, homes. Doubtless, many were homes of which they were well rid; but all experience shows that there must have been far too many of the kind that were well rid of *them*, and to that extent the taxpayers were robbed and the parents and the children pauperized. And that even that other kind were much better off in the long run, their being in the institution did not guarantee. Children, once for all, cannot be successfully reared in regiments within the narrow rules and the confinement of an asylum, if success is to be measured by the development of individual character. Power to regulate or shorten their stay is not vested to any practical extent or purpose in any outside agency. Within, with every benevolent desire to do the right, every interest of the institution as a whole tends to confuse the perception of it. The more children, the more money; the fewer children, the less money. A thousand children can be more economically managed for $110,000 than five hundred for half the money. The fortieth annual report of the Juvenile Asylum (1891) puts it very plainly, in this statement on page 23: "Until the capacity of the Asylum was materially increased, an annual deficit ranging between $5,000 and $10,000 had to be covered by appeals to private contributors." Now, it runs not only the New York house but its Western agency as well on its income.

The city pays the bills, but exercises no other control over the institutions. It does not even trouble itself with counting the children. [31] The committing magistrate consults and is guided more or less by the Officers of the Society for the Prevention of Cruelty to Children, in his choice of the institution into which the child is put. But both are bound by the law that imposes the "faith test." The faith test, as enforced by civil law anywhere, is absurd. The parents of the eighty percent of children in institutions who were not orphans, split no theological hairs in ridding themselves of their support. Backed by the money sacks of a great and wealthy city, it is injurious humbug. This is not the perfection of organized charitable effort for the rescue of the children of which I spoke, but rather the perversion of it.

It is reasonable to ask that if the public is to pay the piper, the public should have the hiring of him too. A special city officer is needed to have this matter in charge. Nearly six years ago Commissioner Lowell submitted a draft for a bill creating a department for the care of dependent children in New York City, with a commissioner at the head whose powers would have been an effective check upon the evil tendencies of the present law. But we travel slowly along the path of municipal reform, and the commissioner is yet a dream. Some day we may wake up and find him there, and then we shall be ready, by and by, to carry out the ideal plan of placing those children, for whom free homes cannot be found, out at board in families where they shall come by their rights, denied them by institution life. Then, too, we shall find, I think, that there is a good deal less of the problem than we thought. The managers of the Union Temporary Home in Philadelphia decided, after thirty-one years of work, to close the House and put the children out to board, because experience had convinced them that "life in the average institution is not so good for children as life in the average home." The intelligence of the conclusion, and the earnestness with which they presented it, guaranteed that their "Home" had been above the average.

"The testimony of two gentlemen on our Board of Council," they reported, "both experienced as heads of great industrial enterprises, is that institution boys are generally the least desirable apprentices. They have been dulled in faculty, by not having been daily exercised in the use of themselves in small ways; have marched in platoons; have done everything in squads; have had all the particulars of life arranged for them; and, as a consequence, they wait for someone else to arrange every piece of work, and are never ready for emergencies, nor able to 'take hold.'" But when they came to actually board the children out, all but the parents of nine were suddenly able to take good care of them themselves, and of the rest three found a way before final arrangements were made. There were seventy children in the Home. Pauperism runs in the same ruts in New York as in Pennsylvania, and the motive power is the same—ill-spent money.

# 16

# THE VERDICT OF THE POTTER'S FIELD

L OOKING BACK NOW over the field we have traversed, what is the verdict? Are we going backward or forward? To be standing still would be to lose ground. Nothing stands still in this community of ours, with its ever swelling population, least of all the problem of the children of the poor. It got the start of our old indifference once, and we have had a long and wearisome race of it, running it down.

But we have run it down. We are moving forward, and indifference will not again trap us into defeat. Evidence is multiplying on every hand to show that interest in the children is increasing. The personal service, that counts for so infinitely much more than money, is more freely given day by day, and no longer as a fashionable fad, but as a duty too long neglected. From the colleges young men and women are going forth to study the problem in a practical way that is full of promise. Charity is forgetting its petty jealousies and learning the lesson of organization and cooperation. "Looking back," writes the Secretary of the Charity Organization Society, "over the progress of the last ten years, the success seems large, while looking at our hopes and aims it often seems meagre." The Church is coming up, no longer down, to its work among the poor. In the multiplication of brotherhoods and sisterhoods, of societies of Christian Endeavor, of King's Daughters, of efforts on every hand to reach the masses, the law of love, the only law that has real power to protect the poor, is receiving fresh illustration day by day.

The Fresh Air Work, the Boys' Clubs, the Society for the Prevention of Cruelty to Children, bear witness to it, and to the energy and resources that shall yet win the fight for us. They were born of New York's plight. The whole world shares in the good they have wrought.

Kindergartens, industrial schools, baby nurseries are springing up everywhere. We have children's playgrounds, and we shall be getting more, if the promised small parks are yet in the future. Municipal progress has not kept step with private benevolence, but there is progress. New schools have been built this year and others are planned. We are beginning to understand that there are other and better ways of making citizens and voters than to grind them out through the political naturalization mill at every election. If the rum power has not lost its grip, it has not tightened it, at all events, in forty years. Then there was one saloon to every 90.8 inhabitants; today there is one to every 236.42. [32] The streets in the tenement districts, since I penned the first lines of this book, have been paved and cleaned as never before, and new standards of decency set up for the poor who live there and for their children. Jersey Street, Poverty Gap, have disappeared, and an end has been put, for a time at least, to the foul business of refuse gathering at the dumps. Nothing stands still in New York. Conditions change so suddenly, under the pressure of new exigencies, that it is sometimes difficult to keep up with them. The fact that it is generally business which prompts the changes for the better has this drawback, that the community, knowing that relief is coming sooner or later, gets into the habit of waiting for it to come that way as the natural one. It is not always the natural way, and though relief comes with bustle and stir at last, it is sometimes too long delayed.

Another mischievous habit, characteristic of the American

people, preoccupied with so many urgent private concerns, is to rise up and pass a law that is loudly in demand, and let it go with that, as if all social evils could be cured by mere legal enactment. As a result, some of the best and most necessary laws are dead letters on our statute books. The law is there, but no one thinks of enforcing it. The beginning was made at the wrong end; but we shall reach around to the other in season.

The chief end has been gained in the recognition of the child problem as the all-important one, of the development of individual character as the strongest barrier against the evil forces of the street and the tenement. Last year I had occasion to address a convention at the National Capital, on certain phases of city poverty and suffering, and made use of the magic lantern to enforce some of the lessons presented. The last picture put on the screen showed the open trench in the Potter's Field. When it had passed, the Secretary of the Convention, a clergyman whose life has been given to rescue work among homeless boys, told how there had just come to join him in his work the man who had until very lately been in charge of this Potter's Field. His experience there had taught him that the waste before which he stood helpless at that end of the line, looking on without power to check or relieve, must be stopped at its source. So he had turned from the dead to the living, pledging the years that remained to him to that effort.

It struck me then, and it has seemed to me since, that this man's position to the problem was most comprehensive. The evidence of his long-range view was convincing. Society had indeed arrived at the same diagnosis some time before. Reasoning by exclusion, as doctors do in doubtful diseases, the symptoms of which are clearer than their cause, it had conjectured that if the "tough" whom it must maintain in idleness behind prison bars, to keep him from preying upon it, was a creature of environment, not justly to blame, the community must be, for allowing him to grow up a "tough." So, in self-defense, it had turned its hand to the forming of character in proportion as it had come to own its failure to reform it. To that failure the trench in the Potter's Field bore unceasing witness. Its claim to be heard in evidence was incontestable.

Now that it has been heard, its testimony confirms the judgment that had already experience to back it. There is no longer room for doubt that with the children lies the solution of the problem of poverty, as far as it can be reached under existing forms of society and with our machinery for securing justice by government. The wisdom of generations that were dust two thousand years ago made this choice. We have been long in making it, but not too long if our travail has made it clear at last that for all time to come it must be the only safe choice. And this, whether from the standpoint of the Christian or the unbeliever, from that of humanity or mere business. If the matter is reduced to a simple sum in arithmetic, so much for so much—child rescue, as the one way of balancing waste with gain, loss with profit, becomes the imperative duty of society, its chief bulwark against bankruptcy and wreck.

Thus, through the gloom of the Potter's Field that has levied such heavy tribute on our city in the past—even the tenth of its life—brighter skies, a new hope, are discerned beyond. They brighten even the slum tenement, and shine into the home which just now we despaired of reaching by any other road than that of pulling it down. Tireless, indeed, the hands need be that have taken up this task. Flag their efforts ever so little, hard-won ground is lost, mischief done. But we are gaining, no longer losing, ground. Seen from the tenement, through the framework of injustice and greed that cursed us with it, the outlook seemed little less than despairing. Groping vainly, with unseeing eyes, we said: There is no way out. The children, upon whom the curse of the tenement lay heaviest, have found it for us. Truly it was said: "A little child shall lead them."

# Register of Children's Charities

**AS PUBLISHED BY THE CHARITY ORGANIZATION SOCIETY**

In addition to the charities given here, seventy-eight churches of all denominations conduct weekly industrial and sewing classes, generally on Saturdays, for which see the Directory of the Charity Organization Society, under Churches, where may also be found the register of thirty-two fresh air funds not recorded below, and of some kindergartens and clubs established by various churches for the children of their congregations.

## NURSERIES
*(AGES RECEIVED)*

Ahawath Chesed Sisterhood, 71 East 3rd St.
*(3 to 6 years)*

Bethany Day Nursery, 453 East 57th St.
*(2 weeks to 6 years)*

Beth-El Society, 355 East 62nd St.
*(2½ to 6 years)*

Bethlehem Day Nursery, 249 East 30th St.
*(1 week to 7 years)*

Children's Charitable Union, 70 Ave. D
*(3 to 7 years)*

Day Nursery and Babies' Shelter, 118 West 21st St.
*(1 to 5 years)*

École Française Gratuite and Salle D'Asile
69 Washington Square
(*2 to 11 years*)

Emanu-El Sisterhood, 159 East 74th St.
(*3 to 6 years*)

Grace House Day Nursery, 94 Fourth Ave.
(*1 to 8 years*)

Hope Nursery, 226 Thompson St.

Jewell Day Nursery, 20 Macdougal St.
(*2 to 5 years*)

Manhattan Working Girls' Association, 440 East 57th St.
(*2 weeks to 10 years*)

Memorial Day Nursery, 275 East Broadway
(*1 to 6 years*)

Riverside Day Nursery, 121 West 63rd St.
(*1 month to 8 years*)

St. Agnes' Day Nursery, 7 Charles St.
(*8 days to 6 years*)

St. Barnabas' House, 304 Mulberry St.
(*4 weeks to 8 years*)

St. Chrysostom Chapel Nursery, 224 West 38th St.

St. John's Day Nursery, 223 East 67th St.
(*1 to 6 years*)

St. Joseph's Day Nursery, 473 West 57th St.
*(2 weeks to 7 years)*

St. Stephen's Equity Club, Kindergarten and Nursery
59 West 46th St.

St. Thomas' Day Nursery, 231 East 59th St.
*(— to 6 years)*

Salle D'Asile et École Primaire, 2 South 5th Ave.
*(3 to 8 years)*

Silver Cross Day Nursery, 2249 Second Ave.
*(2 weeks to 10 years)*

Sunnyside Day Nursery, 51 Prospect Pl.
*(2 weeks to 7 years)*

Virginia Day Nursery, 632 5th St.
*(6 months to 6 years)*

Wayside Day Nursery, 216 East 20th St.
*(2 months to 7 years)*

West Side Day Nursery, 266 West 40th St.
*(18 months to 7 years)*

Wilson Industrial School Day Nursery, 125 St. Mark's Pl.
*(1 month to 6 years)*


### KINDERGARTENS

Ahawath Chesed Sisterhood Free Kindergarten
71 East 3rd St.

All Souls' Church Free Kindergarten
70th St. East of Lexington Ave.

Beth-El Society Free Kindergarten
355 East 62nd St.

Central Presbyterian Church Free Kindergarten
454 West 42nd St.

Cherry Street Kindergarten
340 Cherry St.

Children's Charitable Union Kindergarten
70 Ave. D

East Side Chapel and Bible Women's Association Kindergarten
404 East 15th St.

East Side House Kindergarten
Foot of East 76th St.

Emanu-El Sisterhood Kindergarten
159 E. 74th St.

Free Kindergarten Association of Harlem, No. 1 School
2048 First Ave.

Free Kindergarten of St. John's Chapel
Varick near Beach

French Free School
69 South Washington Sq.

Hebrew Free School Association
East Broadway and Jefferson St.

Kindergarten of Madison Square Presbyterian Church House
Third Ave. and 30th St.

Kindergarten of St. George's Ave. A Mission
253 Ave. A

Kindergarten of St. George's Chapel
130 Stanton St.

Kindergarten of Shearith Israel Congregation
5 West 19th St.

Ladies' Bikur Cholim Society Kindergarten
177 East Broadway

Neighborhood Guild Kindergarten
146 Forsyth St.

N. Y. Foundling Hospital Kindergarten
175 East 68th St.

N. Y. Kindergarten Association Schools:

No. 1, 221 East 51st St.

No. 2, Alumnae Kindergarten, corner 63rd St. and First Ave.

No. 3, 228 West 35th St.

No. 4, 348 West 26th St.

No. 5, Shaw Memorial, 61 Henry St.

No. 6, Mcalpine, 62 Second St.

No. 7, Ave. A and 15th St.

St. Andrews' Free Kindergarten
2067 Second Ave.

St. Bartholomew's Kindergarten
209 East 42nd St.

St. James' Free Kindergarten
Ave. A and 78th St.

St. Mary's Kindergarten
438 Grand St.

Shaaray Tefilla Sisterhood Kindergarten
127 West 44th St.

Silver Cross Sisterhood Kindergarten
2249 Second Ave.

Society for Ethical Culture Kindergarten
109 West 54th St.

Temple Israel Sisterhood Kindergarten
125th St. and 5th Ave.

Trinity Church Association Kindergarten
209 Fulton St.

Wilson Industrial School Kindergarten
125 St Mark's Pl.

## INDUSTRIAL SCHOOLS

Abigail School and Kindergarten, 242 Spring St.

American Female Guardian Society Office, 32 East 30th St.

Home School, 29 East 29th St.

Industrial School

| | |
|---|---|
| No. 1 | 552 First Ave. corner 32nd St. |
| No. 2 | Rose Memorial, 418 West 41st St. |
| No. 3 | 124 West 26th St. |
| No. 4 | 34 Willett St. |
| No. 5 | 220 West 36th St. |
| No. 6 | 125 Allen St. |
| No. 7 | 234 East 80th St. |
| No. 8 | 463 West 32nd St. |
| No. 9 | East 60th St. and Boulevard |
| No. 10 | 125 Lewis St. |
| No. 11 | 52nd St. and Second Ave. |
| No. 12 | 2247 Second Ave. |

Children's Aid Society, Office, 24 St. Mark's Pl.
*Industrial Schools —*

Astor Memorial, 256 Mott St.

Ave. B, 607 East 14th St.

Cottage Place, 208 Bleecker St.

Brace Memorial, 9 Duane St.

East River, 247 East 44th St.

East Side, 287 East Broadway

Eleventh Ward, 295 Eighth St.

Fourth Ward, 73 Monroe St.

Fifth Ward, 36 Beach St.

Fifty-Second Street, 573 West 52nd St.

German, 272 Second St.

Henrietta, 215 East 21st St.

Italian, 156 Leonard St.

Jones Memorial, 407 East 73rd St.

Lord, 135 Greenwich St.

Park, 68th St. near Broadway

Phelps, 314 East 35th St.

Rhinelander, 350 East 88th St.

Sixteenth Ward, 211 West 18th St.

Sixth Street, 632 Sixth St.

West Side, 201 West 32nd St.

West Side Italian, 24 Sullivan St.

*Night Schools —*

German, 272 Second St.

Italian, 156 Leonard St.

Brace Memorial (Newsboys), 9 Duane St.

Eleventh Ward, 295 8th St.

East Side, 287 East Broadway

Lord, 135 Greenwich St.

Jones Memorial, 407 East 73rd St.

Fifty-Second Street, 573 West 52nd St.

West Side, 400 Seventh Ave.

Church Society for Promoting Christianity among Jews
(Industrial School for Girls)
68 East 7th St.

Eighth Ward Mission School, 1 Charlton St.

Five Points House of Industry, 155 Worth St.

Five Points Mission, 63 Park St.

Free German School, 140 East 4th St.

Hebrew Free School Association
East Broadway and Jefferson St.

Italian Mission (P. E. School for Girls), 809 Mulberry St.

Industrial Christian Alliance, 113 Macdougal St.

Louis Downtown Sabbath and Daily School (Hebrew)
267 Henry St.

Mission of the Immaculate Virgin
Lafayette Pl. and Great Jones St.

Mission School of All Souls' Church, 213 East 21st St.

New York Bible and Tract Mission (School for Girls)
422 East 26th St.

New York House and School of Industry, 120 West 16th St.

Sisterhood of the Good Shepherd (P. E.), 419 West 19th St.

St. Barnabas House, 304 Mulberry St.

St. Vincent De Paul Industrial School, 346 West 43rd St.

St. Elizabeth Industrial School, 235 East 14th St.

Spanish Industrial School, 1345 Lexington Ave.

Trinity Industrial School, 90 Trinity Pl.

St. George's Industrial School, Teutonia Hall

Trinity Chapel Industrial School, 15 West 25th St.

St. Augustine's Chapel Industrial School, 105 East Houston St.

St. Mary's Lawrence St., Manhattanville

West Side Industrial School, 266 West 40th St.

Wilson Industrial School, 125 St. Mark's Pl.

United Hebrew Charities (Industrial School for Girls)
128 Second Ave.

Zion and St. Timothy Industrial School, 332 West 57th St.

## FRESH AIR WORK

The Tribune Fresh Air Fund, Tribune Building

Bartholdi Créche, 21 University Pl.

Children's Aid Society
        Health Home, West Coney Island
        Summer Home, Bath Beach

The King's Daughters Tenement House Committee
77 Madison St.

New York Infirmary for Women and Children, 5 Livingston Pl.

New York City Mission and Tract Society, 106 Bible House

St. John's Guild, 501 Fifth Ave.
        Floating Hospital (every weekday but Saturday)
        Seaside Hospital, Cedar Grove, Staten Island

Sanitarium for Hebrew Children, 124 East 14th St.

Society for Ethical Culture, 109 West 54th St.

New York Association for Improving the Condition of the Poor (ocean parties), 79 Fourth Ave.

St. Barnabas Fresh Air Fund, 38 Bleecker St.

The Little Mothers' Aid Society, 305 East 17th St.

New York Bible and Tract Mission, 416 East 26th St.

New York Society for Parks and Playgrounds for Children
36 Union Square

American Female Guardian Society
Summer Home at Oceanport, N. J.

Summer Shelter, Morristown, N. J.
(apply to Charity Organization Society), 21 University Pl.

## BOYS' CLUBS AND READING ROOMS

Ascension Memorial Chapel (P. E.), 330 West 43rd St.

Avenue C Club, 65 East 14th St.

Bethany Church, Tenth Ave., between 35th and 36th Sts.

Calvary Parish, 344 East 23rd St.

Chapel of the Comforter, 814 Greenwich St.

Christ Chapel, West 65th St., near Amsterdam Ave.

Church of the Archangel (P. E.)
117th St. and St. Nicholas Ave.

Church of the Redeemer, Park Ave. and 81st St.

College Settlement, 95 Rivington St.

Covenant Chapel, 310 East 42nd St.

Dewitt Chapel, 160 West 29th St.

East Side House, foot of 76th St. and East River

Free Reading Rooms:
        8 West 14th St.
        330 Fourth Ave.
        590 Seventh Ave.

Grace Mission, 640 East 13th St.

Holy Communion (P. E.) Church, 49 West 20th St.

Holy Cross Lyceum, 43rd St., between Eighth and Ninth Ave.

Holy Cross Mission, 300 East Fourth St.

Lafayette Club (Middle Collegiate Church), 14 Lafayette Pl.

Mission Chapel of Madison Ave. Church, 440 East 57th St.

Madison Square Church House, Third Ave., corner 30th St.

Manor Chapel, 348 West 26th St.

Memorial Baptist Church, Washington Square, South

Monday Night Club (Church of Holy Communion)
49 West 20th St.

Neighborhood Guild, 147 Forsyth St.

New Jerusalem Church, 114 East 35th St.

North Side Boys' Club, 79 Macdougal St.

St. Bartholomew's Parish House, 207 East 42nd St.

St. George's (P. E.) Church (Memorial House)
207 East 16th St.

St. Luke's M. E. Church (Knights of St Luke)
108 West 41st St.

St. Mary's, Lawrence St., Manhattanville

West Side, Vermilye Chapel, 794 Tenth Ave.

Wilson Mission Building ("Ave. A Club"), 125 St. Mark's Pl.

## CHILDREN'S LODGING HOUSES

Brace Memorial, 9 Duane St.

Girls' Temporary Home, 307–309 East 12th St.

Tompkins Square, 295 8th St.

East Side, 287 East Broadway

Forty-Fourth Street, 247 East 44th St.

West Side, 400 Seventh Ave.

Mission of the Immaculate Virgin
Lafayette Pl. and Great Jones St.

## CHILDREN'S HOMES—TEMPORARY AND

## PERMANENT

Asylum of St. Vincent De Paul, 215 West 39th St.

Asylum of Sisters of St. Dominic (House of Reception)
137 Second St.

Berachah Orphanage (Gospel Tabernacle), 692 Eighth Ave.

Bethlehem Orphan and Half-Orphan Asylum
(controlled by thirteen Lutheran churches of New York
and vicinity)
College Point, L. I.

Children's Fold, 92nd St. and Eighth Ave.

Colored Orphan Asylum, West 143rd St. and Boulevard

Free Home for Destitute Young Girls, 23 East 11th St.

Dominican Convent of Our Lady of the Rosary
329 East 63rd St.

Five Points House of Industry, 155 Worth St.

German Odd Fellows' Orphanage (apply at Home)
82 Second Ave.

Hebrew Benevolent and Orphan Asylum
Amsterdam Ave. and 136th St.

Hebrew Sheltering Guardian Orphan Asylum
Eleventh Ave. and 151st St.

Holy Angels' Orphan Asylum
(for Italian Children from New York)
West Park-on-the-Hudson

House of Mercy, 81st St. and Madison Ave.

Ladies' Deborah Nursery and Child's Protectory
        Male Department, 95 East Broadway and 83 Henry St.
        Female Department, East 162nd St., near Eagle Ave.

Leake and Watts Orphan House, Ludlow Station, Hudson R. R.

Messiah Home for Little Children, 4 Rutherford Pl.

Mission of the Immaculate Virgin for Homeless and
Destitute Children
Lafayette Pl. and Great Jones St.

St. Joseph's Home for Destitute Children
House of Reception, 143 West 31st Street

New York Foundling Hospital (Asylum of Sisters of Charity)
175 East 68th St.

New York Infant Asylum, Amsterdam Ave. and 61st St.

Orphanage of the Church of the Holy Trinity, 400 East 50th St.

Orphan Asylum Society, Riverside Drive and West 73rd St.

Orphans' Home and Asylum of Protestant Episcopal Church
49th St. near Lexington Ave.

Roman Catholic Orphan Asylum, Madison Ave. and 51st St.

St. Agatha's Home for Children, 209 West 15th St.

St. Ann's Home for Destitute Children, Ave. A, corner 90th St.

St. Benedict's Home for Colored Children
House of Reception, 120 Macdougal St.

St. Christopher's Home, Riverside Drive and 112th St.

St. James' Home, 21 Oliver and 26 James St.

St. Joseph's Orphan Asylum, 89th St. and Ave. A

Shepherd's Fold (P. E. Church), 92nd St. and Eighth Ave.

Protestant Half-Orphan Asylum, Manhattan Ave., near 104th St.

Home for Seamen's Children, (New York and Vicinity)
West New Brighton, S. I.

Society for the Prevention of Cruelty to Children
100 East 23rd St.

## REFORMATORY INSTITUTIONS

Burnham Industrial Farm, Office, 135 East 15th St.

Hebrew Sheltering Guardian Society, Eleventh Ave. and 151st St.

New York Catholic Protectory, Office, 415 Broome St.

New York Juvenile Asylum, 176th St. and Amsterdam Ave.

St. James' Home, 21 Oliver St.

House of Refuge, Randall's Island

House of the Holy Family, 132 Second Ave.

## CHILDREN'S HOSPITALS AND DISPENSARIES

All Saints' Convalescent Home for Men and Boys
(Holy Cross Mission)
Avenue C and 4th St.

Babies' Hospital of the City of New York, 657 Lexington Ave.

Babies' Ward, Postgraduate Hospital, 226 East 20th St.

Children's Hospital, Randall's Island

New York Infirmary for Women and Children, 5 Livingston Pl.

Five Points House of Industry Infirmary, 147 Worth St.

Good Samaritan Diakonissen (Hahnemann Hospital)
Park Ave. and 67th St.

Infants' Hospital, Randall's Island.

Laura Franklin Free Hospital for Children, 17 East 111th St.

New York Foundling Hospital, 175 East 68th St.

Nursery and Child's Hospital, Lexington Ave. and 51st St.

St. Mary's Free Hospital for Children, 405 West 34th St.

Harlem Dispensary for Women and Children, 2331 Second Ave.

Sick Children's Mission of Children's Aid Society
287 East Broadway

Yorkville Dispensary and Hospital for Women and Children
1307 Lexington Ave.

New York Orthopaedic Hospital, 126 East 59th St.

New York Ophthalmic Hospital, 201 East 23rd St.

### ASYLUMS FOR DEFECTIVE CHILDREN

Crippled Boys' Home (Forty-Fourth Street Lodging House)
247 East 44th St.

Institution for the Improved Instruction of Deaf Mutes
Lexington Ave. and 67th St.

Idiot Asylum, Randall's Island

New York Institution for the Blind, Ninth Ave. and 34th St.

New York Institution for the Instruction of the Deaf and Dumb
Eleventh Ave. and 163rd St.

New York Society for the Relief of the Ruptured and Crippled
Lexington Ave. and 42nd St.

St. Joseph's Institution for the Improved
Instruction of Deaf Mutes
772 East 188th St.

Sheltering Arms, Amsterdam Ave. and 129th St.

Society of St. Johnland (apply at Calvary Chapel)
220 East 23rd St.

Syracuse State School for Feebleminded
(apply to Superintendent of Outdoor Poor)

Children's Aid Society, Haxtun Cottage, Bath Beach, L. I.

House of St. Giles the Cripple, 422 Degraw St., Brooklyn

# Notes

[1] It is, nevertheless, true that while immigration peoples our slums, it also keeps them from stagnation. The working of the strong instinct to better themselves, that brought the crowds here, forces layer after layer of this population up to make room for the new crowds coming in at the bottom, and thus a circulation is kept up that does more than any sanitary law to render the slums harmless. Even the useless sediment is kept from rotting by being constantly stirred.

[2] Report of committing magistrates. See Annual Report of Children's Aid Society, 1891.

[3] The census referred to in this chapter was taken for a special purpose, by a committee of prominent Hebrews, in August 1890, and was very searching.

[4] Dr. Roger S. Tracy's report of the vital statistics for 1891 shows that, while the general death rate of the city was 25.96 per 1,000 of the population—that of adults (over five years) 17.13, and the baby death rate (under five years) 93.21—in the Italian settlement in the west half of the Fourteenth Ward the record stood as follows: general death rate, 33.52; adult death rate, 16.29; and baby death rate, 150.52. In the Italian section of the Fourth Ward it stood: general death rate, 34.88; adult death rate, 21.29; baby death rate 119.02. In the sweaters district in the lower part of the Tenth Ward the general death rate was 16.23; the adult death rate, 7.59; and the baby death rate 61.15. Dr. Tracy adds: "The death rate from phthisis was highest in houses entirely occupied by cigarmakers (Bohemians), and lowest in those entirely occupied by tailors. On the other hand, the death

rates from diphtheria and croup and measles were highest in houses entirely occupied by tailors."

[5] Meaning "teachers."

[6] Even as I am writing a transformation is being worked in some of the filthiest streets on the East Side by a combination of new asphalt pavements with a greatly improved street cleaning service that promises great things. Some of the worst streets have within a few weeks become as clean as I have not seen them in twenty years, and as they probably never were since they were made. The unwonted brightness of the surroundings is already visibly reflected in the persons and dress of the tenants, notably the children. They take to it gladly, giving the lie to the old assertion that they are pigs and would rather live like pigs.

[7] As a matter of fact, I heard, after the last one that caused so much discussion, in a court that sent seventy-five children to the show, a universal growl of discontent. The effect on the children, even to those who received presents, was bad. They felt that they had been on exhibition, and their greed was aroused. It was as I expected it would be.

[8] The Sanitary Census of 1891 gave 37,358 tenements, containing 276,565 families, including 160,708 children under five years of age; total population of tenements, 1,225,411.

[9] The general impression survives with me that the children's teeth were bad, and those of the native born the worst. Ignorance and neglect were clearly to blame for most of it, poor and bad food for the rest, I suppose. I give it as a layman's opinion, and leave it to the dentist to account for the bad teeth of the many who are not poor. That is his business.

[10] The fourteenth year is included. The census phrase means "up to 15."

[11] The average attendance was only 136,413, so that there were 60,000 who were taught only a small part of the time.

[12] See Minutes of stated Session of the Board of Education, February 8, 1892.

[13] Meaning evidently in this case "up to fourteen."

[14] Report of New York Catholic Protectory, 1892.

[15] If this were not the sober statement of public officials of high repute it would seem fairly incredible.

[16] Between 1880 and 1890 the increase in assessed value of the real and personal property in this city was 48.36 percent, while the population increased 41.06 percent.

[17] *Philosophy of Crime and Punishment,* by Dr. William T. Harris, Federal Commissioner of Education.

[18] Seventeenth Annual Report of Society, 1892.

[19] *English Social Movements,* by Robert Archey Woods, page 196.

[20] The Superintendent of the House of Refuge for thirty years wrote recently: "It is essential to have the plays of the children more carefully watched than their work."

[21] Report for 1891 of Children's Aid Society.

[22] In this reckoning is included employment found for many big boys and girls, who were taken as help, and were thus given the chance which the city denied them.

[23] It is inevitable, of course, that such a programme should

steer clear of the sectarian snags that lie plentifully scattered about. I have a Roman Catholic paper before me in which the Society's "villainous work, which consists chiefly in robbing the Catholic child of his faith," is hotly denounced in an address to the Archbishop of New York. Mr. Brace's policy was to meet such attacks with silence, and persevere in his work. The Society still follows his plan. Catholic or Protestant—the question is never raised. "No Catholic child," said one of its managers once to me, "is ever brought to us. A *poor* child is brought and we care for it."

[24] The Society pleads for a farm of its own, close to the city, where it can organize a "farm school" for the older boys. There they could be taken on probation and their fitness for the West be ascertained. They would be more useful to the farmers and some trouble would be avoided. Two farms, or three, to get as near to the family plan as possible, would be better. The Children's Aid Society of Boston has three farm schools, and its work is very successful.

[25] I once questioned a class of 71 boys between eight and twelve years old in a reform school, with this result: 22 said they blacked boots; 36 sold papers; 26 did both; 40 "slept out"; but only 3 of them all were fatherless, 11 motherless, showing that they slept out by choice. The father probably had something to do with it most of the time. Three-fourths of the lads stood up when I asked them if they had been to Central Park. The teacher asked one of those who did not rise, a little shaver, if he had never been in the Park. "No, mem!" he replied, "me father he went that time."

[26] The lodging houses are following a noteworthy precedent. From the Society for the Prevention of Pauperism, organized in the beginning of this century, sprang the first savings bank in the country.

[27] That is the average number constantly in asylums. With

those that come and go, it foots up quite 25,000 children a year that are a public charge.

[28] Report upon the Care of Dependent Children in New York City and elsewhere, to the State Board of Charities, by Commissioner Josephine Shaw Lowell, December 1889.

[29] Mrs. Josephine Shaw Lowell on Dependent Children, Report of 1889.

[30] Anna T. Wilson: *Some Arguments for the Boarding Out of Dependent Children in the State of New York.* This opposition the Superintendent explains in his report for 1891, to be due in part to the lying stories about abuse in the West, told by bad boys who return to the city. He adds, however, that "oftentimes the most strenuous opposition ... is made by stepmothers, uncles, aunts, and cousins," and is "due in the majority of cases not to any special interest in the child's welfare, but to self-interest, the relative wishing to obtain a situation for the boy in order to get his weekly wages."

[31] It will do so hereafter. This autumn the discovery was made that the city was asked to pay for more children than there ought to be in the institutions according to the record of commitments. The comptroller sent two of his clerks to count all the children. The result was to show slipshod bookkeeping, if nothing worse, in certain cases. Hereafter the ceremony of counting the children will be gone through every six months. Nothing could more clearly show the irresponsible character of the whole business and the need of a change, lest we drift into corporate pauperism in addition to encouraging the vice in the individual.

[32] In 1854, with a population of 605,000, there were 6,657 licensed and unlicensed saloons in the city, or 1 to every 90.8 of its inhabitants. At the beginning of 1892, with a population

of 1,706,500, there were 7,218 saloons, or 1 to every 236.42. Counting all places where liquor was sold by license, including hotels, groceries, steamboats, etc., the number was 9,050 or 1 to every 188.56 inhabitants.

# Index

by Tanja Bekhuis, PhD

Pages in **bold italics** indicate figures, mainly photographs. Stories or anecdotes about children are indexed by name of child and again under 'stories of children.' TExtract® was used for semantic analysis and development.

# About the Author

*Jacob August Riis (1849–1914)*
*Source: Library of Congress, United States*

Jacob Riis emigrated from Denmark to New York in 1870. Like many immigrants, he was at times homeless and penniless. Eventually, he found work as a police reporter and later as a newspaper journalist. He wrote about the social and environmental effects of the urban slum and its challenges to survival. He is sometimes referred to as a "muckraker"—a term for early investigative journalists—because of his revelations and tireless efforts to educate the public about poverty. To do so, he gave lectures with magic lantern slides depicting the hard lives of immigrants using his own flash photographs as well as those of other photographers. He also published illustrated magazine articles and books. His ardent prose coupled with images revealed an unknown world of suffering to people of privilege. In an exhaustive study of the "tenement house problem," Riis' work was cited as having "done more to educate the general public on this question than the writings of any other person. To his active efforts are due the tearing down of the worst slum New York City ever saw, the old 'Mulberry Bend,' and also the destruction of a number of unsanitary rear tenements." (DeForest and Veiller, 1903)

His book *The Children of the Poor* (1892) is replete with moving portrayals of orphans and outcasts, as well as "little toilers" who worked to keep families afloat, sometimes earning more than their parents. He describes everyday lives, both sorrows and joys, and gives an unflinching account of child labor at the expense of an education. Riis saw *The Children of the Poor* as a companion to his better known *How the Other Half Lives* (1890). Taken together, the books help readers understand what life was like in a nineteenth century slum and the need for reforms during the Progressive Era.

## RESOURCES FOR FURTHER STUDY

1. Riis, Jacob A. *The Making of an American.* New York: Macmillan, 1901. [Autobiography. Available at www. bartleby. com.]

2. Riis, Jacob August, and Alexander Alland. *Jacob A. Riis: Photographer & Citizen.* Aperture, 1974, 1993. [Biography with photographs modifed by Alland for exhibition; foreword by Ansel Adams, renowned photographer.]

3. Jacob Riis: Revealing "How the Other Half Lives." [US Library of Congress online exhibit. Background information, biography, and commentary with photographs and excerpts from diaries and notes. Links to many primary resources. Available at www.loc.gov/exhibits/jacob-riis.]

4.  DeForest, Robert W., and Lawrence Veiller (eds), New York State Tenement House Commission. *The Tenement House Problem: Including the Report of the New York State Tenement House Commission of 1900.* Macmillan, 1903. [In-depth study of living conditions in urban slums. Architectural design, building laws, disease, and crime discussed as they relate to tenement housing. Importance of Jacob Riis' work acknowledged. Available at https://books.google.com.]

5.  Tenement House Museum, 103 Orchard Street, New York, NY 10002. [History of immigration seen through the eyes of people who lived and worked in the Lower East Side. The tenement, built in 1863, was home to thousands of immigrants. *See* www.tenement.org.]

6.  Yochelson, Bonnie, and Daniel Czitrom. *Rediscovering Jacob Riis: Exposure Journalism and Photography in Turn-of-the-Century New York.* University of Chicago Press, 2014. [Critical analysis of Riis as a reform-minded investigative journalist. Discussion of Riis' collaboration with other photographers, consequent attribution problems, and misperceptions of the 'artistry' of his photographs given modern archival efforts. Both authors are historians.]

*~ Tanja Bekhuis, PhD*

CPSIA information can be obtained
at www.ICGtesting.com
Printed in the USA
BVHW072135031218
534641BV00009B/193/P